Islam and the Veil

Theoretical and Regional Contexts

Edited by Theodore Gabriel and
Rabiha Hannan

B L O O M S B U R Y
LONDON · NEW DELHI · NEW YORK · SYDNEY

Bloomsbury Academic
An imprint of Bloomsbury Publishing Plc

50 Bedford Square	175 Fifth Avenue
London	New York
WC1B 3DP	NY 10010
UK	USA

www.bloomsbury.com

First published by Continuum International Publishing Group 2011
Paperback edition first published 2012

British Library Cataloguing-in-Publication Data
A catalogue record for this book is available from the British Library.

ISBN: HB: 978-1-4411-8735-2
PB: 978-1-4411-3519-3

Library of Congress Cataloging-in-Publication Data
Islam and the veil : theoretical and regional contexts / edited by Theodore Gabriel and
Rabiha Hannan.
p. cm.
ISBN 978-1-4411-8735-2
1. Hijab (Islamic clothing) 2. Veils–Islamic countries. 3. Women in Islam. 4. Muslim
women – Clothing. 5. Islamic clothing and dress. I. Gabriel, Theodore P. C. II. Hannan,
Rabiha. III. Title.
BP190.5.H44I85 2011
297.5'76–dc22
2010046125

Contents

Notes on the Contributors

Rajnaara Akhtar is a graduate in law and a qualified solicitor specialising in Human Rights Law. She is currently a doctoral student at the University of Warwick, School of Law, researching on British Muslims and the evolution of the practice of Islamic personal law with particular reference to dispute resolution.

Dr. Alison Scott Baumann is Reader Emeritus in Cultural Hermeneutics at the University of Gloucestershire, and England representative for the 'Ricoeur Foundation' in Paris, reflecting international work as a Ricoeur scholar. Her major research interests lie in philosophy and the application of philosophy to social justice projects, including over ten years of work with British Muslim groups. This includes work in developing partnerships with the Markfield Institute of Higher Education, Al Mahdi Institute and Ebrahim Community College. She is a trustee of Kashmir Education Foundation (UK) and works in Pakistan on girls' education and teacher training for women. Recent and current research include a project on global citizenship funded by the Department For International Development (DFID 2000–3), and serving as a member of the working party for Islam at Universities in England, commissioned by the British Government and chaired by Dr. Siddiqui. She is the author of, *inter alia*, *Collaborative Partnerships as Sustainable Pedagogy: working with British Muslims in collaborative partnerships* (2007).

Rev Dr. Marcus Braybrooke is President of the World Congress of Faiths, Patron of the International Interfaith Centre, Co-founder of the Three Faiths Forum and Peace Councillor and prolific author. He has published over forty books on world religions and Christianity, including *Pilgrimage of Hope, Faith and Interfaith in a Global Age, Time to Meet, How to Understand Judaism, What We Can Learn from Islam*. His latest book is *Beacons of the Light: 100 holy people who have shaped the history of humanity.*

Dr. Katherine Bullock completed her Ph.D in political science at the University of Toronto in 1999. She has taught a course on the 'Politics of Islam' at the University of Toronto for the last several years. She is the Editor of the *American Journal of Islamic Social Sciences*. Her monographs include *Muslim Women Activists in North America: Speaking for Ourselves* (University of Texas Press, 2005) and *Rethinking Muslim Women and the Veil: challenging historical and modern stereotypes* (IIIT Press, 2003). She has also published articles on Muslim women and the media, and Islam and political theory. Dr. Bullock is a community activist and lectures frequently, to both Muslim and non-Muslim groups. She has worked for the Islamic Society of North America as a media spokesperson and is a founding member of the Federation of Muslim Women, and Beacon, a group dedicated to supporting new Muslims. Originally from Australia, she now lives in Mississauga, Canada, with her husband and children. She embraced Islam in 1994.

Dr. Simonetta Calderini is Reader in Islamic Studies at Roehampton University, London. Her research is focused on Women in Islam, particularly the Isma'ili community. She has published widely and spoken at many conference venues on these issues. Her latest publication is *Women and the Fatimids in the World of Islam*, Edinburgh University Press.

Dr. Sariya Contractor is a Research Assistant at the University of Gloucestershire. She carried out her doctoral research on British Muslim women at the University of Gloucestershire, leading to her Ph.D thesis on 'Muslim Women in Multicultural Britain: exploring the inter-play between Islam, ethnic culture and integration'. She has also been involved in the government-funded project on Islam in British universities.

Dr. Javaid Ghamidi is an internationally known eminent Pakistani scholar of Islam and exegete of the Qur'an and *Hadith*. He is the founder of the al Mawrid Institute of Islamic Sciences, Lahore. He is the author of the magnum opus *The Mizzan*, a comprehensive treatise on Islam (2001).

Malika Hamidi is Director General of the Brussels-based think tank European Muslim Network (EMN), which is working on issues related to Muslim identity in Europe. She is also the Vice-President of the International Study Group of Reflection on Women in Islam (GIERFI). Malika Hamidi is a Ph.D candidate in sociology at the École des Hautes Études en Sciences Sociales (EHESS) in Paris. Her current research explores the emergence of a transnational Islamic feminist movement of thought and action in the West. She is also qualified as a social worker. For the last 11 years she has been involved and active in various organisations at grassroots level in the issue of Women and Islam in the West.

Khola Hasan is a writer, broadcaster and public speaker. She holds a Master's degree in International and Comparative Legal Studies from the School of Oriental and African Studies, University of London. She is currently Director of Albatross Consultancy Limited, which is involved in research and outreach programmes on issues related to Muslim women. She is also an executive member of the East London Three Faiths Forum, and involved in Scriptural Reasoning with St. Ethelburga's Centre for Peace and Reconciliation. She is a regular contributor to BBC Radio 4's 'Beyond Belief' series of programmes, and a debate that she took part in in 2005 with Irshad Manji on the subject of Women in Islam later won the Sony Gold Prize for Best Speech Programme. She also took part in one of the renowned Doha Debates on the issue of equality for women.

Dr. Usama Hasan, a physicist, is a Senior Lecturer at Middlesex University, a part-time Imam and author and speaker on Islam. His latest publication is *The Way of the Prophet: a selection of hadith* (Islamic Foundation, 2009).

Dr. Roy Jackson is a Senior Lecturer in Religious Studies and Course Leader for Religion, Philosophy and Ethics at the University of Gloucestershire. He specialises in Philosophy of Religion, Nietzsche, and contemporary Islamic thought in relation to ethics, philosophy and politics, and has written a number of books on Nietzsche, Plato, Philosophy of Religion, and Islam. More recently he has published *Fifty Key Figures in Islam* (Routledge, 2006) and *Nietzsche and Islam* (Routledge, 2007)

Notes on the Editors

Dr. Theodore Gabriel is an Honorary Research Fellow in Humanities at the University of Gloucestershire, where he was Senior Lecturer in Islamic Studies from 1986 to 2000. His research expertise is on Islam in South and South East Asia and Inter-Religious Relations. He has published widely and his latest monograph is *Christian Citizens in an Islamic State: the Pakistan experience* (Ashgate, 2008). He is also the editor of *Islam in the Contemporary World* (Vikas, 2001) and Co-Editor of *Islam and the West Post 9/11* (Ashgate, 2004).

Rabiha Hannan holds an MA in Muslim community studies, with a specialisation in gender issues. She has worked in the voluntary sector for over ten years, supporting a variety of local and national projects that aim to enhance dialogue and understanding between people. She is Co-Director of the Community Relations Initiative, a consultancy that works on research, educational and practical projects aiming to bring communities together. She has been Vice Chair and Chair of the Leicester SACRE (2007–9) and was on the implementation team leading to the formation of the national Christian–Muslim Forum. She is married, has four children, and lives in Leicester. She is currently acting as Consultant to the Muslim Burial Council of Leicester and is a Community Governor for a local Primary School. She is a qualified pharmacist by training.

Acknowledgements

We are grateful to the University of Gloucestershire, and especially to Dr. Shelley Saguaro, Head of Humanities, for her encouragement and support for the annual Islam conference that made this volume of essays possible. Secondly we are most thankful to the learned scholars who contributed the well-informed and clear analyses of issues relating to Islam and the Veil. We appreciate the time, research and thought devoted by the contributors to the preparation of these articles.

We acknowledge with thanks the publisher Continuum Books, and especially Ms. Kirsty Schaper, Commissioning Editor for Religious Studies of this prestigious publishing house, for her interest in the subject, for accepting the book for publication and for the timely and detailed guidelines provided for preparation of the manuscript.

Introduction

Theodore Gabriel and Rabiha Hannan

The issue of the veiling of Muslim women has often been the subject of political controversy, hot debate in the media, and much public interest in the West in recent times. Quite a few incidents involving veiled Muslim women in the workplace, in school classrooms and similar public scenarios have been the subject of disputes and even litigation. Jack Straw, former UK Home Secretary, stirred up a hornet's nest when he remarked in October 2006 that the veiling of Muslim women made community relations more difficult. Furthermore, France's ban on the headscarf in schools in 2004, and more recently French President Nicholas Sarkozy's remarks on the face-veil as being 'not welcome in France', gave rise to yet more apprehension and distrust.[1] Now France has banned the *niqab* (complete veiling) outright!

Why does this subject exercise the concerns of people in the West so much? The issue has not invited as much public attention in other multi-religious regions, such as India, Pakistan or Malaysia, though the veiling of women does become the focus of public attention and debate in predominantly Muslim nations such as Turkey, Iran or Afghanistan from time to time, and is part of feminist movements in such nations. In Egypt from colonial times the veiling, or rather the unveiling, of women has been part of the general social metamorphosis. Turkey and Iran have occasionally banned it, while in some Muslim nations (e.g. Afghanistan under the Taliban) it has been rigorously enforced. In Saudi Arabia even non-Muslim women must wear the veil in public. But it is in the West that the issue of Islamic veiling has now become controversial.

Perhaps no other religious symbol is more overtly visible or controversial than the veil. But why is it that this small piece of cloth can exercise the concerns of so many people? Does it really go against the grain of feminism and undo the work of the suffragette movement? Does it hamper the quest for equality between man and woman? Or could it instead be a tool of liberation, redefining a woman's sexuality and enabling her to become more than merely an object of physical desire?

One of the problems in the West is that much of the debate has not proceeded from a well-studied or even a well-informed position. This is a significant drawback for any meaningful discussion of a controversial and even emotive issue such as veiling. This is the case in general in discussions of the status of women in Islam, but in the issue of Islamic veiling the debate has been particularly vociferous but ill-informed and ill-thought-out. The veil is often portrayed as a symbol of the oppression of women in Islam. But the issue is complex and needs knowledge of both the faith and the cultures associated with the Muslim diaspora in the West. It is quite easy to acquire misconceptions and distortions of the facts when trying to understand this important phenomenon in Islamic practice. Without carefully examining the motivations of veiled Muslim women, which can be multifarious, and without being cognisant of the implications of veiling for Muslims as well as other societies, it is easy to dismiss the practice as a superstition, or a symbol of cultural backwardness and Muslim male hegemony over women, and in short to arrive at unbalanced and subjective conclusions which are far from the reality. Much empathy is needed, as well as effort, to obtain an informed view of the practice, rather than merely to judge it from the perspective of a sceptical external observer.

It is also true that political developments on the world stage involving Islam have generated a substantial amount of Islamophobia in the West. The wars in Iraq and Afghanistan, and acts of terrorism such as 9/11 and 7/7, however far these may be from the precepts of Islam, the ongoing Israel–Palestine confrontation, and violent incidents transpiring from these problematic situations, have meant that to some extent the image of Islam in Western eyes is that of extremism, militancy and conflict. This is, of course, a total distortion of the truth, but the concerns about and hostility towards the veiling of Muslim women partly arise from these factors, the 'veil' being the most visible identification of the faith. Such concerns and hostility have sometimes resulted in the abuse of veiled women.

Religious practices cannot be examined in isolation. There are scriptural, theological, social and historical factors involved in this Muslim practice. In modern times the casting aside of the *hijab* has become for some a symbol of liberation. On the other hand, uneducated criticism and attempts to curtail the practice of Islamic veiling have implications for religious liberty, intercommunal relationships and cultural interaction. Motivations for wearing the veil can be several. It can be a symbol of piety, of religious identity, of women's need for anonymity and security; it can also signify protest against social or political injustice; it may even indicate social hierarchy. To many in the West the veil can be a symbol of alienness, opposition to cultural integration, even of covert evil intention. It arouses

Islamophobia, and aversion to the veil can be a symptom of Islamophobia. At the same time, much of Western comment on the veil ignores instances of veiling in Western cultures themselves – for instance in Christian monasticism, in high society, and in funerary rituals.

Ironically the two factors of stereotyping and discrimination have led to a wave of rediscovery of Islam for many Muslims in Europe. In an attempt to forge a symbol of Muslim pride and identity, the veil has sometimes been used as a tool to demonstrate that one can be both European and religious!

This volume of essays seeks to provide well-studied, knowledgeable analyses of the practice. Some of the essays are concerned with examining the practice in general, looking into the social, psychological, scriptural and theological issues involved in veiling. Others highlight the practice as manifested in regional contexts. The authors include philosophers, female Muslim scholars who practise veiling, and non-Muslim academics who are well versed in the research and teaching of Islamic Studies. On the whole they provide a well-rounded overview, and provide diverse perspectives and discussion on the practice. This sensitive issue is handled well in the essays, and the analyses and conclusions are objective – though it is obvious that the subjective element cannot entirely be laid aside. The volume on the whole comes out as a well-balanced discussion of veiling. But it is the diversity of views and opinions that is important at this juncture; it is a well-known Islamic principle to allow disagreement and discussion to occur, so that you come to the best conclusion. In this case there may not be one conclusion, but at the very least it will allow diversity of opinion to remain relevant to people.

A paradigm often referred to has been the prophetic times, and the actions and sayings of the Prophet have often been cited in the arguments. This has the effect of simplifying, clarifying and illuminating the concepts involved in the discussion.

Studies from the Indian subcontinent, the United Kingdom, France and Canada are evidence of the regional diversity in the veiling debate. The focus of this book is largely, though not exclusively, on the Muslim diaspora in the West. The chapter contributed by Roy Jackson relates to the Indian subcontinent, while the contributions by Marcus Braybrooke, Javed Ghamidi and Theodore Gabriel make general points about the issue of veiling without a regional focus.

We have arranged the book into three parts. The first sets the scene and provides a background to the labyrinth of ideas around the topic. It includes a chapter from Marcus Braybrooke on the importance of embracing diversity as well as respect and understanding towards others, even when it might appear to differ from your own way of doing things; and one from Theodore Gabriel, reflecting on the injunctions in the Qur'an and ahadith (sayings and actions of the Prophet Muhammad pbuh) regarding apparel (for Muslim men as well as women) and examining the diverse implications it can have for Muslims and others. A critique by Roy Jackson of Maududi's work on female seclusion demonstrates how some Muslims have used the veil as a tool to limit the Muslim woman's involvement in the public sphere. In contrast, Alison Scott-Bauman explains how Orientalism in reverse can sometimes lead to negative conclusions of the 'other', without just cause. Simonetta Calderini reveals that veiling is an issue in the Isma'ili community, and discusses tensions on this account between the community's traditionalists and its reformist/'progressive' sections.

The second part is an exploration of the primary texts in Islam, their meaning and their interpretation and how they impact on the female dress requirements for today. Khola Hasan explains how the Qur'an liberates women through the use of the veil and modest behaviour. Javed Ghamidi looks at the way that the importance of modesty and guarding morality is at the heart of the issue, more than the extent of dress. Usama Hasan shows how scholars in history too differed on the extent and purpose of dress. With Rabiha Hannan, they make a thorough examination of the verses in the Qur'an, as well as relevant ahadith that seem to allude to the issue of attire. This has the effect of simplifying, clarifying and illuminating the concepts involved in the discussion.

The final part reviews the impact of veiling on human rights and freedom. Katherine Bullock and Sariya Contractor have made use of interviews with practitioners of the veil to explore reasons behind why women choose to wear it, thereby demonstrating time and again that – in the West, at least – it has been the woman's own personal choice and inner religious conviction to adopt the veil. Rajnaara Akhtar explores issues of democracy in Europe, and argues for the right to dress as one chooses, whilst Malika Hamidi further demonstrates the inequalities and sense of injustice felt by women who merely want to practise their faith.

We should clarify that the authors of individual papers present their own opinions and not those of the editors. These may sometimes differ in perspective to those of other contributors, but they serve to demonstrate the richness of the discussion.

Part One

Theoretical Contexts

Chapter 1

Respect in a Plural Society

Marcus Braybrooke

The subject of the Veil, like the issues raised by the Archbishop of Canterbury in his lecture on *Shari'a* and British Law are complex and important. How do we strike the right balance between allowing faith communities a proper freedom and affirming our shared life together? What should be the balance between multiculturalism and social cohesion or Britishness? My ideal would be that of the Chief Rabbi – 'a community of communities' – respect for the beliefs and practices of particular faith communities and the recognition of the values that we share and which provide the basis for the society to which we all belong.

Perhaps I can approach the subject under the headings of xenophobia, human rights and the plural society.

A couple of years ago I saw a production at Stratford of a play that may have been partly written by Shakespeare. It was about the Evil May Day riot in 1517, when the citizens of London rose against the Lombard immigrants who had settled in the city and were taking the locals' jobs. Huguenot immigrants in the seventeenth century were no more popular; nor were the Jewish immigrants at the end of the nineteenth century, at which time there was talk of immigration quotas. For example, to quote from the Royal Commission on Alien Immigration, early in the last century:

> A foreign Jew will take a house and he moves in on a Sunday morning, which rather, of course, upsets all the British people there. Then his habits are different. You will see the houses with sand put down instead of oilcloth or carpet.[2]

So the situation today is not unparalleled. I believe the British approach of allowing national and religious groups to maintain their own identity within the overarching framework of British Law is right. In India, the East India Company prevented Christian missionaries from coming to the country, until it was overruled by Parliament in 1813. Even so, unlike

French and Portuguese imperialism, there was no intention on the part of the British to interfere with Hindu or Muslim religious customs, as Queen Victoria reiterated after the Mutiny. When in 1803 Lord Wellesley, in the name of universal moral law, suppressed the sacrifice of children, he was criticised for unjustified interference with Hindu custom. As a result he did not dare try to stop *suttee* – the practice of a widow immolating herself on her dead husband's funeral pyre. Later, however, the principle of equality of all subjects before the law was affirmed in defiance of traditional privileges for members of the high castes.

Enough of the history lesson!

But perhaps it reminds us that the issues are not new.

Xenophobia, in the form of resentment of newcomers – especially if they are thought to take jobs or lead to overcrowding – is common and will often express itself in dislike for the characteristics that make people different.

The question of human rights is more complicated, especially if the differences between cultures seem to the majority to be immoral – such as with *suttee*, female circumcision or forced marriage. If a practice contravenes a basic human right (though I am certainly not suggesting that wearing a veil does so), then it is right to challenge it; but not on the basis of one religion claiming the moral high ground, rather in the name of the values that we share. This is why I think the attempt to articulate a Global Ethic is so important, such as the Declaration drawn up at the 1993 Parliament of the World's Religions.[3] Based on the fundamental demand that every human being must be treated humanely, the 1993 Declaration affirms four 'Irrevocable Directives':

1. Commitment to a culture of non-violence and respect for life
2. Commitment to a culture of solidarity and a just economic order
3. Commitment to a culture of tolerance and a life of truthfulness
4. Commitment to a culture of equal rights and partnership between men and women.

My primary concern, therefore, would be to ask whether the law and practices of a faith community and of a nation measure up to the universal values which are grounded in our belief in God and which are to be found, with or more or less clarity, in all religious traditions. I am not sure that the treatment of women in any of our faith communities measures up to a culture of equal rights.

Religion is tied up with identity. Why did the Jewish immigrants move house on a Sunday? Because their religion did not allow them to do such work on the Sabbath; thereby they violated the great British tradition of a Sunday lie-in or 'church-going'.

For many people, religion is a question of practice and identity as much as of belief. I remember my initial surprise when I first read this passage by the Religious Studies scholar Richard Gombrich:

> For most people in the modern world religion is first of all an identity, a label, badge of allegiance of a group. What is your religion? it says on the form, and the terrorist asks the same question. Protestant and Catholic in Ulster, Hindu and Sikh in the Punjab ... In this sense religion cannot be quite separated from politics or indeed from racism.'[4]

I realized I had seen 'religion' too much through Western eyes. Gombrich goes on to say that, in defining a religion:

> The first answer which occurs to someone from a Christian background is likely to be that religion is a matter of belief, particularly of belief in God. But half the world does not think in these terms. For them, religion is first and foremost what you do, not what you think.[5]

Now, I welcome maximum freedom for all faith communities in Britain within the context of British law and universal moral law. And British law continues to adapt itself. Many changes have taken place in my lifetime. People can take the oath in court on any of the world scriptures. Most school meals offer a vegetarian option. Firms allow workers time to observe holy days, including Good Friday. There are Jewish and Muslim as well as Christian faith schools.

I think there should be further accommodation of Muslim concerns. For example, as you know, a marriage in church is both a religious and a legal occasion. If a couple gets married in a mosque, a civil marriage at the registry office is also required. Provided that the British law that marriage is intended to be lifelong and monogamous is affirmed, I see no reason why both the religious and the civil marriage should not be held in a mosque.

There will, of course, be points of tension. How far should people to able to opt out from the law of the land on the grounds of conscience? Less than a hundred years ago, conscientious objectors against war were imprisoned. Doctors can refuse to take part in abortions. Sikhs on motorcycles do not have to wear crash helmets. Should Catholic Adoption Agencies be required to treat gay couples like married couples? My instinctive answer would be 'no'. But what if we changed the sentence to 'should they be required to treat black couples like white couples'?

My sadness is that, instead of trying to find compromises that respect the conscience and convictions of others – even when we do not agree with them – we often tend not to deal with the actual issue but to turn it into a battle about identity. In contrast, let me mention what happened when the TV programme *Songs of Praise* was filmed at the West London Synagogue. A choir from one of the black churches was asked to take part. Now, as you know, men cover their heads in a synagogue, but for the choir this would be to contravene the teaching of the New Testament, and they said they could not take part. The Rabbi suggested that they sat in a gallery, and the TV cameramen agreed not to film the top of their heads – so that Jewish viewers would not be offended.

You will think I am avoiding the Veil. Let me go back to my three topics.

In terms of xenophobia, I think we have to do all we can to overcome prejudice and ignorance in the host community – which is a large part of the work of interfaith organisations. Above all we need to encourage people of different faiths to meet. Should the minority community make concessions? After the 7/7 London bombings, the distinguished Muslim leader Dr Zaki Badawi, fearing possible reprisals against Muslims, suggested that Muslim women should not wear the veil if to do so was likely to put them in danger of hostility or attack. Some Muslim women reacted angrily to his suggestion. If a person feels their identity to be threatened it often makes them more defensive and determined to affirm their beliefs and practices.

In terms of human rights, there is clearly a public feeling that the veil, and even more the *burqa*, is a sign that women are treated as 'second class' in Muslim society, and this, of course, offends feminists. The South African Muslim Farid Esack said that when he visited Uzbekistan in 1988 – when it was still part of the Soviet Union – his guide said to him, 'You will be delighted to know how alive Islam is; you will not see a single woman on our streets.'

For many Muslim women, wearing the veil is, I gather, a rejection of the sexual promiscuity of British society, something of which many Christians are equally critical. Hudda Khattub, who wrote the *Muslim Woman's Handbook*, said, 'Muslims don't keep shifting their goalposts. Christianity changes, like the way some people have said pre-marital sex is OK if it's with person you are going to marry. It seems so wishy-washy. Islam was constant about sex and about praying five times a day.' A Muslim man, who has returned to the practice of his faith, said his whole attitude to women had changed. 'When I meet a Muslim woman nowadays with full *hijab*, covered up, I can talk to her, really communicate – it's no longer about sex.' Other Muslims say they have 'equality of status', whereas Western women's equality seems to be about imitating men.

In terms of living in a plural society, practising Christians are also a minority. Indeed, society is made up of numerous minorities. As we get to know each other better and communicate more, we can learn to value our differences and to see them as an enrichment rather than as a problem. If we are too defensive, we build up barriers in society; the more open and welcoming we are, the less tension there will be.

There is growing awareness of the importance of interfaith understanding and cooperation. Very recently the Queen accepted an award for her contribution to interfaith cooperation, which she has often highlighted in her Christmas messages. In Britain the number of local interfaith groups has nearly doubled since the year 2000. The number of international interfaith conferences has also increased rapidly. Very recently, religious leaders from Uzbekistan – Muslim, Russian Orthodox and Jewish – visited this country and spoke about the good interreligious relations that exist there, partly because Soviet oppression has forced them to support each other. The head of theological training in Morocco has said that the study of other religions is now being introduced at all levels of his curriculum.

We need to know more about how much our cultural and intellectual traditions owe to each other and to the wisdom of the East, to hear in them the word of God.

The most fruitful approach however, is often not to focus on theology, but to concentrate on issues that are of common concern, such as medical ethics. This helps to involve a wide range of people who may be hesitant to talk about their religion but keen to discuss, say, problems of communities

In conclusion, there is a great responsibility on those of us engaged in interfaith work to help communities understand each other – especially those who practise a faith but accept second-hand teachings. Interfaith is always a call to faith communities for internal reform as well as better interfaith relations. We need also to commend the shared moral values that derive from our belief in God. Rather than striving for special exemptions for our faith group, we should together seek by democratic means to ensure that the laws of the country reflect the universal values to be found in the teaching of our respective faiths.

Chapter 2

Reflections on Sartorial Injunctions in Islam

Theodore Gabriel

The question of the *hijab* is a hotly debated issue in modern times, especially in the West. Most of the debate, in the media, by politicians and by the general public, is not well informed, does not fully consider all aspects of the issue and does not examine what the religion of Islam says about the dress of men and women.

There are also injunctions in the faith regarding the dress of men. Men, like women, should cover their *awrah*, the private parts (24:30). The *awrah* in this case refers to the area between the navel and the knees. There is also an injunction that the dress should not be tight-fitting and reveal the shape of the *awrah*. The dress should not be made of very thin material. Then there is the command that the dress should be clean and without staining (74:4). White clothes are preferred, as they will show up dirt clearly and lead to the garments being cleaned. Also the *Shari'ah* declares that Muslim men's dress should be distinctive and differ from that of non-Muslims.

There are Muslim men who are veiled. The Tuareg are a prime example of this. These inhabitants of the Sahara go about veiled and are known as *Kel Tagelmust* (People of the Veil).

The command to lower the gaze, that is, not to stare at members of the opposite sex, applies equally to men as to women (24:30).

However, the issue of male dress never enters this debate about Islamic dress. Is it because the female veil, *khimar* and *jilbab* are taken to indicate that Islam oppresses women? Is this a convenient ploy to denigrate Islam? Fadwa el Guindi agrees, and states that harem, veil and polygyny are words that have come to evoke Islam and are synonymous with female weakness and oppression in the Islamic community,[6] even though they are also part of many other cultures.

In colonial times the *hijab* was taken as a symbol of cultural inferiority, and could almost justify the Western powers conquering and ruling Muslim territories so as to bring about cultural reform and liberate Muslim women oppressed by their men – forgetting how badly the women in their own home cultures were faring. Even now in the West, the *hijab* is often taken as a symbol of Muslim oppression of women, and Katherine Bullock is right to assert that this attitude is to be found among both the intelligentsia and the unlettered in Western society.[7] Sadder still, this view is also adopted by some liberal Muslim women, to whom discarding the *hijab* seems to symbolise female liberation from male oppression.

So this coalescence of Muslim dress and culture has been an effective device to belittle Islam and affirm the inferiority of Muslim culture. The language of colonialism and feminism followed the same trajectory. The alleged oppression of women in other cultures became the *raison d'être* for subjugating them and for imposing Western culture on them – this even at a time when many Western women also wore veils, and women's rights and feminist movements in the West were derided. Victorian female attire covered all parts of the body except the head and the hands. Catholic nuns still cover their hair, and women often veil their faces, for instance at funerals, and no one ever expresses any reservations about this. El Guindi points out that, in Egypt, both Muslim and Christian women wore the Habarah – a long skirt, head cover and a *burqu'* (a cloth covering the lower part of the nose and the mouth and falling to the chest).[8]

I cannot understand why there should be so much misgiving and even apprehension in the West about veiled women. How is this a threat to anybody? I would be more wary of an unveiled person who might be carrying a knife or a gun than a veiled Muslim woman going innocently about her business behind her veil. Of course it might be argued that the veil could be camouflage for a terrorist, as has sometimes happened. But these are rare abuses of the veil.

Also I cannot understand why, in nations where individual liberty and freedom are so much extolled, Muslim women should not be free to wear the garments they prefer and are comfortable with. Is it not religious discrimination, is it not undemocratic, to desire that every woman should conform to the Western notion of correct female dress that consists of skimpy clothes exposing much of their flesh? I agree with Katherine Bullock when she points out that it is a funny kind of equality when we expect male business executives to wear full-length trousers and long-sleeved shirts and jackets, but their female counterparts to be clad in short skirts and low-cut tops.[9]

Do not such attitudes reveal a deep-seated hostility against and fear of Islam, rather than a desire for uniformity, conformity or cultural integration? We usually like diversity, and the matter of dress is no exception. It is only in the horror world of science fiction movies that everyone is dressed alike.

The Qur'an enjoins modesty in the matter of dress. 'Bedizen not yourselves with the bedizance of the time of ignorance', it says (33:33). So modesty in dress is one of Islam's and the Prophet's reforms in the time of *Jahiliyya*. The whole idea is to prevent immodest thoughts from entering one's mind when seeing a person of the opposite sex. It echoes Jesus's injunction that it is better to pluck out your eye than to enter eternal fire with both eyes (Matthew 5:29). Prevention is better than cure. This seems to many to be a very hard teaching, but to a believer it is a serious matter. So the *hijab* and Khalwat[10] and such regulations are part of the salvific process in Islam. Perhaps it could be argued that it is instinctive and natural in a woman to display her adornments, both natural and otherwise. Is this ingrained in our biological evolution? However, we are also endowed with intelligence and senses of morality and ethics to counter our purely natural instincts. This is what distinguishes human beings from animals. The Prophet is said to have stated that people who display their charms wantonly will not even get a smell of paradise.[11]

Motivation

Most non-Muslims in the West presume that the *hijab*, or *khimar*, *niqab* or *jilbab*, has been forced on Muslim women by their men. They do not attempt to examine the motivations of the women themselves for wearing it. These can be many.

First of all, the veil can be a symbol of a Muslim woman's identity. This is particularly true in non-Muslim environments such as the West, when Muslim women (and men) might feel a need to reinforce their religious identity with scripturally ordained apparel. Moreover, just as Muslim men are enjoined in Islamic law to be distinct from non-Muslims in dress, Muslim women also desire to look different and wearing the *hijab* can achieve this distinctiveness. The Sikhs have their turban, Hindu women have their *bindi*, Christian women might wear a crucifix. Why the furore only about the *hijab*?

It is also to be pointed out that the Prophet stated that it is not forbidden to look at the hair and hands of non-Muslim women.[12] This seems to imply that the veiling of Muslim women is not simply a matter of practical necessity or a matter of gender, but has a significance related to their faith and religious identity.

It can be a symbol of piety. Women who wear the *hijab* are often extremely committed to their faith. They may feel that they are obeying God's words explicitly and therefore acquiring merit towards their salvation. They may consider the *hijab* to be a symbol of their moral status. Who are we to criticise such feelings? The Qur'an seems to indicate that the first man and woman, Adam and Havva, were clothed with garments sent down from heaven and did not at all see each other's *awrah* (7:26). It was only after they yielded to Satan's temptation that their private parts were revealed to each other (7:20). Katherine Bullock mentions that some women thought that wearing the veil might need some moral preparation.[13] It is almost a form of sacrament to them. Many women may think it is *fard* (an obligatory religious duty) to wear the veil. It may also enable them to work outside the home without any concerns that they are going against the tenets of Islam and Islamic society.

So it was not the Prophet or Islam who introduced veiling. Scholars aver that the practice of female veiling existed in Mesopotamia and the Mediterranean region long before the advent of Islam.[14] In pre-Christian Greek society, free women were secluded so that they would not be seen by men who were not close relatives.[15] Some women were so modest that they would not allow themselves to be seen even by relatives.

The veil could also be a symbol of class hierarchy. I was struck by this when I lived in the Lakshadweep Islands, a Muslim territory of India. There, most of the women just wore a loose head-covering called the *tattam* and were clad in full-sleeved shirts and sarongs. The veiling was therefore very light. But there were some groups in the islands, especially those who were called Pattanis, probably of North Indian origin and speaking Urdu instead of the local dialect, whose women were completely covered from head to toe. They were from a higher economic and social class and their women rarely came out of their houses. El Guindi remarks on the fact that, in Assyria (modern Iraq), there was prohibition against slave girls being veiled.[16] Moreover, women of noble birth were obliged to be veiled; even the servant girls who accompanied them had to be veiled, but only by virtue of being their escorts. McLeod suggests that, in Egypt, the *hijab* might be a device of the middle classes by which to differentiate themselves from lower classes.[17]

There is also be the possibility that the *hijab* could be decorative and could be produced in different styles and with differing ornamental designs to augment its attractiveness, just as with any other female garment, and its use thus falls within the feminine penchant for enhancing their attractiveness. Of course, this approach might not conform to the Prophetic injunction to wear simple dress and hide their *zeena* (adornments). Of course, in such a case, wearing the *hijab* might not be solely a social invention, but practised in combination with some the other factors mentioned above, including those of religiosity.

The *hijab* might be prompted by security concerns. The wearing of the *hijab*, as I have already discussed, is to avoid the contingency of lustful thoughts or liaisons and even of *zina* (fornication). In addition, some women have remarked that being partially incognito in this way gives them a feeling of security. It may gain them respect from men, and the anonymity might confer less chance of undesirable attention from men of loose character, such as wolf-whistling or unsavoury and unwanted remarks. Fedwa Malti Douglas cites the instance of a Muslim woman who commented that a male glance felt as if a scorpion had stung her, testifying to its possible intensity and how violent a mere look could be.[18] So the *hijab* may enable women to move about more freely in society, avoiding the attention of aggressive males, and maintaining their privacy even in public space.

The word *hijab* might indicate something that protects. It is in this sense that it is used in anatomy: for example the term *hijab al-jawf* translates as *hijab* of the stomach (i.e. the diaphragm). Many who wear the *hijab* might consider it protection of their privacy and their dignity.

The *hijab* might be used as a form of political protest, though this may not apply to the Western context. It could very well be a reaction to the Westernisation of Arab societies, to the failure of Arab governments to counter Israeli high-handedness, even to discrimination against women in the wider society, a circumstance that is somewhat paradoxical. In Turkey, as Malti Douglas points out, it has been adopted by highly public women, such as film stars, participating in the transnational discourse on women and veiling.[19] The *chador* had become a powerful symbol of opposition to the Shah of Iran by the Fedayeen and the Mujahideen. It implied anti-imperialism, anti-moral decadence, anti-corruption and opposition in general to the Shah's regime and his programme of Westernization.

The True Meaning

Now we will look into the true meaning of *hijab*. The word *hijab* does not really mean a veil. *hijab* means a curtain, and *hajaba*, the related verb, means to hide. Fatima Mernissi suggests that the space behind a *hijab* is forbidden space. The Qur'an specifically instructs disciples of the Prophet to speak to the Prophet's wives from behind a curtain. The incidence of the verse of the *hijab* is related to the marriage of the Prophet to Zainab bint Jahsh. Three impolite guests, instead of leaving after the wedding meal, lingered on, and the Prophet became increasingly annoyed. Then the Prophet drew a *sitr* (curtain) between himself and his disciple Anas, who came to announce the departure of these vexful guests, at the same time reciting the following ayah:

O you who believe, do not enter the prophet's homes unless you are given permission to eat, nor shall you force such an invitation in any manner. If you are invited, you may enter. When you finish eating, you shall leave; do not engage him in lengthy conversations. This used to hurt the prophet, and he was too shy to tell you. But God does not shy away from the truth. If you have to ask his wives for something, ask them from behind a barrier. This is purer for your hearts and their hearts. You are not to hurt the messenger of God. You shall not marry his wives after him, for this would be a gross offence in the sight of God (33:53).

So the function of the apparel is to create a forbidden space, presumably a sacred space, between lascivious gaze and people of the opposite sex. It is significant that the context for this revelation indicates that the reason for the *hijab* is respect, not oppression or coercion. So why do some individuals presume that the *hijab* symbolises the oppression of women? It is to be remembered that the Qur'anic verse refers to the wives of the Prophet. They were often called *Umm al Muslimeen* (Mother of the Believers). The wearing of the veil would thus indicate that all Muslim women to some extent share the great honour that the wives of the Prophet were accorded. Thus the wearing of the veil would be a mark of respectability and dignity, not of oppression, enslavement nor restriction of freedom. We must remember that slaves were specifically forbidden to wear the veil. Indeed the idea of the *hijab* and *sitr* was also applied to some Caliphs, who sat behind a curtain or veil to escape the gaze of the members of their court.[20] So the space behind their *hijab* had some thing of sanctity and regality about it too.

Fatima Mernissi points out that the *hijab* has three dimensions – visual, spatial and ethical. The problem is that most people, when they see a veiled woman, are aware only of the visual. They remark upon the looks of the woman, or rather the inability to see her looks, but the ideas related to space and the ethics behind wearing the veil are mostly overlooked. If they would consider these other two dimensions they would understand better the rationale for wearing the veil – that the space behind the *hijab* has a special dignity or even sanctity, and that there are ethical aspects to a woman's decision to wear it.

So the *hijab* descended in order to separate public space and the sanctified presence of the Prophet and his wives. In other contexts the Qur'an has used the term to denote separation of the saved from the damned on the Day of Judgement (7:46) and protection for the elite from the awesome brilliance of the divine countenance that could burn them up (42:51). So basically the *hijab* indicates the separation of the sacred from the profane, rather than merely a scrap of cloth used by men to oppress women. Some early Christian missionaries used to think of Muslim women as being 'buried alive behind the veil,'[21] a perspective that is not entirely absent in the West nowadays. This type of discourse on the veil is detrimental to the real liberation of women, liberation from inequality in wages, lack of freedom to study and enter the professions, or to participate in public offices, as it distracts and distorts the facts, hiding them behind a façade of criticism of Islamic practices rather than looking at women's rights in society as a whole.

It is also a fallacy to consider that Islam is a killjoy kind of religion. When some complained to the Prophet that their husbands shunned meat and perfume and distanced themselves from their wives, the Prophet went to the pulpit and cried out: 'What should I do with my friends who shun meat, perfume and women? I myself eat meat, smell perfume and receive pleasure from my wives.'[22] It is apparent that such pleasures are not forbidden within the boundaries of moral behaviour. It is certain that the Prophet did not advocate celibacy or extreme asceticism. When a group of faithful followers asked him permission to castrate themselves, he dissuaded them, saying that such an act is forbidden in Islam.[23] It is reported that he said '*La rahbanniya fi Islam*' (There is no monkery in Islam). He enjoined his followers to marry and enjoy a family life. Islam comes out as a caring religion fully cognisant of human needs. So the intention of the veil is not to prevent sexual relations but to discourage adultery and promiscuity, and to confine sexual relations within the boundaries of matrimony, thus avoiding society's descent into sin and *fitna* (chaos).

Of course there are certain contexts in which wearing the *niqab* might be counter-productive. There are situations in which seeing a woman's face is a necessity for communication. Teaching children is one such context. A child cannot communicate or learn from a teacher who is fully veiled. Of course, children are in a sense *mahram* to the teacher and anyway the teacher acts in a quasi-parental role in the school. Thus this does not contravene the regulations of Islamic veiling. A female teacher can wear the *hijab* and show her face and hands in a school. A hospital or doctor's surgery is a similar situation in which a *niqab* might not be appropriate. Seeing a face can be very reassuring in such circumstances. But to insist that a woman can never wear the face veil is a denial of individual liberty.

The wider concept of privacy is enshrined in the Qur'an in the passage where God commands believers to seek permission before entering a house (24:58–60). This passage also indicates that a woman has two garments, an outer one and an inner one. By wearing the *hijab* she is actually extending her privacy beyond the confines of the house and into public space. This is the privilege of women who desire such privacy, and who are we to question this? Here we have ethical boundaries that govern how men and women interact, and the *hijab* ensures that such boundaries are observed and decent behaviour ensues when the two sexes meet. It should not descend to unlimited freedom and trespassing on morally and ethically sanctioned boundaries. This is the essence of the sartorial injunctions in Islam.

It can be argued that such privacy and boundaries can be achieved without becoming a *muhajabba*, but this is not possible for all individuals. The veil of the heart is for the exceptional. Moreover, the *hijab* is worn for the sake of men, not women. This cannot be overlooked in any discourse of the veil.

Chapter 3

Unveiling Orientialism in Reverse

Alison Scott-Baumann

Why does the *hijab* arouse such passion? The woman and her hair, her neck, her earlobes, all have become a battleground between cultures, where both sides assert their identity by showing how different they are from each other, demonstrate weaknesses and blame them on the woman too. I will consider these issues as a woman philosopher, with some reference to my empirical research. It seems to be a characteristic of humans that we think in terms of opposites, or pairs, and we often choose to see them as mutually exclusive. Those who insist upon creating binary systems to explain the world have had to accept that communism and capitalism no longer provide a useful polarisation, and they have selected the pairing of Islam versus the West. The *hijab* has become one of the symbols of this polarisation that I wish to contextualise within the idea of Orientalism in reverse, as developed by Achcar. He asserts that there is a trend in both the Muslim and the non-Muslim worlds towards the idea that Islam holds the key to its own salvation, and that only truly Islamic solutions to life's problems will be both authentic and effective. I will argue that this is one, although not the only, motivator for the passion that surrounds the *hijab*, from both the side of the Western secularist and that of the devout Muslim. In this context I pay less attention to the political aspects of Achcar's exposure of Orientalism in reverse, and focus more on Western attitudes towards the female as object. Finally I will suggest a third way, as recommended by Said himself, the critic of Orientalism, in his plea that we should look towards a different interpretation of the relationship between knowledge and power: he believed we should ask how we can study other cultures and peoples from a non-repressive and non-manipulative perspective.[24]

In order to consider how to develop such a perspective I will also use my research on the French hermeneutical philosopher Paul Ricoeur (1912–2005) because of his writing on the hermeneutics of suspicion and our responsibility to be suspicious of our own motives as well as those of others. The work of Ricoeur provides a clear way of looking at this debate because he analyses humanity by seeking similarities and he recommends a faith-based attempt at effective conciliatory social action. In the second half of his essay, 'Freedom in the Light of Hope', he discusses Immanuel Kant, one of the greatest European philosophers. Ricoeur shows us that Kant sowed the seeds for the hermeneutics of suspicion in three significant ways: in terms of doubt about the self, the limits of reason and the doubts about institutional religion. Ricoeur was also influenced strongly by Hegel, Husserl, Freud, Nietzsche and Marx. Ricoeur ascribed to Marx, Nietzsche and Freud an emphasis on a pervasive suspicion, telling us that we hide our true desires (for sex, power and money respectively) behind false consciousness, and should endeavour to be more open with others and ourselves. Ricoeur believed this to be an unduly pessimistic distortion of human life, but welcomed the stimulus provided by these three masters of suspicion as their ideas helped him to propose a more honest way of living together in a complex, multinational world. He also believed that some veiling of the truth might be necessary, in order that life still holds some mystery.

For Ricoeur, the hermeneutics of suspicion is invaluable as it leads to the destruction of old beliefs and old illusions and it must then lead to a hermeneutics of recovery. Before applying his approach, it is necessary to analyse the dominant discourse about the *hijab*, which consists mostly of strident opinions expressed by those who may have an exclusively secularist agenda and who do not talk to British Muslims. Every word in this debate has special meaning: the term 'secularist' alone could take up a whole chapter – in this context it is often used in contrast with faith. In his essay 'Urbanization and Secularization', Ricoeur describes it as having two main characteristics: the transfer of power from the churchman to the civil servant, and the 'erasing of the distinction between the spheres of the sacred and the profane'.[25] Current debate includes rhetoric in the media, in policy-making circles and among intellectuals, analysing the discourse around faith, secularism, democracy and freedom of choice. We need to take personal responsibility for this process, which is often blamed on journalists. Ricoeur argued that suspicion is vital, but that it must be proportionate to the situation. He also argued for attestation, which will form part of my concluding argument. If we do not speak for ourselves and also fail to speak with others, there is a chance that we may retreat into Orientalism or Orientalism in reverse, or even into the comforting strong place of sceptical doubt, the scepticism which Cavell describes as the overbearing conviction that we know more than other people do about themselves and that we are therefore able to stand back and judge.[26]

The Muslim woman and her *hijab* demonstrate very clearly the power of this sceptical doubt, as I will show. The *hijabbed* Muslimah is seen by different people as symbolising a range of different ideas. I wish to contextualise how these ideas often represent themselves as conflicting polarities involving freedom and oppression, and between knowledge and power. It will be necessary to set the scene briefly for Britain, as this is my main area of activity.

The Context

The *hijab* as a head covering is reasonably well tolerated, if not accepted, in daily British life. Britain provides a more *hijab*-friendly environment than many European countries, such as France, where the *hijab* is censured as a sign of religious identity and forbidden in schools and within the civil service. However, in Britain there are pressures; these conflicting ideas of freedom and oppression form part of the rhetoric about Muslims in the media at a time when the modern state is striving for homogeneity. Jackson and O'Grady perceive this in the apparent hardening of attitudes against Muslims in some government pronouncements about multiculturalism, such as that of Ruth Kelly in 2006, leading, as they see it, to more strident expressions of racism in the media. Indeed, civil society in Britain is currently characterised by pervasive and divisive media coverage of Islam as the alien 'other', and by cultural traditions living side by side but never meeting.[27] This was exacerbated by the 2001 riots in Blackburn and elsewhere, the catastrophe of 9/11, and the horror of the 7 July bombings in London in 2005.

Half a million of the approximately two million Muslims in Britain are of school age. This is a young and, relatively speaking, very religious group; this applies to both their faith observance and their identity politics (Mukadam and Scott-Baumann 2010).

Orientalism

Several attempts have been made by the UK government to resolve what they see as this inability within Muslim communities to cope in modern society, and the *hijab* is taken to indicate an unwillingness to engage with secular life. The government has had some impact but risks the increase of friction between policy implementation and various Muslim communities, although many of the Muslim women we interviewed feel this is one of the best countries for Muslims to live in.[28] The government established a policy on social cohesion, and the London bombings of 7 July 2005 led to the establishment of a Muslim working party called Working Together to Prevent Extremism. In 2006 Bill Rammell, Minister for Higher Education at the Department for Education and Science set up a working party to look at 'Islam in Higher Education', chaired by Dr Siddiqui. Siddiqui made it clear that he would be prepared to investigate two areas: the teaching of Islam in universities and the pastoral support provided for Muslims on campus. His recommendations included the need to update the teaching of Islam, make it more relevant to the diversity within British Islam, and ensure that Islamic experts with theological as well as secular understanding teach Islam. He also recommended the appointment of Muslim prison chaplains. Working parties have been created to look at such issues, including the establishment of the Mosques and Imams National Advisory Board (MINAB) and the National Muslim Women's Advisory Groups (NMWAGs).[29] The Government has also commissioned independent research such as the Muslim Faith Leader Training Review, which I co-chaired with Dr Mohamed Mukadam (2008–2010).

Counter-terrorism policies are dominant in current official attitudes, even when those attitudes are apparently based upon the desire for social justice and equity within the UK for all communities. In this context, competing cultural positions depict the *hijab* as a sign that has become a double symbol, symbolising on the one hand veiling as a way of guarding *against* evil (guarding against the arousal of an impregnating male?), and on the other hand veiling *as* evil itself (denying the male his right to arousal?). In *The Symbolism of Evil*, Ricoeur explores how an object or a phenomenon in our lives can become a symbol that gives rise to thought. Of course, he asks us to consider how an object becomes a symbol in the first place; I will consider that briefly here.[30]

Public rhetoric about the *hijab* and terror conveys to me that feeling of a closed debate, one that can also be clarified by Ricoeur's work on ideology and utopia … he shows us that ideology cannot be argued with as it permits no possibility for discussion or challenge; using Marx's concept of ideology as a 'total structure of the mind',[31] almost everyone I know (who is not a Muslim) tells me that women who cover up are oppressed, and the implication is that they are oppressed by men who threaten the free choice of the woman to be uncovered. I ask them why women who wear clothing that is very revealing are not also oppressed? Often I am pitied for my naivety when I ask such questions. Western culture presents a strange equation between showing the body and showing that one is free, perhaps from rape; but this challenges the concept of freedom. The woman herself, whether she is *hijabbed* or not, may benefit from a healthy suspicion about what freedom is or can ever hope to be.

How does Orientalism fit in here? Edward Said's 1978 book *Orientalism* shows the tendency among Western observers to see the exotic (literally and metaphorically) in the Muslim world. From this comes the associated tendency to perceive Islam as so different as to be incommensurate with one's own culture. Said's ideas have been contested and indeed can be demonstrated to be stereotypes in their own right. Despite its weaknesses, Said's thesis leads us to an interesting discussion of the position that 'only we can understand us'. While he denies that it is tenable to argue that only *we* (whoever we are) can understand *ourselves*, it clearly forms a key role in Said's argument, and must be true to a certain extent.

Orientalism in Reverse From an 'Orientalist' Perspective

Gilbert Achcar takes Said's idea of Orientalism and critically analyses its reversal: that Islam sees itself alone as containing the power to understand itself. Through this reversal, Islam is seen as arguing that only Muslims can resolve their own problems. Islamism, therefore, is the only possible agent of modernisation, and the religion of Islam is the essential language and culture of Muslim peoples. Islamism can be seen variously as a form of purism, as a form of religious authenticity, as a flight from Western modernisation or a consistent development of a new future for Islam; and in its various permutations I believe it helps us to understand the *hijab* debate. In particular Achcar charts the adoption of Orientalism in reverse by various French intellectuals, who then abandon it. He is critical of both the adoption and the abandonment of Orientalism in reverse, preferring to hope for a more nuanced approach. Just to complicate matters, there is a version of Orientalism in reverse as proposed by the Muslim world and a different one as proposed by the world of those who are not Muslim. I will take the second one first: Orientalism in reverse, as proposed by the 'Western' world. Exaggerated representations of Muslims are rooted in the belief that Muslims seek solutions that are alien to 'us'. This has the added advantage, of course, of giving the illusion that 'we' are identifiable as similar to each other and therefore able to show solidarity, in being unified against the alien Other, the exotic oriental. Reverse Orientalism forms part of the British dilemma, because non-Muslims are encouraged to perceive only those aspects of UK Muslim life to which they can attribute the embodiment of extreme versions of Islam, such as honour killings and terrorist acts. What needs to be acknowledged is that most Muslims reject these acts, as do most of those who are not Muslim. However, what we actually focus on is the determination to see Muslim solutions to problems as alien, and even the problem itself is seen as alien and therefore not a problem: Muslims' concerns over British foreign policy are often dismissed as overreaction, Muslims' concerns about their women are generalised, seen as totally inappropriate and therefore not a response to a legitimate problem.

In order to see whether the idea of Orientalism in reverse is useful for understanding the *hijab*, we need to explore how Westerners interpret the ways in which Muslims think about their women. This may show us, as Yegenoglu puts it, 'the cultural representation of the West *to itself* by way of a detour through the other'. The detour can be made via the exotic 'other', and may lead to a feeling of superiority. Orientalist thinking is predicated upon asymmetries of power, whereas Ricoeur's approach to self-understanding depends upon seeing how similar one is to the other, not how different. The covering of the head, *hijab*, and the covering of the face, niqab, are seen by many as demonstrations of oppression; the woman waits submissively for permission to have some agency granted by her males. May she go out? May she communicate with others? May she even accept the 'veiling' of her voice in that she will decide not to communicate with men outside her family and marriage circle? We know from the prevalent media discourse that the *hijab* is perceived in Western Europe as a symbol of oppression, in support of which there are news stories about horrific honour killings and forced marriages. We whose heads are uncovered rejoice in our freedom of choice and emancipated womanhood when we see such oppression, without considering that we may also experience oppression of a different kind. Hirji shows us how the idea of the oppressed exotic woman may even feed the fantasy of the white colonial male that he is needed to rescue the Muslim woman from this oppression, as recently in Afghanistan. With regard to Afghanistan, this fantasy disregards the complex historical reasons for the position of Afghan women in their society, which includes incursions over the centuries by foreign powers. In their analysis of Orientalism in films, Shohat and Stam apply this to the colonial mind and its conquered lands: 'The Western imagery metaphorically rendered the colonialised land as female to be saved from her environmental disaster.' This distorted understanding of ours is not good enough to persuade the thoughtful person that the *hijab* is truly a sign of oppression. However, it is good enough for many Europeans. I believe we need to understand how this came to have such a dominant position in the modern psyche; the *hijab* seems to me to be a symbol for many things, depending on who you are.

Being Over-suspicious, Creating Pre-terrorist Ideas

From the secular viewpoint of an Orientalist approach, theologically driven behaviour in a secular society almost seems to be thought of as suspicious in its own right. Such religious behaviour can then seem conducive to pre-terrorist activity, by which I mean activity that indicates sympathy with terrorism. In this way the 'precogs', young people with special powers in the film 'Minority Report', identify a 'not-yet-thought-about' crime before it has taken place. The police in this science-fiction film are able to use information from the precogs to track down the person who *will have* the desire to murder, and prevent them from executing the crime. This is a situation where thought can be evil: instead of being presumed innocent until proven guilty, the precogs' society shows us the dangers of humans as thinking, knowing and acting beings.

Many philosophical issues arise here, such as whether we have free will, and whether we can be held responsible for our thoughts. Toscano draws our attention to a famous case in France, known as the Tarnac Nine, in which young activists were labelled by the state as terrorists, even though their actions were acts of civil disruption and fell far short of legal definitions of terrorism. We know also that the police stop and search procedure has been amended in the fear of terrorist attacks, so that people can be stopped and searched even without reasonable suspicion.[32] I wish to consider whether a girl dressed in black, wearing a *hijab*, seems to arouse fears of pre-terrorist activity, similar to the identification of evil intent before the action is committed. Guilt by association would thus be attributed because of a dress code, and generalised to a group of people who dress similarly. We note this from our research; a Muslim prison chaplain told us about her – otherwise good – training programme:

Bi-monthly meetings for counter-terrorism, it's quite a knock on your self-esteem. Also they ask me, tell us please, do the women prisoners say they are happy when British soldiers die in Iraq or Afghanistan? I mean, what can I say? Why would they?[33]

Of course there is potential for friction, given certain aspects of British foreign policy, yet such assumptions create concern about the way in which many non-Muslims perceive Muslims. Achcar provides one way of understanding this apparent paradox: his work on Orientalism in reverse explains the belief that Muslims develop Islamic solutions to problems. By Orientalist definitions, the solutions that Muslims choose are incomprehensible to non-Muslims: in this case the celebration of modesty, the principle of the *hijab*. Westerners can deny the importance of modesty and then construe such solutions as alien. By a strange form of argument, it then seems acceptable to look at extreme and alien behaviours (e.g. suicide bombing, honour killings and forced marriages) and decide that they fit the Orientalism-in-reverse argument (even though other groups of people who are not Muslim, e.g. the Tamil Tigers, use suicide bombing). Then we can activate suspicion, thinking like the precogs, believing that we know more than most people do (which is true of the precogs in their science-fiction world) and attributing these acts *potentially* to all Muslims. Using the same way of thinking, it can be argued that Muslim clothing reflects the behaviour of those who hold beliefs that are alien to 'the West' and, therefore, that this clothing must signify alien cultural habits.

Using clothing to symbolise values is not unusual, and we probably accept that we think in ways that reflect and support what we want to believe. Kant, with his universality, showed that our viewpoint and our perceptions are determined by the way we are, what we already know. Ricoeur admired Kant's insight into the way we think, and saw how dangerous it can be: he cautioned us to be suspicious about the Kantian sequence, thinking, knowing and acting; thinking and knowing have the potential to be possessive, territorial and potentially avaricious acts that can allow us to possess an image of the world so that we perceive it as we wish to see it. Ricoeur took it even further by emphasising the potency of knowing, our capacity to think we know more than other people do, and to be suspicious in certain circumstances, even when we have no evidence. Ricoeur wished to show that this is not inevitable, although I argue that it may seem so with a concept such as pre-terrorist activity. Ricoeur argued that we only understand life in dualisms, because each of us is destined to be out of step with ourselves, out of step with the person we want to be and the one we think we are; out of step with what we want to achieve and what we can realistically attain. It is in language that we can find the key to meaning and understand ourselves better, to deal with these discrepancies and also, arguably, deceive ourselves. I will argue that the Orientalist *hijab* story (about the *hijab* being an instrument of oppression that may even represent the desire to oppress 'us' with terrorist acts) has no substance in reality, only in language. I wish also to argue that the use of language takes on its own life and becomes part of the ideology of the lives we live; as Ricoeur argues, ideology has no opening for debate. Ricoeur explored in the 1950s the idea that our understanding of evil is a special case, because we find it difficult to conceptualise evil and we have to use images and myths to represent evil. Oppression by one human of another is an example of evil, and I suggest that the *hijab* is used as a symbol to represent a form of evil.[34]

The Symbol Gives Rise to Thought: Signifier, Signified and Evil

The Symbolism of Evil (1967) describes Ricoeur's belief that we cannot represent evil to ourselves, because it is so complex and so ambiguous, so we have to develop a shorthand, symbolic representation. The method used in *The Symbolism of Evil* involves immersion in the full richness of language and culture in order to analyse a hermeneutics of evil, as we represent it to ourselves in myth, symbol and sign. In Christianity evil pre-dates us (as we see with the serpent, the evil 'other' that was there before Adam and Eve). Evil also cannot be grasped in its essence but only by representation; defilement, sin and guilt are the three ideas, and they occur in verbal imagery such as the stain, the fall and blinding respectively: 'Life is a symbol, an image, before being experienced and lived', and the work now is to decipher the wrongdoing wrapped up in the symbol.[35] In myth and religious stories, there are certain strong images that become symbolic: stain becomes the representation of evil because the stain itself represents dirt and defilement. Another example is the Biblical fall: falling down represents falling into sin, because falling is a deviation from the straight pathway that avoids temptation. The danger is that we then use the shorthand without thinking seriously about the original idea. Ricoeur also shows us how the linguistic analysis that Ferdinand de Saussure developed can help us to understand how we come to certain conclusions. Saussure, great linguist and one of the first to develop systematic analysis of language and meaning, analysed language through the use of the signifier, the signified and the referent. The signifier is the term used and recognised (*hijab*), the signified is the meaning of the term (agent of oppression) and the referent is the object (material used by Muslim women to cover their head). In this way the *hijab* has been adopted by Western press and media as a symbol for evil, and Ricoeur warns us of the dangers of letting the signifier and the signified become so interlocked that they have no need of a referent; in other words they do not need to check out in reality their resemblance to the phenomenon that they originally represented.

The symbol gives rise to thought, Ricoeur argues. This raises the deeper question about why the symbol is already one of evil: I need to look further back, to challenge the very idea that a head covering is evil; how did we reach this way of thinking? There must be a range of different factors; one will not be enough, but it is likely that several factors react with each other to create the idea that the *hijab* is bad. One factor is likely to be the preoccupation with terrorism and the way in which the European public seem to be encouraged to see terrorism as synonymous with Islam. Such a view can be reflected in, for example, the research conducted by Insted described earlier in a note. There are exceptions such as Bunting, whose writing takes a more positive approach.[36]

These two polarities, faith versus secularism and Islam versus the West, create a hermeneutics of suspicion, which is 'an integral part of an appropriation of meaning,' the '"deconstruction" of prejudices that prevent the world of the text from being allowed to be'; in other words, suspicion functions as a challenge to our beliefs. However, we become stuck in ignorant prejudice if we accept the information that strengthens our suspicions, instead of challenging our suspicions to ensure that we are being fair and accurate.

Orientalism in Reverse From an Imagined Muslim Perspective

Clearly, as a non-Muslim I can only imagine how to discuss this, and hope to be challenged if I get it wrong: there are many different ways of being a woman, and a Muslim. I hope to avoid the Orientalist perspective, and the reverse one too! Not all Muslim women wear the *hijab*. For those who wear it, the *hijab* provides a practical manifestation of concealment as modesty, and modesty in the form of the *hijab* principle; the veiling of the head and neck, which can extend to veiling the body such that one is modest. The interpretation of modesty may also cause one to avoid seeking out the company of men. It is possible to provide a protected environment, such as we attempted between 1999 and 2002, providing teacher training for Muslim women who sought a Muslim-friendly environment in which to train (Scott-Baumann and Khan Cheema 2001, Scott-Baumann 2003a). These trainee teachers could not veil the voice, as they were required to do a placement in a mainstream school as well as a Muslim one. The *hijab* principle can also become the veiling of the voice, the desire to avoid speaking to others, as the voice is an extension of a woman's beauty. Another factor that may determine the debate about the *hijab*, therefore, surrounds the customs and practices around women's clothing and behaviour. Muslim girls and women who do not wear the *hijab* may be considered less authentic than those who do, just as girls who reveal too little when going out with friends may be considered less authentic members of a group than those whose clothing reveals more. For religious groups, the concept of authenticity is necessary, and some of our interviewees believe that, historically, Islam as expressed in the Qu'ran is fair to women, but that this fairness can become overlaid by customs and practices that may have a less desirable effect.

The main thing in Islam is that at the time of the prophet girls were well-educated. But more cultural issues can be seen as important, and sometimes people mix religion and culture and confuse them with each other.[37]

In secular space there is an unexamined tendency among Western women to believe that authenticity is about attaining consumerist targets through being visibly fashionable and attractive, which currently means wearing less and less clothing and displaying more and more skin, or revealing curves and cleavages through tightness of clothing. It would be understandable to predict dissolute behaviour from such a dress code, which suggests that the Western woman may unwittingly appear to be a contaminant, with which contact is a risk. There is a tendency among many Muslim women to wear more and more clothing and to cover up their curves and cleavages. It is possible that each group is reacting to the other. This increasing polarisation between the majority and the minority in Britain reveals and perpetuates some sort of tension that goes beyond clothing and fashion, places British citizens at odds potentially with each other, and forces them to take up positions to do with identity, chastity, modesty and fertility. Yet they are not, on the whole, talking to each other as mothers, daughters, sisters; they are using their clothing as a symbolic presentation of their position. Look at my *hijab*, I am free to move modestly. No, look at my skin, I am free to show it to everyone. It can be argued, as Modood does, that the debate is polarised not between Christianity and Islam, as might appear to be the case, but between those who believe there is a place for religion in secular society and those who don't.[38] The urgency of dialogue is great, and we know that it happens already in some places, as demonstrated by the research of Laurence and Heath, of Holden and of Pennent.

Even though the *hijab* angers those who insist upon woman's freedom to display her body, I propose that the revealed body is a potentially dangerous way of demonstrating one's womanhood, one based on an ideal of freedom that is perpetuated by forces that we should be able to challenge as useful in their own way, but limited and limiting: fashion houses, press and media, advertising, pornography. There is a limit to how much a woman can comfortably reveal without becoming subordinate, as an individual, to her body as a sexual object. This can create over-reaction. Recently even the female face has become an issue. In Britain the niqab, the face covering that leaves only the eyes revealed, is gaining popularity among women who wish to keep themselves safe from the contamination of Western ways. Some use it only out in the street or in other situations with strange males:

> The niqab? I enjoy wearing it. I feel comfortable when I am out in the street. It must be used carefully; it is not something to be used without thought. When I am here talking to you two women friends in your room at the university I don't need it. When I am at work as a prison chaplain I can take it off when I am inside the prison and working, I take it off because I know the men there as colleagues. I believe it should not be worn with children, like when you are teaching.[39]

There are others who seek to challenge secularist ways with the niqab, and I will address this in my conclusion, with some practical suggestions.

From Suspicion to Attestation

Ricoeur proposes that we must accept absolutely that the only way to understand ourselves is through understanding others: in his masterful *Lectures on Ideology and Utopia* and in *Oneself As Another* he presents the imperative that we learn about ourselves critically through exercising suspicion of others and of ourselves, and seek to explain clearly our motives for thought and action. He invites us to bear witness, to attest to what we believe in, in order to make it clear to others and to facilitate dialogue that may resolve misunderstandings:

In conversation we have an interpretive attitude. If we speak of ideology in negative terms as distortion, then we use the tool or weapon of suspicion. If, however, we want to recognise a group's value on the basis of its self-understanding of these values, then we must welcome these values in a positive way, and this is to converse.[40]

This approach can lead to pluralist visions of integration and identity, but this will only happen if women get together to talk and to deconstruct their views about each other. I believe so-called democracies should not accuse other ways of thinking of being unclear about what they stand for; Halstead has commented on 'an even greater reluctance in the democratic liberal tradition to spell out what the shared values implied in their positions actually are'.[41]

Contractor has developed an important step towards such dialogue about shared values, by helping young Muslim women to make digital stories about themselves and showing them to girls and women who are not Muslim.[42] The change in attitude towards the *hijab* and related issues is significant in Contractor's findings. If we apply suspicion to our own ideologies (which is extremely difficult to achieve), I believe we will discover that women of all faiths and of none face difficulties about identity: the oppression that we assume is facing Muslim women may be there, and there is also oppression that I detect among young secular women. There is contradictory pressure to be modest, there is pressure to be promiscuous, to be slim, even to be thin, to cover up, to uncover, to follow the latest fashions, to refuse to reflect the fashions.

I do not believe that items of clothing should become symbols for values, and I have suggested that the *hijab* is being taken inappropriately, perhaps by both sides in this polarised debate, as a symbol of Orientalism in reverse, as a sign of protection against contamination and as a symbol of supposedly pre-terrorist sympathies. Values are not directly related to dress code; perhaps dress code is a reflection of behavioural patterns. Behaviour reflects the pressures that girls and women feel, to be a particular type of person, to gain approval, to be accepted as a woman. The biological identity of a woman is notoriously difficult to combine with her intellectual identity; being a mother and a worker is still very difficult. This is particularly interesting if we consider the high fertility and childbearing levels among many *hijab*-friendly cultures that seek to restrict male and female access to each other, and the decline in levels of fertility and childbearing among *hijab*-phobic cultures that seem to encourage unfettered male interest in the female as commodified object. We have the statistics regarding sexual health, such as the 63 per cent increase in all new diagnoses of sexually transmitted diseases between 1998 and 2007.[43] It would be naïve to attribute such increases only to better identification of disease. Alcohol consumption is known to play a role in promiscuity, and it seems reasonable to be suspicious of a culture in which alcoholism, obesity and infertility are accepted and are on the increase. Yet it seems to be difficult to face and tackle these problems; Halstead recorded a prevalent definition of democracy as a society in which 'people can do what they want unless there are good reasons for not allowing them to do so'.[44]

Why might a culture reject the behaviour of another culture, when one of them seems to be on a self-destructive mission towards not replacing its population and the other is healthy and reproducing well? We see in the media the arguments against Islam: oppression, lack of choice, and conservativism. There may be truth in that, and here is the irony: when Ricoeur invites us to find out more about ourselves by the way we are reflected in others, he hopes that we will benefit from looking, yet there is also the possibility that we transfer onto others the aspects of ourselves that we wish to disown – that we happily find them unattractive in others but we do not see them in ourselves. Consumerist cultures can surely also be considered to manifest oppression, lack of choice and conservatism.

However, this is where Ricoeur's approach becomes very potent: we need to be suspicious, doubting and challenging about our own behaviour, yet without going as far as Cavell's scepticism, which gives us overbearing confidence:

> [My] deployment of suspicion also invites us to *personalize* concepts. No longer can we pretend that laws, books, works of art and opinions based on racial stereotyping or cultural habits are impersonal representations of natural justice and beauty and nothing to do with us – Ricoeur urges us to challenge them as products of our own personal human action and therefore open to suspicion.[45]

The pro-*hijab* and anti-*hijab* ideology that surrounds us like a striped wallpaper of the mind is easy to ignore and difficult to challenge (pro, anti, pro, anti, go the stripes: we should be suspicious of this dualistic simplicity). I suggest that oppression comes in many forms and is entrenched in the human tendency to refuse to be self-critical. I have shown how Orientalism in reverse can serve to mislead people into seeing the other as the exotic alien, whether Muslim, of another faith or of no faith. Orientalism in reverse can lead to false attribution of pre-terrorist motives, as with the precogs' ability to predict evil, and it is inappropriate to use such thinking to condemn women who cover their hair. Some sort of secularism in reverse is also in play: how can I defend freedom of choice as an inalienable democratic right if it leads to generations of children being too fat, too thin, too drunk or infertile? I have presented here the polarised, dualist way of thinking that makes it difficult for women of different cultural backgrounds to trust each other enough to talk together freely, sharing problems and solutions. There are practical lifeskills at stake here; how can different cultures live together? If I may take two extreme forms: the underdressed young woman who attracts attention to her body parts is as likely to be a dysfunctional interlocutor as the young woman with her face covered by her niqab. With one we see too much to be able to concentrate on a productive conversation; with the other we see too little to be able to communicate clearly. However, I don't believe that the *hijab* is an inhibitor. The concept of the *hijab*, as modest dressing, is useful and practical. Yet if protestations continue, the *hijab* debate will continue to be a distraction that obscures the problems that should unite women in their attempts to find solutions to the great problems that face us all, whether *hijabbed* or not.

References

Achcar, G. (2008), 'Orientalism in Reverse', *Radical Philosophy* 152, 20–30.

Halstead, J. M. (1986), *The Case for Muslim Voluntary-aided Schools. Some Philosophical Reflections.* Cambridge: The Islamic Academy.

Hirji, F. (2009), 'The War for Women's Freedom: Orientalist Imaginaries of Rescue in Afghanistan', paper presented at annual meeting of the International Communication Association, New York. Available online at www.allacademic.com/met/p14796_index.html

Holden, A. (2009), *Religious Cohesion in Times of Conflict. Christian–Muslim Relations in Segregated Towns.* New York and London: Continuum Books.

Insted (2008), The Search for Common Ground: Muslims, non-Muslims and the UK Media. London: Greater London Authority.

Jackson, R. and O'Grady, K. (2007), 'Religions and Education in England: Social Plurality, Civil Religion and Religious Education', in R. Jackson et al. (eds), Pedagogy in Religion and Education in Europe. Developments, Contexts, Debates. Münster: Waxmann; pp.181–202.

Laurence, J. and Heath, A. (2008) 'Predictors of community cohesion: multi modelling of the 2005 Citizenship Survey', in Race, Cohesion and Faiths Summary No.3 Communities and local Government Publications. Available online at www.communities.gov.uk

Mukadam, M. and Scott-Baumann, A. (2010), Muslim Faith Leader Training. Independent research conducted for the Department for Communities and Local Government.

Parekh, B. (2000), Rethinking Multiculturalism: Cultural Diversity and Political Theory. Basingstoke: Macmillan.

Pennant, R. (2005), Diversity, Trust and Community Participation in England. Research, Development and Statistics Directorate (RDS), Home Office Findings. Available online at www.homeoffice.gov.uk.rds/pdfs05/r253.pdf

Ricoeur, P. (1967), The Symbolism of Evil, transl. E Buchanan. Boston: Beacon Press.

— (1974a), 'Urbanization and Secularization', in D. Stewart and J. Bien (eds), Political and Social Essays (originally published in French, 1956). Athens: Ohio University Press; pp. 176–97.

— (1974b), Freedom in the Light of Hope The Conflict of Interpretations, transl. D. Ihde. Evanston, Ill: Northwestern University Press; pp. 411–24.

— (1992), Oneself As Another, transl. K. Blamey. Chicago: Chicago University Press.

Sahin, A. (2005), 'Exploring the religious life-world and attitude toward Islam among British Muslim adolescents', in L. J. Francis, M. Robbins and J. Astley (eds), Religion, Education and Adolescence. Cardiff: University of Wales Press.

Scott-Baumann, A. (2003a), 'Teacher Education for Muslim Women: intercultural relationships, method and philosophy', Ethnicities 3(2), 243–61.

— (2003b), 'Citizenship and Postmodernity', Intercultural Education 14(4).

— (2007), 'Collaborative Partnerships as Sustainable Pedagogy: working with British Muslims', in C. Roberts and J. Roberts (eds), Greener by Degrees: Exploring Sustainability through Higher Education Curricula. Geography Discipline Network (GDN), University of Gloucestershire. Available online at www.glos. ac.uk/shareddata/dms/FF071DBEBCD42A039FF8B1E4A2EE4606.pdf

— (2009), Ricoeur and the hermeneutics of suspicion. London and New York: Continuum Books.

Scott-Baumann, A. and Khan-Cheema, A. (2001), 'A case study in widening participation with British Muslims'. Journal of Learning and Teaching 6(1), 6–8.

Shohat, E. and Stam, R. (1994), Unthinking Eurocentrism: Multiculturalism and the media. London: Routledge; p. 156.

Siddiqui, A. (2007), Islam at Universities in England: The Siddiqui Report. London: Department of Innovation, Universities and Skills.

Toscano, A. (2009), 'The War Against Pre-Terrorism: The Tarnac 9 and The Coming Insurrection', Radical Philosophy 154, 2–7.

Yegenoglu, M. (1998), Colonial Fantasies. Cambridge: Cambridge University Press.

Chapter 4

Mawdudi, *Purdah* and the Status of Women in Islam

Roy Jackson

Who was Mawdudi, and why is he important today?

Sheikh Sayyid Abu'l-A'la Mawdudi was born on 25 September 1903 in the city of Aurangabad in Maharashtra state, India. Various other spellings of Mawdudi are Maudoodi and Maududi, and he is also known as Mawlana (or Maulana). When considering how much authority a person possesses, that person's name and honorific title can reveal much. Mawdudi is one such person. The title 'Mawlana', for example, means something like 'our lord' or 'our master', and is usually a form of address to a sovereign, although more commonly used in the Indian subcontinent for respected religious leaders. In addition, the title 'Sheikh' (Sheik, Cheikh, Shaikh) literally means 'elder' in Arabic, and was originally the traditional title given to Bedouin tribal leaders, whilst the title 'Sayyid' has no direct comparison in the Western sense, although perhaps 'Lord' gives some indication of the nobility that the title possess, and it is given to males who can trace their lineage right back to the Prophet Muhammad in the sixth century AD.

To this day, the name of Mawdudi is often spoken with respect and authority by Muslims throughout the world. Mawdudi wrote more than 120 books and pamphlets, on many subjects, covering ethics, politics, religion, slavery, human rights, *shari'a*, the Prophet Muhammad, sociology, literature, and the Qur'an – to name but a few. Many of these writings are undoubtedly intelligent, persuasive and insightful. However, Mawdudi can also be accused of engaging in the rhetoric of a misguided intellectual, with dated attitudes that have no place in or relevance for modern society. His views on women unfortunately fall into this latter category, in particular the views expressed in his book *Purdah and the Status of Woman in Islam*. It would be preferable if this unfortunate text on women could simply be put aside and ignored. However, as a 'traditionalist', Mawdudi's views on women can tell us much about contemporary traditionalist writing on gender that sets out to respond to Western images of women, and, although written in 1939, it has been repeatedly reprinted and is still often quoted as an authoritative source, as are so many of Mawdudi's works. As Malise Ruthven notes:

> In his [Mawdudi's] hands 'Islam' becomes much more than a succession of hair-splitting legal judgements emanating from an archaic social system. It is a full-blown 'ideology' offering answers to every human and social problem. It is mainly this reason that, despite its rigidity, Maududi is widely admired by Muslim radicals from Egypt to Malaysia [...] Along with Sayyid Qutb, he is the most widely read theoretician among young Sunni activists.[46]

Mawdudi was brought up during the time of the break-up of the old Mughal empire and the imposition of British colonial rule. Mawdudi spent his childhood and early youth in Hyderabad, where the extremely wealthy and powerful Nizam-ul-Mulk ('Administrators of the Realm') effectively ruled, independently of the Mughal emperors. The state was 80 per cent Hindu and only 10 per cent Muslim, but was none the less largely Muslim in shape. The Mawdudis were just one family that had enjoyed the noble patronage of the Paigah nobility, who claim their descent from Umar, the second rightly-guided Caliph. The court had its chamberlains, household troops, Arab mercenaries with daggers and muskets, rajahs and maharajahs. It was in this feudal and somewhat magical place that Mawdudi's character was formed. It is no surprise that the change in regimes to British rule would have a profound psychological effect on Mawdudi and many other Indian Muslims. The decline of Mughal rule coincided with the decline of Muslim rule. As Europeans replaced Muslims in positions of authority, land was transferred from Muslims to Hindus, nobles were deprived of taxes, and unemployment increased. Mawdudi was a Sunni Muslim who had a strong ethical position in the face of immense social, political and religious change. In addressing this decline in Muslim power, he looked to Islamic tradition for answers, although, at the same time, he can be described as a modern thinker, not merely burying his head in that tradition. Importantly, he did not see modernity as a final nail in the coffin for Islam, but rather saw modernity – at least certain aspects of it – as an opportunity to revitalise Islam. Mawdudi was concerned with how to be a Muslim in the modern age, and he devoted his life to communicating what he considered to be the best way to be a Muslim. In that way his message is strongly ethical in the philosophical sense of the term: what does it *mean* to be good?

In 1918, at the age of only 15, Mawdudi decided he had to make a living in order to support his family. He went to the cosmopolitan, lively and politically vibrant city of Delhi to pave a career for himself, going into journalism. He became editor of the monthly journal *Al-Jami'at* in 1925 and came to the attention of the public with the publication of two books, *al Jihad fil Islam* (1926) and *Towards Understanding Islam* (1930). This latter book was so well known that it became a prescribed textbook in schools, resulting in a generation of Muslims knowing Mawdudi's name. In 1932, he became editor of the monthly journal *Tarjuman al-Qur'an* which he continued for the rest of his life. Mawdudi's activities were not restricted merely to writing, however. Early on, he became involved in two political movements: the Swaraj (home-rule) and the Khilafat (preservation of the caliphate). He gradually became a recognised figure amongst Muslim radicals and, in 1941, established the religious political party *Jamaat-i-Islami*, which exists in Pakistan to this day. A constitution was established for the *Jamaat*, and this tells us much about Mawdudi's own political views. The *Jamaat* originally consisted of men only[47] (a Women's Wing was set up in February 1948), with an elected Amir (leader) being Mawdudi himself, who selected a *Majlis-i-Shura* (consultative council). The members of the *Shura* were expected to abstain from non-Islamic activities (professions yielding interest, or to do with alcohol, dance and music, gambling, etc.) and not to serve under any government that did not accept *shari'a*. The party structure was strictly hierarchical, with the Amir the final arbiter of all organisational and ideological affairs.

The party was set up initially with the intention of promoting Islamic values within India, and Mawdudi was hostile towards Jinnah's intentions of establishing a separate Islamic state. But as it became clear that India was going to be partitioned, he was won over to the idea of Pakistan and moved there himself in 1947, where he remained politically active, spending time in prison and even being sentenced to death for his outspoken views on which direction Pakistan should take. Whereas Jinnah considered Pakistan to be a (secular) country in which Muslims can live, Mawdudi considered Pakistan to be a country that should be Islamic. The death sentence was annulled after popular protest, and Mawdudi died of a kidney ailment on 22 September 22 1979, at the age of 76.[48]

What is *Purdah?*

Purdah is considered by some Muslims, scholars and laypersons alike, to be binding upon women in Islam because of its injunctions in the Qur'an.[49] However, *purdah* – literally meaning 'curtain' or 'veil' – can be interpreted in many different ways. In the sense of attire, *purdah* can be a reference to the veiling of the entire body by wearing a robe called a *burqa*, or only parts of the head and face by the wearing of a veil or a scarf (in the Qur'an, the term used is *khimār*). In the sense of seclusion, *purdah* refers to restrictions on women's movements outside of the home, so that a woman could be unveiled but still be in a state of *purdah* by being secluded in the home. In the somewhat exclusive society that Mawdudi grew up in, women were secluded in the *mahal khānah* (the 'palace') or, more commonly, the *zanānah* (the women's place), and grown men were excluded from it. It was the duty of men to go out into the evil world once they were old enough to no longer need the protection and nurture of the *zanānah*. The *zanānah* was not just the abode of the mother, but could also possibly include the child's grandmother, aunts and sisters and, if wealthy enough, a wet-nurse.

Mawdudi's Views on *Purdah*

Mawdudi's views on women and *purdah* need to be seen in the wider context of his political and moral philosophy. His book *The Ethical Viewpoint of Islam*, published in 1947, gives us a clear indication of his stance on society as a whole and Islam's position within it. He sees the world, both the Western world and the Islamic world at the time, as being in a state of sickness and decay and, therefore, in need of a cure:

> Thus the moral vices, which the greatest part of humanity was nurturing within itself for ages, now stand fully exposed before us ... Only the stark blind can now harbour the delusion that all is well with the diseased humanity ... We see whole nations exhibiting, on a huge scale, the worst morals which the conscience of humanity has always condemned with one voice ... Every nation, by its own free choice, selects its worst criminals and places them at the helm of its affairs ... There is no form of villainy ... which these nations have not been guilty of, on a huge scale and with the utmost shamelessness ... It is obvious that collective vices make their appearance only when individual vices have reached their nadir ... mankind is passing through a period of intense moral decadence which grips by far the greatest majority of human beings. If this state of affairs continues a little longer the time is not far when humanity will meet with a colossal disaster, and long ages of darkness will supervene.[50]

With a world so full of vice, and facing the prospect of a new dark age, Mawdudi looked for a radical transformation that involved the antithesis of contemporary values. Values such as pluralism, atheism, sexual equality and promiscuity, emphasis on the individual, humanism and so on were the vices, the diseases from which society must be cleansed. For the cure:

> The conclusion to which I have been led is that there is only one correct basis for morality and that basis is supplied by Islam. Here we get an answer to all the basic ethical questions and the answer is free from the defects noticeable in philosophic replies and untainted by other religious creeds which create neither firmness and integrity of character nor prepare man to shoulder the immense responsibilities of civilised life.[51]

The only way to live an ethical life – synonymous with being a Muslim – is to live in a truly Islamic state. In Mawdudi's view, 'the sex instinct is the greatest weakness of the human race'[52] and 'It is only Islam which can provide a wholesome atmosphere for the development of high morals and noble traits of character and which can guarantee true progress of man's intellectual, spiritual and physical abilities.'[53] An Islamic state, therefore, would 'prevent the sexual urge from running wild, to moderate and regulate it in a system.'[54]

Mawdudi's theocracy[55] would necessarily lack pluralism or individualism, as all would be subject to the will of God as understood primarily thorough the Qur'an and the *sunna* of the Prophet Muhammad. The question of human rights, let alone women's rights, in a theocratic state is a fascinating one and, whilst Mawdudi makes use of such terms as 'democracy' and 'equality', we find that his actual views are far removed from how these terms are commonly understood.

Mawdudi divided his conception of an Islamic state into four groups: male Muslims, female Muslims, *zimmis* ('People of the Book') and non-Muslims (followers of religions not recognised as *zimmis*, such as the Ahmadis and atheists). Presuming that women would constitute approximately half the population of Mawdudi's Islamic State, the subject of women's authority within it is of considerable importance. As shall be shown, in practice, however, only the first category would have the opportunity to be full citizens in his state, and even then there were a number of provisos. In the hierarchy of categories, female Muslims would be second-tier: better than *zimmis* and other non-Muslims, at least.

Mawdudi begins *Purdah and the Status of Woman in Islam* by outlining the status of women in different ages and civilisations. This short opening chapter provides a series of generalisations concerning the cultural attitudes towards women in Ancient Greek, Roman, Christian Europe and modern Europe. One common theme runs through each of the accounts of these civilisations: the increase in what is perceived by Mawdudi to be sexual perversion and corruption coincides with (and, presumably, is the cause of) the decline in these respective civilisations. With the advent of the twentieth century in Europe, Mawdudi identifies three 'doctrines'[56] of Western society:

1. Equality between the male and female. Mawdudi's concern is not so much that woman obtains moral equality, but that woman is allowed to work in the job market on equal terms. This Mawdudi sees as a 'wrong concept of equality'[57] because the woman becomes so absorbed in economic, political and social pursuits that she neglects her obligation to care for the family.
2. Economic independence of woman. As women have become economically independent, they no longer feel any obligation to have a husband or family: 'Hundreds and thousands of young women in every Western country like to live unmarried lives, which they are bound to pass in immoral, promiscuous and sinful ways.'[58]
3. The free intermingling of the sexes. This has led to 'an ever-growing tendency towards showing off, nudeness and sex perversion'.[59] Men are growing more voracious in their sexual appetites, while women put aside all moral restraint to attract the opposite sex.

Before stating that women in the pre-Islamic era (*jahilliyah*) and in Western society up to the modern period had no freedom, rights or dignity, Mawdudi paints what he sees as a dark and satanic picture of a decadent and corrupt Western society. For example, there are 'members of the same sex ... involved in homosexuality to the extent that they have lost all interest and desire for the opposite sex',[60] and people reading '... magazine articles providing contraceptive information'.[61] Considering such things to be wrong gives the reader a hint of Mawdudi's attitude. He put much of this moral decline down to 'the depraved moral condition of women which is reflected by their attire, nudity, increasing smoking habits and their free and unrestricted intermingling with men'.[62] He then goes on to quote an American committee of moral reformers known as the Committee of Fourteen, which states that it has 'revealed that almost all ballrooms, night clubs, beauty salons, manicure shops, massage rooms and hairdressing shops in America have turned into houses of prostitution'.[63]

Also, according to an 'estimate'[64] (although Mawdudi does not quote his source), 90 per cent of the American population is afflicted with venereal diseases. It is unfortunate that Mawdudi's choice of sources generally lack academic credence, and his own personal attitudes shine through blatantly in a dogmatic and, frankly, somewhat bizarre manner. This needs to be emphasised to show that there is much more than a mere suspicion that, in Mawdudi's Islamic state, female liberty would be a misnomer.

> Some nations have given woman the position of governor over man. But no instance is found of a nation that raised its womanhood to such a status and then attained any high position on the ladder of progress and civilisation. History does not present the record of any nation which made woman the ruler of its affairs, and won honour and glory, or performed a work of distinction.[65]

Where woman has attained at least some degree of equality with man, 'it has already corrupted community life'.[66] Although Mawdudi insists that, as human beings, man and woman are equal, he adopts his usual approach to such egalitarian principles by qualifying them:

> It has been established by biological research that woman is different from man not only in her appearance and external physical organs but also in the protein molecules of tissue cells.[67]

Thus, this 'equality' only exists in the sense that man and woman are both 'human beings', but that is where it both begins and ends; he states that women are, in a sense, 'disabled' to such an extent during menstruation that it affects her powers of concentration and her mental abilities. At such a time,

> ... a lady tram conductor ... would issue wrong tickets and get confused while counting the small change. A lady motor driver would drive slowly as if under strain, and become nervous at every turning. A lady typist would type wrongly, take a long time to type and omit words in spite of care and effort, and would press wrong keys inadvertently ...[68]

And so on. In short, a woman's mental and nervous system becomes 'lethargic and disorderly'.[69] She loses her mental balance and is even more likely to commit a crime or suicide!

During pregnancy, a woman is 'mentally deranged' and, after delivery, 'exposed to various troubles'. During the period of suckling, the 'best of her body is turned into milk for the baby'. There follows the lengthy period of bringing up the child, which requires her 'fullest attention'.[70] Consequently, Mawdudi allows for little time left in life for the woman to partake in society outside of rearing children, and no mention is made of man's role in this particular process, except:

> For the continuance of the race man's only function is to impregnate the female. He is then free to have any pursuit in life. In contrast to this, the woman has to bear the whole burden of responsibility. It is to bear this burden that she is fashioned right from the time when she is a mere clot of blood in her mother's womb.[71]

Consequently, Mawdudi has moved on from talking of 'equality' to the qualified 'equipotential', and then to determining woman's burdensome destiny from the moment of her conception. Mawdudi does not consider it to be 'fair play' to require women to undergo the hardships of the economic field; to shoulder social responsibilities that man must so reluctantly bear; to take part in promoting the cause of industry and commerce, agriculture, administration of justice and defending the country.

> Above all [he asks], will it be just and right to require her to allure men's hearts also by her presence in mixed gatherings and provide them with means of entertainment and pleasure?[72]

We know Mawdudi's answer to this: to allow such a thing would be unfair and 'sheer inequality'! A woman, burdened so heavily 'by nature' should not have such additional duties in society. Besides which, even if she had equal duties, 'she cannot in fact be expected to perform them with manly vigour'.[73] As an example of woman's abilities:

> Imagine for a while the plight of a land or naval force which wholly consists of women. It is quite possible that right in the midst of war, a fair number of them might be down with the menstrual discharge, a good number of delivery cases forced to stay in bed, and a fair percentage of pregnant ones fuming and sulking uselessly.[74]

Mawdudi describes woman as 'tender', 'plastic', 'soft', 'pliable', 'submissive', 'impressionable', 'yielding', 'timid' and, basically, incapable of functioning in spheres of life demanding 'firmness and authority, resistance and cold-temperedness, and which requires the exercise of unbiased, objective judgement and strong will-power'.[75]

Mawdudi then proceeds to qualify his earlier remarks that men and women have 'equipotential' by stating that, in fact, men and women do not have equipotential in all aspects of life. In the same way that Mawdudi looks at history in an attempt to justify his notion that no nation has prospered under a woman ruler, he now states that no woman's genius is as great as the likes of such men as Aristotle, Kant, Hegel, Shakespeare, Napoleon, Salah-ud Din and so on. His ignorance of social conditions is quite remarkable, and his attempt to balance such apocryphal remarks by proclaiming that no man could ever be as great a mother is rather typical of anti-feminist rhetoric.

From what we have seen of Mawdudi's opinions so far, it seems fairly self-evident that woman's authority in his Islamic state will be somewhat restricted. For Mawdudi, the men are naturally generals, statesmen and administrators, and women are the wives, mothers and housekeepers: 'This is the division of labour which nature herself has devised between the sexes.'[76]

His outlining of woman's authority can be categorised into four parts:[77]

1. Man is to carry out the 'laborious' social duties of earning a living, and his education should be designed to prepare him for this.
2. Women are to look after domestic affairs and make home-life 'sweet, pleasant and peaceful'. Likewise, her education should gear her towards these duties.
3. Woman is to 'maintain the family system and save it from confusion'. The man must be the leader of the family.
4. There must be 'safeguards in the social system' to prevent individuals from 'confusing and mixing up the different fields of activity of the two sexes'.[78]

It is evident that Mawdudi does not envisage equal education for both sexes: the woman should only be taught how to cook, sew and rear children. Therefore she would already be disabled and discriminated against should she wish to engage in activities outside of the home – not that she would be given the opportunity in the first place in Mawdudi's state:

They are allowed to go out under necessity. But this permission is neither unconditional, nor unlimited. Women are not allowed to move about freely and mix with men in social gatherings.[79]

Regarding the political role of women, Mawdudi states in *Human Rights in Islam* that 'In Islam there is a functional distribution between men and women and according to which the field of politics and administration belongs to the men's sphere of responsibility.'[80] He also quotes the well-known *hadith*: 'A nation that entrusts its affairs to a woman can never prosper.' This *hadith* is a perfect example of the use of an unreliable source to substantiate Mawdudi's personal political philosophy; it is the kind of dogmatic quote that goes completely against the spirit of the Qur'an.[81]

Woman's political representation is equally circumscribed; although he appears willing to extend the right to vote to women, he considers the present system of universal adult franchise harmful and would like therefore to qualify it with a certain level of education,[82] and yet he has previously stated that women will not, in fact, be given access to such an education. The election of women to the legislative assemblies 'is absolutely against the spirits and precepts of Islam … active politics and administration are not the field of activity for womenfolk'.[83] The best Mawdudi will do is to provide a separate Assembly made up of women only who are elected by women only: its role to 'look after the affairs of women such as female education, female hospitals, etc.'[84]

The Need for a *Weltanschauung*

The arrival of Islam did not create new systems, institutions, ideas and theories out of nothing; rather it presented a new approach to existing systems. In the development of civilisations, intellectual disciplines and schools of thought, a general pattern can be perceived as a progress from a particular worldview to a distinct intellectual school of thought, and only then to achieve a new mode of social organisation. That is to say, a *weltanschauung* is required that culminates in institutions which capture the spirit and message of the original philosophy in some concrete and workable form.[85] Although the Qur'an may contain this *weltanschauung* in its ideality, bringing it into reality is another matter.

Throughout Mawdudi's political philosophy he adopts the approach of being overly influenced by past commentaries of the primary source, the Qur'an. As a result he fails to relate the Qur'anic spirit – its *weltanschauung* – to contemporary circumstances. Traditional *tafsir* were all written by men and, consequently, the opinions and experiences of women within the text have been largely buried beneath male scholarship. It is only quite recently that scholars – almost exclusively female – have been returning to the Qur'an to rectify this imbalance. Yet Mawdudi's state would result in such stasis for women that she would neither have the time, the confidence nor the education to engage in such exegesis. Mawdudi's occasional rhetorical utterances along the lines of the equality of man and woman are utterly meaningless when he actually begins to elaborate. Mawdudi's Islamic state would be in its purest form, beyond the metaphysical and impersonal to the political. Thus, Mawdudi attempts to justify the Pure Islamic state by referring to the Qur'an as a legitimate legal code of political conduct. But such sovereignty alone would not only be impractical in today's complex society – for the Qur'an is limited in its political expression – but also Mawdudi's interpretation does not seem to hold up to scrutiny. Mawdudi frequently adopts an atomistic, unintegrated approach that does not take account of the social conditions existing today. Qur'anic significance rests upon the reader's ability to deduce general principles to Qur'anic solutions to rulings upon specific and concrete historical issues:

> In building any genuine and viable Islamic set of laws and institutions, there has to be a twofold movement: First one must move from the concrete case treatments of the Qur'an – taking the necessary and relevant social conditions of that time into account – to the general principles upon which the entire teaching converges. Second, from this general level there must be a movement back to specific legislation, taking into account the necessary and relevant social conditions now obtaining.[86]

If one believes in the basic justice of Islam, then the Qur'an's holistic message must surely reflect that. This requires a different methodology in the exegesis of the Qur'an: in the case of particular *ayat* which apply to specific circumstances in existence at the time of the revelation it is necessary to determine the principles or moral values underlying them, rather than apply it literally to the present day. As the Qur'an's basic principle is social justice, it seems contradictory to suggest that the woman's place is in the home, unless one can genuinely show that this is a universal truth as clearly defined in the Qur'an, and that the modern conception of social justice is an aberration. Men in history have attempted to do this, but more modern scholars are revealing the anti-hierarchical nature of the Qur'an in the relation to the roles of man and woman:

> ... although the Qur'an has established a universal rule for determining if deeds performed by individuals are valuable, it has not decided on the deeds between genders in any explicit way. This contradicts the assumption that there are specific roles for women determined by the Qur'an.[87]

Mawdudi's views are important because he reflects a genuine concern amongst many, Muslims and non-Muslims alike, that modernity, and 'post-modernity', have led to alienation and meaninglessness. This need not result in a complete rejection of tradition, but nor should it result in Mawdudi's attempt to recreate a romanticised conception of the Islamic state as it seemingly existed under the Prophet Muhammad. The fact that women are able to read the Qur'an for themselves, as well as other sources of authority such as *hadith*, allows old words to evoke new responses, together with an understanding that all societies, past and present, are imperfect in some way or other. In addition, Mawdudi was unwilling and unable to accept that human beings, women included, are able to exercise reason and should be trusted in their individual responses to traditional narratives.

References

Jackson, Roy (2009), *Mawdudi and Political Islam.* London: Routledge.

Mernissi, Fatima (1991), *Women and Islam: An Historical and Theological Enquiry.* London: Blackwell.

Nasr, Sayyid-Vali Reza (1992), *Islamization of Knowledge.* Islamabad: International Institute of Islamic Thought.

Rahman, Fazlur (1982), *Islam and Modernity: Transformation of an Intellectual Tradition.* Chicago: University of Chicago Press.

Ruthven, Malise (2000), *Islam in the World,* 2nd edn. London: Penguin Books.

Wadud-Muhsin, Amina (1992), 'Understanding the Implicit Qur'anic Parameters to the Role of Women in the Modern Context', *The Islamic Quarterly* 34(2).

Books by Mawdudi

The Ethical Viewpoint of Islam. Lahore: Markazi Maktaba Jam'at-i-Islami; 1947.

The Meaning of the Qur'an, vol. 4. Lahore: Islamic Publications Ltd.; 1971.

Human Rights in Islam. Leicester: The Islamic Foundation; 1980.

Purdah and the Status of Woman. Lahore: Islamic Publications Ltd.; 1986.

Chapter 5

Female Seclusion and the Veil. Two Issues in Political and Social Discourse

The reforms of Sultan Muhammad Shah

Simonetta Calderini

In her seminal work *Women and Gender in Islam* (1992), Leila Ahmed convincingly argued that the issue of the condition of Muslim women, as exemplified by the wearing of the veil, had by the end of the 19th century become part of a colonial narrative/discourse of Western superiority, aptly used to reinforce cultural assumptions and justify political action. Such a narrative had been embraced by a number of Muslim modernist reformers, such as Egyptian intellectual Qasim Amin (*The Liberation of Woman*, 1899) for whom the veil and female segregation symbolised the 'backwardness' of Islamic societies. In turn, the denunciation and rejection by other Muslim intellectuals of what they saw as an uncritical acceptance of the Western model of progress led to the emergence of an Islamic narrative of resistance, which made use of the same discourse on gender, as epitomised by Mawdudi's booklet *Pardah and the Status of Woman in Islam* (1939).

To this day, the discourse of the veil is filled with contested meanings and agendas for Muslims and non-Muslims alike. On the one hand, Muslim 'modernists', human rights activists, feminists and the Western media invoke the issue of the veil to critique oppressive religious, cultural and social norms, while (mainly) Western politicians appeal to it in order to critique specific Islamic regimes. On the other hand, many Muslim women have embraced the veil as a visible tool of self-assertion, of national or religious identity and of ideological defiance against the West, Western-backed governments or more broadly against secularism and consumerism.

In this chapter I aim to show a lesser-known side to the discourse of the veil: that of those Muslim women for whom *not wearing the veil* is a means of expressing their distinctive religious and communal identity. The example I will provide is of the Shi'i Imami Nizari Isma'ili women, whose former imam, Sultan Muhammad Shah (1877–1957, 48th imam of the Nizari Isma'ilis), also known as Aga Khan III,[88] made full use of the 'colonial discourse' of the veil to critique the Muslim societies of his time and enthusiastically embraced the reformist agenda of female education and suffrage. At the same time, in his position as Muslim leader, he was able to present arguments drawn from his understanding of Islamic history and his interpretation of the Qur'an to support his critique. In this chapter I am going to present some of his arguments and his reforms on the veil alongside the broader discourse of women's seclusion.

Seclusion and *Pardah*: The Terms, the Concepts, the Argument

Despite being expressed by the same terms in languages such as Arabic, Persian and Urdu, female seclusion and the wearing of the 'veil', though interconnected issues, can nevertheless be seen as separate and not necessarily consequential topics to be raised when addressing the status of women in Islam. In the case of the Aga Khan's modernist critique, and his consequent directives on women issues, female seclusion and female dress were in several instances not only addressed in a distinctive manner but were also adapted for the diverse audiences to which the Aga Khan spoke.

In this chapter I am going to refer to terms such as *hijab* and *pardah* and their different meanings and understandings. The Qur'anic use of the term *hijab* is that of a screen or a barrier to create separation and privacy. In fact, of the seven times the term occurs in the Qur'an, only once does it refer to separation between men and women. In Surat al-Ahzab (The Confederates) 33.53, in a passage exhorting the Prophet's companions to respect his privacy and domestic intimacy, *hijab* indicates the curtain or screen, whether interpreted as being physical or metaphorical, which should separate the Prophet's wives from his companions or fellow-Muslims. Earlier verses addressed to the prophet's wives in the same *sura* (33.32–3) had advised them to 'abide in your homes', thus providing some past and present commentators with the justification for the confinement of all Muslim women to their homes.[89]

In addition to the Qur'anic meanings of the term, in modern parlance *hijab* has come to indicate the veil worn by Muslim women, usually referring to the wearing of a headscarf and loose garments. Similarly to *hijab*, the term *pardah*, of Persian origin, can mean a curtain, a partition, but also veil; therefore a woman in *pardah* (*pardanashin/purdanashin*) can mean a veiled or a secluded woman. Particularly in reformist discourse of the end of the 19th and beginning of the 20th century, in areas of the Indian subcontinent, the term *pardah* was used to broadly refer to the practice of female seclusion.

Aga Khan III

The main figure of this chapter is Sultan Muhammad Shah, the 48th imam and spiritual leader of the Imami Shi'I Nizari Isma'ilis, the largest communities of whom, during his lifetime, were to be found in India (and later Pakistan), greater Syria (Syria/Lebanon) and East Africa (the then states of Tanganyika, Uganda and Kenya). At the death of his father in 1885, Sultan Muhammad Shah, at the tender age of 8, became the spiritual leader, or imam, of the Isma'ilis with the title of Aga Khan III. This honorific title had first been bestowed upon his great grandfather Hasan Ali Shah by the Qajar monarch Fath 'Ali Shah. Aga Khan III's Persian mother, who was 35 at the time of his succession, became his effective guardian until he reached the age of 16. As customary among women of her origin and status, she wore the veil. She looked after her son's financial interests as well as the administrative side of the Isma'ili communities, which she organised in local councils. Even after the Aga Khan reached maturity, she continued to be influential, especially in maintaining and reinforcing links with the local Isma'ili Indian communities while the Aga Khan was away in his travels.

In his lifetime, the Aga Khan witnessed crucial political and territorial upheavals: the end of the Ottoman empire, two world wars, the end of the British Empire in India, its partition and the creation of Pakistan. He also witnessed the rise of women's rights movements in the West and parts of the Islamic world, and was instrumental in fostering social changes in education and women's participation. During the 72 years of his imamate, he strove for leadership status beyond his community and came to be recognised as an advocate of Muslim interests in India first and the whole subcontinent after partition, as a sponsor and supporter of educational projects and a keen advocate of female education. Internally, in consultation with local Isma'ili community representatives, he promulgated constitutions for the Isma'ilis of specific regions. These and other changes shaped the Isma'ili communities in accordance with the modern era in matters of trade, education, ritual, dress, communal representation and other spheres, while, at the same time, a more rational communal and legal structure served to consolidate the imam's authority among his communities.

With reference to the status of women in Pakistan, the Aga Khan's modernist and reformist outlook is summarised in a speech he made in Pakistan in 1953, when he stated:

Ladies, believe me, if Pakistan does not rise to the modern era of the equal position of women, you will find not only Europe but all the other countries of Asia going ahead of you ... To begin with, the women here, to my horror, are forbidden taking part in the religious life of the country. In practically every Muslim country the women are allowed to go to mosques for Friday prayers and there are proper wings divided by 'pardahs' [here with the meaning of screens] from the men where they conduct Friday prayers ... The first thing to agitate for, is to get your right for your prayers, which women enjoy in practically every Muslim country.[90]

Making use of a language that still reflects the colonialist discourse linking the status of women with social progress, the Aga Khan critiques attitudes to women found in Pakistan. He is not (yet) envisaging a removal of the screen separating men and women at the congregational prayer, 'not side by side with men but in reserved quarters attached to all the mosques',[91] but he is showing that its very existence is proof of women's mobility (i.e. of coming out of a broader *pardah*, or female seclusion) and, fundamentally, of women's right to attend prayer in mosques '... so that the habit of praying in public and self-respect and self-confidence becomes general amongst women'.[92] In this and similar addresses, Sultan Muhammad Shah is showing the women of Pakistan, both Isma'ili and non-Isma'ili, that women's restrictions are not only unjustified, but, in view of the practice in most Islamic countries of this time, fully unacceptable.[93] What he describes as a feeling of 'horror' epitomises his decades-long call for reforms in the Islamic world involving women's status and education.

When analysing the speeches and actions of the Aga Khan, we need to keep in mind the different registers and audiences he addresses: on the one hand he projects himself to the wider public, usually the Indian Muslims but also the Hindus, the British, and Muslims in general, while on the other he appeals to his own Isma'ili communities. As far as the Isma'ilis are concerned, the type, extent and timing of reforms as envisaged by the Aga Khan varied considerably due to the diverse geographical, social, political and religious contexts in Asia and Africa where Isma'ilis were living as minorities.

Pardah as Seclusion and Female Education

Aga Khan III to the Muslim public

In 1902, on the occasion of the All India Muhammadan Educational Conference in Delhi, a young (25-year-old) Aga Khan outlined in his presidential address his vision of the reforms needed for Muslims in India and indicated what he believed to be the reasons why Muslims were lagging behind Western societies. One of the most important was what Aga Khan III considered to be the appalling and unjustifiable status of women. In this respect, he stated: 'There is absolutely nothing in Islam, or the Koran, or the example of the first two centuries, to justify this terrible and cancerous growth that has for nearly a thousand years eaten into the very vitals of Islamic society.'[94] He further clarified that '*pardah*, as now known, itself did not exist till long after the Prophet's death and is no part of Islam'.[95] His use of the term *pardah* here goes far beyond that of curtain or veil; rather, he is referring to the practice of female seclusion, as evidenced by his examples of the roles of women during the time of prophet Muhammad and his companions when, far from being confined to their homes, they would be present on the battlefields to tend the wounded.

In a 1918 book on the political status of India, which Aga Khan III wrote as a way of contributing to the hoped-for implementation of self-government/self-determination for India, he positively remarked that Indian society was progressing and that one important issue of society, the *pardah* system (here to be understood as female seclusion) was 'disappearing' among the upper classes, 'faster than many in England or even Englishmen in India realise'.[96] Nevertheless, a year later, the Southborough Committee on Franchise was to use the issue of *pardah* to justify its rejection to extend the vote to women in India, on the basis that women would not exercise their right and go to the polling booths. The Aga Khan strongly rejected this argument, by stating that, first, the British officials who made such statements were not aware of social changes and the diminishing number of Indian women in *pardah*. Second, the issue was one of social justice, not of numbers, and that the right to vote, irrespective of how many women would in fact exercise it, would give women their deserved human and legal dignity.[97]

Aga Khan III to the Isma'ilis

What was a strongly supported platform for reforms before Muslim audiences, especially in India, was translated into directives for the Isma'ili communities in territories such as India and East Africa. With reference to *pardah* in the broader sense of seclusion, in his 1926 constitution for the Isma'ilis of East Africa, the Aga Khan gave priority to improving education and to building schools. His emphasis on modernising and expanding educational facilities and curricula had been a constant call since the early years of his imamate. But while for Indian Muslims at large the figure of the Aga Khan was that of a Muslim modernist and supporter of the educational aims and activities of the Aligarh Muhammadan Anglo-Oriental college, which in 1920 had become an autonomous Muslim University,[98] for his own communities, on the strength of his authoritative role, his plans and projects were soon to become specific rulings ready for implementation.

As far as female education was concerned, in a speech to Isma'ili school-girls of Kandi Moholla, Bombay, in 1913, he enjoined Isma'ili parents to send their daughters to school, to the extent that if, due to limited financial means, parents had to choose between educating a son and educating a daughter, they should opt for schooling the daughter. In his own words: 'We command parents that they must send their daughters to school. We make this *wajib* [a duty/compulsory] upon you ... these girls will be able to earn their living in future and administer better care and guidance to their children ...'[99] Not only was he 'commanding' Isma'ili parents to send their daughters to school, but he was also insisting that girls were to remain in school at least until the age of 14.[100] It goes without saying that such an instruction was also aimed at curbing the practice, common among Indian families, of early marriage. Furthermore, education was in the Aga Khan's view to be a mark of pride of the Isma'ili community; 'there should be no Isma'ili girl who is not educated and literate'.[101]

Three decades later, in a 1945 *firman*[102] to the East African communities, the Aga Khan reiterated the priority of female education and its outcomes both for the benefit of the children's education and for future employment.[103] In the eventuality of the latter, which was seen more as the result of financial need than, for instance, of career or personal fulfilment (a pioneer and a modernist reformer, but still a man of his own times!), the Aga Khan made sure that both traditional female roles and community cohesion were maintained. In a 1954 *ta'liqa*[104] on the extent to which a child's education can be affected by a mother working outside the home, the Aga Khan emphasised the importance for the woman of contributing to the family budget yet, at the same time, the necessity for the child to receive appropriate and suitable care and guidance. These, in his directives, were to be imparted by a woman who was not in need and who belonged to the Isma'ili community.[105] Hence, by implication, by following the Aga Khan's rulings, not only was community life and Isma'ili identity maintained but the cohesion of the Isma'ili community was reinforced by means of voluntary work by the better-off to help those in need. At a family level, the Aga Khan explained, for a woman to be able to work meant that she could be self-sufficient were her husband to become lazy or unemployed.[106]

Analysis of Context

The Aga Khan's pioneering approach to modernisation with regard to female education and work cannot be fully appreciated without a glance at the wider context.

The early years of the Aga Khan's imamate broadly coincide with the coming to the fore of modernist ideas, culminating, in Turkey, with the 1876 Ottoman Constitution and the climax and end of the Tanzimat period (the reformation of the Turkish Empire, 1839–76). In the Middle East as well as in India, this was put into practice by the efforts of individual men and women alike to uphold the educational and legal rights of women. The Aga Khan's language and his references to the status of women were also in tune with the broader Western political colonial discourse, which was adopted by a number of Muslim intellectuals, as mentioned earlier.

Different degrees of women-focused reform programmes and motivations were present in the Middle East and India, from Egyptian Muslim activist Huda Sha'rawi, who formed the Egyptian Feminist Union in 1923, to more inclusive organisations such as the All-India Women's Conference, established in New Delhi in 1927. In India, there had also been a small princely state in Bhopal (now capital of Madhya Pradesh) where, since 1819, women's political influence had reached its fulfilment thanks to a series of female rulers, whether regents or sovereigns in their own right. One such ruler had been Shah Jahan Begam, whose daughter, Sultan Jahan Begam, who reigned between 1901 and 1926, was to be the last Begam of Bhopal. Sultan Jahan was an outspoken reformist and, writing in 1918, noted that the two 'most interesting and important' problems facing Muslim women were *pardah* and education.[107] Her significance in the reform process, particularly for women's legal rights, did not pass unnoticed by the Aga Khan, who corresponded with her by addressing her as 'mother'.[108] Female reformist voices had also emerged in India in the form of satire and outright criticism of the strict custom of *pardah*, which came to be seen more as a social than a religious custom.[109]

While the Aga Khan was voicing and representing concerns, which were widely discussed during his times, to fully appreciate the reformist extent of his views about *pardah* one can look at comparable contemporary opinions.

For a telling contrast, one such example is that of the well-known revivalist Sayyid Abul-A'la Mawdudi (1903–79), who in 1939 wrote a book(let) to justify the custom of *pardah*. In it, he provided arguments in favour of *pardah* from different approaches: scriptural, theological, historical and social. For the doctrinal and theological grounds he used textual arguments and maintained that the sacred texts of Islam were clear enough about the extent of separation between the sexes and the modesty of women. However, as far as the face veil is concerned, Mawdudi's argument is far from clear and, while he cannot deny that the Qur'an itself is not specific about the covering of the face, he nevertheless states that the veil 'is Qur'anic in spirit'.[110]

Contrary to the opinion of those Muslim modernists[111] who consider female seclusion and the veil as a social practice which emerged after the time of the Prophet, Mawdudi claims that the veil 'was indeed devised by the Qur'an itself and established by the Holy Prophet himself as a social custom'.[112] Mawdudi's position on *pardah*, to be understood both as veil and female seclusion, was part of his wider anti-Western ideological and political agenda, which made him present the loss of *pardah*, and the resulting female participation in society, as a loss of Muslim identity, an open door to immorality and corruption resulting from an empty and dangerous desire to emulate the West. So as to avoid the consequences of this dangerous emulation, he strongly believed that 'the conditions prevailing in India demand that the law of *pardah* should be strictly enforced, and not relaxed'.[113]

Suffice it here to contrast the above statements with the Aga Khan's outright condemnation of female restrictions; in the 1950s he stated that in Muslim countries can be found the 'worst vice of slavery of women in *pardah*, *burqah* and *zenana* [*zenana*, in Muslim India indicate the women's quarters, the equivalent of *harim*, hence seclusion] where women are reduced to the moral insignificance of vegetables and physical wrecks, of diseases such as tuberculosis'.[114]

Other contemporary modernist Muslim voices were also not as far reaching as that of the Aga Khan in terms, for example, of female education. When the great Indian Muslim modernist Sayyid Ahmad Khan (d. 1898), the principal figure of the Aligarh movement and of modern education in India, had established in 1875 the Mohammedan Anglo-Oriental College, it was for the benefit of young men only. It was well after his death that the all-female Aligarh Zenana Madrasah was opened in 1906. In other words, the ideal of most modern reformers in India still remained for women to be privately educated in their home.

Aga Khan III to the Isma'ilis on *Pardah* as Veil

While the Aga Khan's pronouncements above were conceived to be of wide appeal to Indian women and to Muslim women, his status as spiritual leader of the Isma'ilis gave him the authority to implement his reformist vision among his own communities. This included pronouncements about the other meaning of *pardah*: the veil. As early as 1905, in a *firman* during his second visit to Zanzibar, the imam had stated:

> ... the external *burqa* [veil] is not for you, but [better] for you is a veil of the heart [*dhill*], have modesty [*aya*: shyness, modesty] in your heart, fill your heart with modesty all the time. You [women] should not cast your eye on other men except your husbands; do not have any thoughts for other men.
>
> If in your mind there is desire for other men, you will not gain from your prayers.[115]

As the legitimate and most authoritative living interpreter of divine revelation, in the views of the Isma'ilis, the imam could be seen here as providing *ta'wil*, or allegorical interpretation of the Qur'anic verse on modesty and dress (*surat al-a 'raf*, 7.26: 'O children of Adam! We have bestowed upon you from on high garments to cover your nakedness ... but the garment of piety (*libas al-taqwa*)/God consciousness is the best.'

Through the above statements on modesty and dress, according to Isma'ili believers, the Aga Khan, as the repository of a special esoteric knowledge, was explaining the inner dimension (*baitin*) of the Qur'anic verses. By virtue of his authority, his statements, wherever possible, were to be implemented by his followers.

However, the timing and extent of the implementation of his reformist views on *pardah* as veil were to be dependant upon the different contexts in which the Isma'ili communities were living. For instance, while in East Africa his directives about marriage, female work and, specifically, female dress were overall very successful, in Pakistan they came to be implemented much later and to a lesser degree. One main reason for this difference is to be found in the diverse religious and legal fabric of the countries. In

East Africa the Isma'ilis, as one of the Muslim minorities, had the right and authority to legislate on matters relating to family and personal law. On the other hand, in Pakistan, notwithstanding the debates on the state's ideological character, the law of the land, broadly based on *shari'a*, was to be extended to all Muslims, including the Isma'ilis, who therefore found themselves in a less flexible position.[116] Another reason to account for the diverse emphasis in the directives and their degree of implementation among Isma'ilis in various countries was the Aga Khan's constant appeal to Isma'ilis to respect the customs and laws of, and show allegiance to, the country they were residing in.[117] Though a sensible way to successful integration and business transactions with the host country, such an appeal was nevertheless not meant to imply an uncritical acceptance of all the local customs, as he believed this would inevitably lead to over-assimilation and eventually to a lack of understanding of both their own individual and communal identity.[118]

On the basis of his speeches, *firmans* and letters, it transpires that the Aga Khan chose to refer again to female dress at a much later stage. The 1946 Constitution for the Isma'ilis of East Africa includes a statement suggestive of the 'abolition of the veil' that reads: '… the bride shall take her seat open faced next to the bridegroom'.[119] In the same year, in a *firman* pronounced in Nairobi, the Aga Khan encouraged women to wear a more Western, 'colonial-style' dress, which he presented as 'ready-to-wear' attire, and enjoined Isma'ili leaders to set an example for the rest of the community. In 1952, having discussed the matter with Isma'ili representatives from Africa, the Aga Khan spelt out a dress policy for Isma'ili women resident in East Africa, and encouraged them to adopt a simple 'colonial frock' for 'political and economic reasons'.[120] Not only was this type of dress more practical and economical than the traditional elaborate Indian sari, but it would also help Isma'ilis to integrate with the local population of East Africa and not set them apart. Dress was only one aspect of a much broader trend of removing the most patent Indian traits and customs among the Isma'ili communities there, from sumptuous marriages to the language used in ritual prayers, from Gujarati to Arabic.[121] It is reported that a change in dress among the Isma'ili women of East Africa was visible within a few weeks of the imam's directives.[122]

With the 1947 partition of British India and the formation of Pakistan, many Isma'ilis migrated from India to Karachi and to East Pakistan.[123] In a state where Islam was its uniting factor, both as an ideological force and as a moral code for its society, the veil became a symbol of religious identity, of national pride and ideological opposition to the colonial West.

As contemporary Indian academic, literary critic and novelist Eunice de Souza (b. 1940) argues in her book on *pardah*, during and following partition the issue of *pardah* became entangled with political agendas: 'for Muslim women, more than for most women, coming out of *Pardah* was fraught with the ideological trap of identity, particularly after 1947'.[124] Moreover, now that the non-Muslim 'other' (the Hindu) was no longer a conspicuous presence, the Muslim 'other' became the object of scrutiny and, as in the case of the Ahmadiyya denomination, the object of criticism, which culminated in 1953 in the anti-Ahmadi agitation. Given the political circumstances of Pakistan, the advertising of denominational diversity was obviously not to be encouraged. Not surprisingly, the issue of the veil was not foremost in the speeches of the Aga Khan directed to Pakistani Muslims and Isma'ilis; however, his reformist educational policies bore their fruits there, as witnessed in the late 1950s by the level of literacy of Isma'ili children up to the age of 14, which was more than double that of non-Isma'ili Muslim children.[125] By then, Isma'ili women, especially the younger generation, would generally not wear the veil, were active participants in their communities (the Isma'ilia Women's Association was founded in 1952 in Karachi), and their circumstances were quite different from those referred to by the Aga Khan in the above-mentioned 1954 speech to Pakistani Muslim women.

For the Isma'ili communities, the Aga Khan's reforms dealt not only with female education, work and dress but also with the most important aspects of family law, particularly marriage and divorce. In line with the reformist ethos of women's organisations all over India and of political leaders of Islamic countries, such as Mustafa Kemal and Reza Shah, the Aga Khan's personal status reforms addressed issues such as polygamy (prohibited in 1952), child marriage (outlawed in 1946) and divorce (granted by the court). Even though radical and far-reaching in theory, the extent of the reforms' implementation was dependant, in practice, upon the authority accorded to local or communal courts, much greater in East Africa than in Pakistan.

In East Africa, implementation was facilitated by the Aga Khan's restructuring of community councils which dealt with family law disputes among Isma'ilis.[126] Overall, the period of reforms and the implementation of communal projects, in fields as diverse as community administration, financial enterprises, health services, housing ownership and educational institutions, coincided with a period of economic prosperity of the Isma'ili merchant communities as well as of wise investment policies of the funds raised during the Jubilees during the Aga Khan's long life (1935, 1946, 1955).[127]

The reform platform devised and implemented by the Aga Khan was well in tune with equivalent reforms in Turkey, Iran and, to some extent, Egypt. In particular, the underlying argument was similar, which equated civilisation with progress and declared that both were exemplified by contemporary Western civilisation. The status of women, their education and overall visibility through behaviour and clothing were of utmost concern to the Aga Khan as well as to Mustafa Kemal, as in both cases the modernising reforms were meant to visibly impact upon both public (community or state) and private domains. Some of their arguments in favour of reform were remarkably similar, for instance holding that traditional items of clothing (such as the fez and the veil) did not, in fact, originate in Islam.[128] Their differences, however, cannot be underestimated: while Kemalism ought to be assessed within broader nationalist, ethnic and secularist ideologies, set as it was within a strong and to some extent rigid state apparatus, the Aga Khan modernist discourse was aimed at different communities held together by religious and cultural, rather than ethnic, territorial or national bonds. Even though the spiritual basis for the Aga Khan's directives made them much more authoritative for their recipients, on account of their applicability to diverse social and geographical contexts, the same directives needed to be capable of a much greater degree of flexibility.

Towards the end of his long life and imamate, the Aga Khan wrote in his *Memoirs* what could be defined as a summary of his gender reforms:

I have always sought to encourage the emancipation and education of women. In my grandfather's and my father's time the Isma'ilis were far ahead of any other Muslim sect in the matter of the abolition of the strict veil, even in extremely conservative countries. I have absolutely abolished it; nowadays you will never find an Isma'ili woman wearing the veil. Everywhere from the first I have encouraged girls' schools, even in regions where otherwise they were completely unknown. I say with pride that my Isma'ili followers are, in this matter of social welfare, far in advance of any other Muslim sect ... I am convinced that our social conditions – education for both boys and girls, marriage, etc. ... are far ahead.[129]

Beyond the personal pride for the implementation of his pioneering reforms, the Aga Khan's words point to a further level of interpretation of the issues of the veil, of female emancipation and the empowerment resulting from coming out of *pardah*: the communal sphere of Isma'ili religious identity. This is the key to a fuller understanding of his modernist discourse of the veil, which sets it apart from similar contemporary reformists. On the one hand, there was the secularist option of political leaders such as Mustafa Kemal, who, as a result of military and political success, had illustrated the implementation of his agenda by abolishing the veil and making education compulsory for all. On the other, reformists such as Mawdudi had used the discourse of *pardah* to further his Muslim revivalist and anti-Western agenda. Instead, the Aga Khan's modernist ideas were instrumental in asserting his role as a Muslim reformist leader but also in strengthening his authority within his communities, thanks to the drawing up, and later the updating, of constitutions for Isma'ilis in different parts of the world and through complex yet efficient community administrative reforms.

Consequently, the Isma'ili communities which he left to his successor the present Aga Khan IV, were in better economic, financial, educational and social shape than most Muslim communities in the Islamic and non-Islamic worlds. The late Aga Khan's conviction that the Isma'ili communities were 'far ahead' proved overall correct, and their progressive outlook was instrumental in their renewed self-identity as well as their survival in different geographical and political contexts.

When contemporary Isma'ili women living in the West are asked about their own understanding of the use of the veil and their practice in this regard, their answers echo the arguments of the late Aga Khan III.[130] They consider the veil to be a sign of backwardness, emphasise the concept of 'veil of the heart' and the importance of integration, or, as a Canadian Isma'ili girl put it, 'to blend into the woodwork'.[131] Isma'ili web discussions on the topic of the veil reveal some degree of confusion as to whether wearing the veil should be understood as 'not compulsory' or as having been 'rejected by the imams', and if it is acceptable for older women to wear it out of cultural custom. It is of interest to notice that wearing the veil is still regarded as acceptable when practising *taquiyya* (hiding your religious identity), with the implication that, in particular contexts, blending is more important than affirming one's identity.[132]

However, in less public contexts, there are some signs of concern within the community coming from questions posed by the modern generations of Isma'ili women, especially those living in the West, who witness a reaffirmation of Muslim identity through the wearing of the veil.

Concluding remarks

To what extent will the reforms of the late Aga Khan stand against the pressure of Islamist revival movements and Muslim 'nationalist' ideologies with their reaction against the Western-inspired 'colonial discourse' of the veil? Thus far, when the local circumstances allow it, Nizari Isma'ilis have experienced an overall continuity with the late 19th and early 20th century reforms of Aga Khan III. The same could not be stated, as far as the wearing of the veil is concerned, about another branch of the Isma'ili community, the Da'udi Bohoras. Under the leadership of the late *dâ'î muñlaq Ŧâhir Sayf al-dín* (1915–65) during a complex period of internal dissent and of pressure for reforms which were spreading throughout India and most Islamic countries, by the mid-20th century *pardah* practices had been gradually abandoned by many Bohora women. Despite no official sanctioning of the lifting of the veil, the leaders of the Bohora religious hierarchy eventually came to turn a blind eye to the numerous cases of Bohora women discarding the veil.[133] However, since 1979 the present *da'i mullaq*, Sayyidna Muhammad Burhanuddin (b. 1915) made it normative for women to wear a type of *burqa* as part of a wider process of the re-appropriation of Islamic identity for the Bohora communities.[134] Such an emphasis on restoring perceived communal Islamic markers has been variously interpreted by scholars as resulting from events of international resonance such as the Iranian revolution, from internal motivations linked to religious authority and leadership or from local circumstances of Bohora communities and the leadership's fear of assimilation.[135]

Moreover, the question of multiple identities will need to be addressed among the various Isma'ili communities, their priorities and the possible contrasting tendencies: being an Isma'ili, a Muslim, a citizen, as well as having an ethnic/cultural identity. If the directives of the late Aga Khan are to be fully implemented and translated to the contemporary context, allegiance to the nation of residence – whether Islamic such as Pakistan or Western such as Canada – would be central to a successful integration.[136] However, this is at variance with the discourse of contemporary Muslim revivalists for whom citizenship, particularly citizenship of a non-Islamic country, is at best secondary or, in more radical cases, outright irrelevant, to personal identity. An issue of primary importance in the understanding of how such identities are to be prioritised is the extent to which Isma'ili identity continues to be shaped by, reaffirmed and expressed through, the acknowledgment of the spiritual authority embodied in the present Aga Khan as imam, guide and spiritual leader of the Nizari Isma'ili communities.

Ever since 1902, when Sultan Muhammad Shah, at the opening speech of the All India Muhammadan Educational Conference in Delhi, identified the improvement of the status of Muslim women as one of the parameters for modern and successful Islamic societies, the discourse of the veil and female seclusion acquired increasing prominence in his speeches and *firmans*. Over time his directives indicated that being an Isma'ili woman should be expressed through participation in education, community and social activities, while keeping modest behaviour and spiritual focus. Up until now, whenever possible, Nizari Isma'ili women have indeed displayed their religious and cultural identities through their visibility and active involvement in economic, educational, social and community activities. Not wearing the veil has been one of the markers of their Isma'ili Muslim identity.[137]

Part Two

Examining the Scriptural Texts

Chapter 6

The Veil: Between Tradition and Reason, Culture and Context

Usama Hasan

Traditional Interpretations Regarding Women's Dress

Of over 6,000 *ayat* of the Qur'an, only about half a dozen refer specifically to the way a woman should dress and/or walk in public. Only two *ayahs* mention items of clothing: the *khimar* (head-cover) and the *jilbab* (outer garment). It is a sad reflection on contemporary Muslim discourse that these issues are usually given far more coverage than these statistics would suggest, with the issue of women's dress blown out of all proportion to the far more fundamental and essential Qur'anic themes of faith, prayer, charity, spiritual purification and progress, and the constant remembrance of God.

The noble Qur'anic term of *hijab*, which in its highest sense refers to the veil between humanity and God that is lifted in the Hereafter for those who purify their souls sufficiently,[138] has been reduced and incorrectly applied in modern discourse to a mere piece of clothing, for which the correct Qur'anic term is *khimar* (head-cover). The term *hijab* has many Qur'anic meanings, none of them to do with dress. The closest meaning to dress is the 'curtain' mentioned in the '*ayah* of *hijab*' that has nothing to do with headscarves or face-veils, but rather with gender-segregation in the Prophet's household.

Traditional interpretations of the two *ayahs* that mention the *khimar* and *jilbab* are analysed here, with a view to arriving at a holistic reading of the issue, which thus provides a link to the theory of *Maqasid al-Shari'ah* or the higher objectives of Islamic law.

The *ayah* of the *khimar* (head-cover)

Say to the believing men that they should lower their gaze and guard their modesty: that will make for greater purity for them: And Allah is well acquainted with all that they do.

And say to the believing women that they should lower their gaze and guard their modesty; that they should not display their beauty and ornaments except what (must ordinarily) appear thereof; that they should draw their veils over their bosoms and not display their beauty except to their husbands, their fathers, their husbands' fathers, their sons, their husbands' sons, their brothers or their brothers' sons, or their sisters' sons, or their women, or the slaves whom their right hands possess, or male servants free of physical needs, or small children who have no sense of the shame of sex; and that they should not strike their feet in order to draw attention to their hidden ornaments. And O ye Believers! turn ye all together towards Allah, that ye may attain Bliss.[139]

Regarding this subject, this part of the *ayah* is often quoted: 'They should not display their beauty and ornaments except what (must ordinarily) appear thereof.'[140]

This part of the *ayah* is understood by the commentators and jurists to classify a woman's *zinah* (adornment, ornaments, especially cosmetic make-up and jewellery) into two types: *zahirah* (apparent adornment) and *batinah* (hidden adornment). The latter type, which she is asked to conceal, is implied by the explicit mention of the former,[141] which she is allowed to reveal, since it is apparent by its very nature.

The following are some of the views of early authorities from the earliest generations of Islam, according to various commentators and jurists.

Imam Tabari[142] quotes a large number of authorities to support his view that this *ayah* means that a woman should cover up in public, except for her face and hands. She is thus permitted to display her face and hands as well as any jewellery or cosmetic make-up that is visible in these parts of the body, such as rings, eye-shadow or eye-liner and henna. Thus, the face and hands, along with the make-up and jewellery worn there, constitute the *zinah zahirah* (apparent adornment) that is ordinarily visible in public. The authorities from whom this view is quoted include Ibn 'Abbas,[143] 'Ata' b. Abi Rabah, Sa'id b. Jubayr, Qatadah, 'Amir b. Shurahil, Ibn Zayd, Dahhak and al-Awza'i. Some later jurists insisted that, if a woman wears make-up or jewellery on her face and hands, these must be covered.[144]

Tabari adds that there are one or two traditions from the Prophet (may Allah bless him and grant him peace), via Qatadah and 'Aishah respectively, that allow a woman to uncover her wrist or half her forearm. Hence, some of the early authorities also extended a woman's 'apparent adornment' to any bangles that she wears.[145]

With the 'apparent adornment' as described above, Tabari asserts that the 'hidden adornment' is therefore the rest of the body, including any cosmetics applied or jewellery worn there, such as necklaces, earrings and anklets. He explains that the command '... and they should draw their veils (head-covers) over their bosoms'[146] also means that women should cover their hair, necks and earrings.

Further, he mentions the other major view about this *ayah*, that is that the 'apparent adornment' refers to a woman's normal (outer) clothing, since clearly this will always be visible in public. This view is that of the following authorities: Ibn Mas'ud, Ibrahim al-Nakh'i and al-Hasan al-Basri. For example, Ibn Mas'ud is reported to have said that the 'apparent adornment' is the shawl or other wrapper worn over the upper body. However, Jassas argues that this view makes no sense since it is the parts of the body that are relevant: it is perfectly permissible to look at women's clothing or jewellery when these are not being worn. The authorities who mentioned eye-shadow and eye-liner, henna or rings were effectively referring to the face and hands, but similar logic cannot apply to the mention of clothing.[147]

Qurtubi states that 'adornment may be apparent or hidden ... As for hidden adornment, it is not lawful to reveal it except to those whom Allah Exalted has named in this *ayah, or their equivalent*'[148] (emphasis added).

Thus, according to Qurtubi, other males besides the close male relatives mentioned in this *ayah* may see the hidden adornment of women. Such males are primarily those mentioned in the penultimate category, in other words those who have no sexual appetite for the women concerned. According to Ibn al-'Arabi, on the authority of several Successors, this category includes the following: the impotent, the insane, the elderly, the starving and the servant.[149] The implication is that the servant has effectively become part of the family.

Ibn Kathir says that, due to the command to believing women to lower their gazes, 'many people of knowledge hold that a woman is not allowed to look at men who are not her close relatives at all, whether or not her glances are lustful', but quotes no such thing with regard to the gazes of men, even though there is an identical *ayah* relating to them.[150] He further says that the command to cover the bosom applies to the chest and midriff.[151]

The *ayah* of the *jilbab* (body wrapper)

O Prophet! Tell thy wives and daughters, and the believing women, that they should cast their outer garments over their persons (when abroad): that is most convenient, that they should be known (as such) and not molested. And Allah is Oft- Forgiving, Most Merciful. Truly, if the Hypocrites, and those in whose hearts is a disease, and those who stir up sedition in the City, desist not, We shall certainly stir thee up against them: Then will they not be able to stay in it as thy neighbours for any length of time.[152]

The traditional commentators are generally agreed that this *ayah* was revealed in the context of sexual harassment by the 'hypocrites, perverts and mischief-makers' towards the women of Madinah, especially female slaves, but including even the wives of the Prophet (may Allah bless him and grant him peace). There is agreement that the commandment in this *ayah* is for free women, whose dress should distinguish them from slaves. This interpretation is affirmed by Tabari, who also attributes it to Ibn 'Abbas.[153]

There remains the issue of what constitutes a *jilbab*. Qurtubi states that the correct view is that it is a garment that covers the whole body: God has commanded all women to cover up, and this can only be done with clothing that is not skin-tight. However, he admits that it is reported from Companions of the Prophet (may Allah bless him and grant him peace) such as Ibn 'Abbas and Ibn Mas'ud that the *jilbab* is no more than the *rida*, a shawl or wrapper for the upper body. He further mentions a minority view that the *jilbab* refers to the head-cover, face-veil or mask.[154] Ibn al-'Arabi repeats the explanations of Tabari and Qurtubi in extremely concise form.[155]

Ibn Kathir adds that the *jilbab* should further distinguish free Muslim women from the women of the Era of Ignorance (*jahiliyyah*), and that it is to be a shawl or wrapper worn over the head-cover, and known as an *izar* (also a wrapper) in his times.[156] He also quotes from Sufyan al-Thawri that it would be allowed in principle to look at the adornment (i.e. bodies and/or jewellery) of *dhimmi* women (non-Muslims under Muslim rule), but that this is forbidden due to the fear of temptation arising, not because their beauty is sacred. His reasoning is that the *ayah* commands only Muslim women to cover up (implying that non-Muslim women need not cover), so that it is known that they are free women, and not slaves or prostitutes.[157]

Qurtubi agrees with Tabari that this *ayah* orders free women, as opposed to slaves, to be known as such from their dress. He goes on: 'It has been said that it is now obligatory upon all women, whether free or slaves, to cover up entirely, including their faces. The woman, all of her, is private (*'awrah*): her body and voice.' He then mentions that the most chaste women he saw on his travels were those of Nablus, where they would only come out of their houses on Fridays, fully-covered, in order to attend the congregational prayer.[158] Interestingly, his fellow Andalusian Ibn al-'Arabi repeats the same statements, almost verbatim, adding that Nablus was thus the best of 'almost one thousand villages' that he had visited.[159] Both Andalusian commentators also mention that they saw 'many chaste women' in spiritual seclusion (*i'tikaf*) in the Furthest Mosque (*Masjid al-Aqsa*) in Jerusalem, remaining there until death.

Ibn al-'Arabi observes that excessive covering would defeat the purpose of being recognised that is mentioned in this *ayah*, and that therefore the point of the *ayah* is not to obligate excessive covering, but for free women to distinguish themselves from slaves who 'walk bare-headed, or with a face-mask only (i.e. without a head-cover or wrapper)'.[160] In contrast, Tabari and Qurtubi remark that it is not the recognition of individuals that is meant here, but of the class of free women as opposed to slaves.

It should be noted that the standard explanation of the context of this *ayah* has been severely challenged by the Andalusian scholars Ibn Hayyan and Ibn Hazm, and by the modern Hadith scholar Albani.

Ibn Hayyan remarks in his commentary on the Qur'an: 'The strongest view is that "believing women" covers both free women and slaves. More temptation is caused by slaves because of their more frequent coming and going compared to free women. Therefore, excluding female slaves from the generality of women needs clear textual indication [which is not found].'[161]

Ibn Hazm says about the standard explanation:

We absolve ourselves of this corrupt explanation that is a slip-up of a person of knowledge, a blunder by a respected, intelligent man or a fabrication by a wicked liar! This is because it says that Allah has given free rein to the perverted to attack the dignity of Muslim maidservants, and this is an eternal affliction! However, no two people of Islam disagree that molestation of, or fornication or adultery with, a slave-woman is as prohibited as that with a freewoman, as are the subsequent criminal punishments, with no difference between the two cases. For this and other reasons, it is incumbent that we must not accept the saying of anyone after the Messenger of Allah, may Allah bless him and grant him peace, unless they attribute it to him, peace be upon him.[162]

Ibn Hazm seems to be referring to Tabari and other traditionalist commentators at the beginning of the above polemic. At the end of it, he is referri to 'Umar b. al-Khattab, since all the commentators quoted in this article agree that he used to forbid slave-women from dressing like freewomen.

On the basis of this counter-argument, Albani refutes an unnamed contemporary author who had argued that the order to wear *jilbabs* was specific to a particular time. For Albani, this argument is dangerous since it leads to abrogation of the necessity of the *jilbab*, since modern Muslim societies no longer have slavery.[163]

The *ayah* of the *hijab* (curtain)

And when ye ask (his ladies) for anything ye want, ask them from before a screen: that makes for greater purity for your hearts and for theirs.[164]

As is clear from its text, this *ayah* obliged the Prophet's wives to be segregated from male visitors to his household.[165] The traditional commentators disagree as to whether or not this applies to all Muslim households, or just to that of the Prophet, may Allah bless him and grant him peace.

The word *hijab* mentioned in this *ayah* clearly refers to a curtain that effects segregation of the sexes.[166] Variants of the word *hijab* used in various *ahadith* also refer to a 'veil' in the sense of a curtain, screen or other means of segregation, but never in the modern meaning of 'head-cover' that is popularly associated with the word '*hijab*'. For example, the Prophet's order to his wife Sawdah bt. Zam'ah to 'veil herself' (*ihtajibi*) from 'Abd b. Zam'ah, an illegitimate son of her father, and to his wives Umm Salamah and 'Aishah (or Maymunah, according to a different narration) to 'veil themselves' (*ihtajiba*) from the elderly, blind Companion, 'Abdullah b. Umm Maktum. In the latter case especially, 'veiling' clearly refers to segregation and not covering, since the point was that they should not be looking at him; he, of course, was unable to look at them. The Hadith scholars Ahmad b. Hanbal and Abu Dawud held that this particular instruction was specifically and only for the Prophet's wives.[167]

The *ayah* of *tabarruj* (flaunting oneself in public)

O Consorts of the Prophet! Ye are not like any of the (other) women: if ye do fear (Allah), be not too complacent of speech, lest one in whose heart is a disease should be moved with desire: but speak ye a speech (that is) just.

And stay quietly in your houses, and make not a dazzling display, like that of the former Times of Ignorance; and establish regular Prayer, and give regular Charity; and obey Allah and His Messenger. And Allah only wishes to remove all abomination from you, ye members of the Family, and to make you pure and spotless.[168]

Ibn al-'Arabi understands the *ayah*, which is primarily directed at the Prophet's household, to mean that all women must stay at home, unless it is necessary for them to come out in public. However, he defends 'Aishah's return journey of hundreds of miles from Madinah to Basra during the incident of the 'Battle of the Camel' as being one of public necessity, since she intended reconciliation and peace in difficult political circumstances, and enjoyed much support from her followers.[169]

As for *tabarruj* (flaunting oneself in public), Ibn Kathir quotes different authorities as saying that this refers to women walking in front of men (*Mujahid*),[170] walking with coquettish or lascivious movements such as the swaying of hips in order to excite sexual passion (*Qatadah*), or to wearing a head-cover that is loose or untied such that her necklaces, earrings and neck are visible (Muqatil b. Hayyan).[171]

The *hadith* of Asma' about revealing only the face and hands in public

This is perhaps the most commonly-quoted *hadith* on the subject: 'Aishah, wife of the Prophet (may Allah bless him and grant him peace), narrated that her sister Asma' visited the Prophet whilst wearing transparent clothing. The Prophet is said to have averted his gaze and observed that an adult woman must cover up in public, except for her face and hands.

Amongst traditionalist jurists, a major disagreement over women's dress is whether or not she must cover her face in public. Hence, this *hadith* is highly controversial in such discussions. In fact, the scholars of *Hadith*, including Abu Dawud, the main transmitter of this report, generally agree that this narration is not authentic, since the narrator from 'Aishah, Khalid b. Durayk, never actually met her.[172]

Furthermore, it is argued that Asma', sister-in-law of the Prophet, wife of the esteemed Companion al-Zubayr b. al-'Awwam and mother of the great Muslim figures, 'Abdullah b. al-Zubayr and 'Urwah b. al-Zubayr, was known to be a woman of great piety: it is unthinkable that she would have appeared in public wearing revealing or transparent clothing. Thus, the jurists who argue that covering the face is obligatory are adamant that this *hadith* is inadmissible in legal discussions of the topic.

On the other hand, the jurists who insist on the legal verdict given in this *hadith* say that the narration is strengthened by numerous others which show that female Companions did not always cover their faces in public, even after the revelation of the *ayah* discussed earlier.[173]

Clearly, many of the early jurists did not regard this *hadith* as authentic and opposed the strict restrictions given therein, so that the *hadith* is ignored by both those who take a stricter view and those who take a less restrictive view than the one it expresses. For example, Imam Abu Hanifah famously did not require women to cover their feet in public. Tabari chose not to quote the 'face and hands' *hadith* as a final arbiter on the subject, but mentioned the *ahadith* that extend this permission to the wrist and half of the forearm.[174]

Since the *hadith* of Asma' is not authentic, and given the diversity of views of the jurists on the topic, it can be argued that the Prophet (may Allah bless him and grant him peace) did not specify exactly which parts of her body every woman should cover or display to every person who sees her, but taught general values and guidelines that would adapt according to time, place, context and culture. This is a holistic reading of the texts that is characteristic of the approach to Islamic law in terms of its higher objectives, the *Maqasid al-Shari'ah*, and is especially relevant to Muslims living as minority faith communities yet full citizens in relatively new contexts such as the modern Western world.

Analysis of Traditional Interpretations

The traditionalist discourse around women's dress is usually restricted to the following alternatives: she must cover from top to toe in public, except possibly for the face, hands and feet. The issue of how she dresses in private in the presence of close male relatives is rarely discussed in detail.

Here it is argued that this traditionalist position is itself a product of *ijtihad*, since there are traditional views that would be dismissed in traditionalist circles as ranging from extremely strict to extremely permissive. Examples of such views now follow:

The *ayah* of the head-cover allows a woman to reveal her beauty and adornment to close male relatives, but does not specify the form that this may take. The jurists have diverse views on this subject, except with regard to the husband, since the general view there is that there is no such thing as 'private parts' between husband and wife.

Jassas reports the following views from different authorities: that a man may look at the hair of his mother, sister, maternal aunt and paternal aunt, but that it is disliked to look at their legs below the knees (Ibrahim al-Nakh'i); it is not allowed for a woman to remove her head-cover in front of her brother (Hasan Basri); it is disliked for a man to look or stare at the hair of his daughter or sister (Tawus and Sha'bi). Jassas then provides the rather far-fetched interpretation that these narrations refer to situations where a man may be afflicted with incestuous temptation.[175]

Tabari reports from Qatadah that she may only uncover her head in front of male relatives. He further reports from Ibn 'Abbas that she may display her earrings, necklace and bangles before them, but as for her anklets, upper arms, neck and hair, these can only be displayed before her husband.[176] Ibn al-'Arabi adds that a similar view is reported from Ibn Mas'ud, and adds another view that a woman should cover her face in public but may uncover it in front of her father.[177] Thus, this view would require a woman to cover her head in front of her father and brothers. Ibn al-'Arabi quotes Sa'id b. Jubayr via Ayyub al-Sakhtiyani as saying that a woman may not display her hair in front of her son-in-law, since he is not mentioned in this *ayah*.[178] In fact, similar views to all these mentioned above were espoused in modern times by Mawdudi.[179]

At the other extreme, Mahalli and Suyuti state in their commentary on the Qur'an that a woman only needs to cover her body between the navel and knees in front of her father, brothers and everyone else mentioned in the *ayah* of the head-cover, and that therefore she may appear topless in front of them.[180] It should be noted that Suyuti was a Shafi'i jurist, and the 'navel-to-knees' view of a woman's *awrah* amongst her household is attributed to some of the students of Imam Shafi'i himself.[181]

Most of the commentators mention under the '*ayah* of the head-cover' that there are two views about what constitutes 'their women' to whom Muslim women may uncover themselves: all women in general, or other Muslim women only.[182]

Tabari also quotes from Ibn Mas'ud that the 'believing women' to whom this *ayah* is addressed refers only to free women, and not to slaves. This interpretation led some jurists to the view that female slaves were only required to cover their bodies between the navel and knees in public, and could therefore walk around topless.[183] The Hanafi jurist al-Jassas says that female slaves are not required to cover their faces or hair, and that even men who are complete strangers may look at their hair, arms, legs below the knees, chests and breasts.[184]

Qurtubi reports on the authority of Imam Zuhri that it is not appropriate for men to look at pretty females, whether they be adult women or young girls.[185] Ibn al-'Arabi suggests that a woman should perhaps cover in front of young boys, since it is possible that the latter might lust after the former or vice-versa.[186]

Regarding the *ayah* of the *jilbab*, Tabari famously quotes from several authorities, including Ibn 'Abbas and 'Abidah, that a woman is required to cover entirely from top to toe, except that she is allowed to uncover one eye, since she needs to see where she is going.[187] The tiny minority of jurists who tried to insist on such a view were perhaps being one-eyed themselves, and unaware of the importance of stereoscopic vision.

Most, if not all, of the primary narrations quoted in this section from early authorities are of disputed authenticity, which partly explains why the jurisprudence based on them is not mainstream. However, assuming that at least some of them are authentic, they would appear to illustrate that early understanding of these *ayat* was strongly conditioned by culture and context: for example, the insistence by some jurists that a woman must cover her head in front of her father and brothers.

The Theory of *Maqasid al-Shari'ah* (Higher Objectives of Islamic Law)

The *Shari'ah* is based on both universal and specific texts, principles and judgments from the Qur'an and the *Sunnah*, the example of the Prophet, peace be upon him. Far from being set in stone, the problem of specifically applying universal principles in Sacred Law has led to a vigorous debate throughout Islamic history and the complex evolution of an extremely diverse body of legal schools and opinions. Within three centuries of the founding of Islam, there were dozens of legal schools, of which about seven remain influential across the Islamic world, both Sunni and Shi'i. An important early debate that continues today was between traditionalists and rationalists over whether the universal principles of God's law were to be known by revelation or reason, or by both. The four main areas covered by classical *Sharia* were: *ibadat* (ritual worship), *mu'amalat* (economics), *munakahat* (marriage, divorce and family) and *jinayat* (crime and punishment).

A significant development in Islamic law between the fifth/eleventh and eighth/fourteenth centuries was the approach to legal purpose known as the theory of *Maqasid*, or the higher objectives of law. Imam Ghazzali (d. 505/1111) argued from a holistic reading of the Qur'an that the purpose of *Shari'ah* was to fundamentally preserve five matters: faith, life, wealth, intellect and family.[188] This development occurred six centuries before John Locke's articulation of a similar approach to law in England. Over the next three centuries after Ghazzali, theologians such as

Ibn Taymiyyah added a number of other 'fundamental purposes' of law: preservation of reputations, neighbourhoods and communities; fulfilment of contracts; moral purity; trustworthiness; the love of God. The culmination of this theory came with Shatibi (of Jativa, Andalusia, d. 790/1388), who explicitly synthesised traditionalist and rationalist approaches,[189] but Islamic legal theory and practice, once centuries ahead of other civilisations, fell into relative decline for the next half-millenium.

The last century has seen a renewed interest in *Maqasid*, especially amongst Muslim reformers, thinkers and revivalists, since this approach avoids legalistic hair-splitting and attempts to holistically recapture the essential spirit of Islamic law. The significance of this approach may be illustrated by the following quote from one of its masters, Ibn al-Qayyim (d. 751/351):

> The Islamic Law is all about wisdom and achieving people's welfare in this life and the afterlife. It is all about justice, mercy, wisdom, and good. Thus, any ruling that replaces justice with injustice, mercy with its opposite, common good with mischief, or wisdom with nonsense, is a ruling that does not belong to the Islamic Law, even if it is claimed to be so according to some interpretation.[190]

Recent thinkers such as Hashim Kamali of Malaysia have suggested that the following are 'legal purposes' that must be protected and promoted by the *Shari'ah*: fundamental human rights and liberties; public welfare; education; scientific and medical research; the environment.[191]

In conclusion, it could be said that *Maqasid* theory derives a set of rational legal principles based upon a holistic reading of tradition. The aim is thus to achieve a perfect balance between tradition and reason.

Relaxation of legal rules in times of hardship

The leading contemporary jurist, 'Abdullah b. Bayyah, has commented on the issue of Muslim women's dress in Western societies, especially when their personal safety may be at risk. He affirms his view that, in normal circumstances, a Muslim woman must cover her hair in public: she is only allowed to uncover her face and hands. However, he quotes Abu Hanifah's view that the feet may be uncovered, and quotes a minority view mentioned by the late master of Qur'an commentary and *Maqasid* at Zaytunah University in Tunisia, Ibn 'Ashur, that a woman may uncover her hair in public.[192] He further states that the obligation to cover her hair during prayer (*salat*) is of a slightly lesser degree, but only according to Imam Malik. Thus, if a woman prayed bareheaded, she would be encouraged (but not obliged) to repeat her prayer with her head covered, as long as the time for that prayer had not expired.[193]

Ibn Bayyah proceeds to discuss the difference in levels of prohibition and obligation, and between means and ends in prohibitions: the latter are more important than the former. After quoting Shatibi, Ibn al-Qayyim, Qarafi and Ibn al-'Arabi on these matters, he concludes: 'The presence of hardship may thus necessitate the uncovering of parts of the body', and mentions the *hadith* of Anas, who 'saw the whiteness of the shins' of the Prophet's wives 'Aishah and Umm Salamah at the Battle of Uhud, as they hurried around the battlefield, giving water to wounded soldiers with their skirts gathered up.[194]

Throughout his discussion, and from his choice of examples and quotes, Ibn Bayyah strongly implies that he would allow a Muslim woman to uncover her hair in public in Western societies if this was to avoid hardship. For example, in addition to the points mentioned above, he quotes Shatibi during his discussion as saying: 'Clear prohibitions may be violated if there is an overriding benefit involved.' However, it is not surprising that he does not explicitly make this statement, given his strong traditionalist background and membership of extremely conservative juristic councils such as the Islamic Fiqh Academy based in Mecca and the European Council for Fatwa and Research based in Dublin.

Such hardship may include the likely effects of harassment, social exclusion, alienation or provocation of resentment amongst neighbours.[195]

The importance of local custom and context

Islamic legal theory, including the principles (*usul*) and higher objectives (*Maqasid*), emphasises the importance of local custom ('*urf*) and context. For example, Ibn al-Qayyim devotes a long chapter in his detailed work on legal theory to the 'Change and diversity of legal judgments (*fatwa*) according to changing times, places, situations, intentions and habits.'[196] Shatibi similarly discusses the issue at great length in his *Muwafaqat*.

An example involving (men's) dress from a recent traditionalist jurist is interesting. The late Shaykh Muhammad b. Salih b. 'Uthaymin, a member of the panel of senior religious scholars of Saudi Arabia, discussed the fact that the Prophet (peace be upon him) would often wear no more than two wrappers for the upper and lower body respectively, plus a turban. He then commented that this was no longer the customary dress of the people of

Arabia, and that it would be inappropriate to wear such clothing now since this would go against the local custom of wearing a white robe and *ghutrah* or head-dress for men.[197]

It should be noted that conforming to local custom in terms of dress is an ancient characteristic of Muslim communities. For example, one reason why the customary public dress in Saudi Arabia and other Gulf states is still limited to a white robe for men and a black *jilbab* for women is to avoid individualism and ostentation in dress: communal life is so important that individuals 'melt into the crowd' even in terms of their dress.

Muslim Women's Dress From a Holistic, *Maqasid*-based Reading of the Qur'an and Sunnah

Based on the above discussions, we are now able to attempt a reading of the Islamic revelation that is holistic, balances tradition with reason and law with spirit, but is yet suited to modern contexts.

The underlying spirit of these texts is clear: it is for men and women to dress and behave with shyness and modesty (*haya'*) in public. The Qur'an mentions that Moses' future wife or sister-in-law came to him, walking bashfully or with shyness and modesty.[198] Further, one purpose of this ethos is to avoid sexualisation of the public space.[199]

The *ayah* of the *khimar* (head-cover)

This *ayah* and the preceding one encourages believing men and women to be careful when looking at the opposite sex, to avoid lustful glances, and to guard their chastity. Furthermore, women are asked to cover their bosoms.

Traditionalist readings require women to cover their hair in public, but, as we have seen, these are strongly conditioned by culture and context: for example, many pre-modern and even modern Western societies had men and women covering their heads in public until the middle of the 20th century, as cinema footage from Europe or the USA will show.

A rationalist reading would argue that uncovered female hair does not generally cause sexual temptation in modern Western societies (and others), and that therefore the requirement to cover the hair should no longer apply. This has been the view of modernist reformers such as Sir Sayyid Ahmad Khan of British India,[200] and the late Sheikh Zaki Badawi, former Imam and Khatib of the Regent's Park Mosque and founder of the Muslim College, both in London.

Another argument in this regard would be that the veil (head-cover) mentioned in this *ayah* is a means, not an end: the purpose is to cover the chest area, not the head. In response to the question as to why God would then mention the head-cover, it is argued that women in Arabia would cover their heads to protect them from the heat of the sun, but sometimes leave their breasts exposed, as found in some Islamic descriptions of the *Jahiliyyah* period and in some Byzantine-era depictions from Syria. Thus, the commandment in this *ayah* comprises a very practical method for covering the bosom with an existing and available piece of clothing: the head-cover.

Furthermore, it could be argued that the grammatical construction of the command involving head-covers is identical to that of another Qur'anic commandment – to strike terror into the hearts of one's enemies during war using horses.[201] If a jurist were to maintain a very literal understanding of the *ayah* of the head-cover, he or she would be forced to say, for consistency's sake, that modern warfare can only be conducted with horses, and not with tanks or armoured vehicles.[202]

The *ayah* of the *jilbab* (body wrapper)

The question as to whether or not this *ayah* was supposed to distinguish between slave-women's and freewomen's public dress is redundant, given the abolition of slavery throughout the world.

We are left with the simple teaching that a woman must cover up, in other words dress modestly, in public. The difference of opinion remains as to which body parts she must cover.

In response to those who obligate several layers of clothing for Muslim women, such as a *jilbab* over and above a *khimar* and other clothing, the view of Qurtubi and Ibn al-'Arabi that the point of the *jilbab* is to cover the body may be quoted.

The context of the Qur'anic revelation needs to be borne in mind as well: many of the Prophet's companions had very little clothing, and often only one garment or piece of cloth that was insufficient to cover the whole body. Recorded examples are those of 'Amr b. Salamah,[203] Mus'ab b. 'Umayr[204] and the Prophet's daughter, Fatimah.[205] Even whole rows of men were in this position whilst praying, their short garments tied above their shoulders such that their private parts were barely covered, and their legs bare: the women in the rows behind were commanded not to raise their heads from prostration until the men were sitting with folded legs.[206] Needless to say, underwear was virtually unknown. Hence, when the Prophet was asked whether it was acceptable to pray in one garment, he replied, 'Does each of you have two garments?'[207]

In similar vein, Bukhari heads a chapter: 'In how many garments may a woman pray?'; and begins with the statement of Ikrimah: 'If she covers her body with a single garment, it is sufficient.'[208]

The above analysis partly explains why many women of that time would largely stay at home – they simply did not have enough clothing to venture out in public, and the Prophet had forbidden, for example, the pre-Islamic practice of naked circumambulation of the Ka'bah.[209] Hence the Prophet only obliged them to come out twice a year: to attend the Eid congregation, even if they would not be praying due to menstruation. It was for these Eid occasions that the Prophet advised women who did not have a *jilbab* to borrow one from a friend,[210] since the *jilbab* is simply a cloth than can be used to cover the whole body.

Thus, this *ayah* simply means in modern times that women (and men) should be dressed modestly in public, without being provocative or drawing attention towards themselves. For example, a (modest) top, blouse, jumper, blazer, jacket, coat or similar garment would all suffice for a woman to achieve the purpose of wearing a *jilbab*.

The *ayah* of the *hijab* (curtain)

This *ayah* encourages gender segregation wherever appropriate and/ or possible or desirable, but does not obligate it, since many traditional authorities hold that it applies only to the Prophet's household.

The *ayah* of *tabarruj* (flaunting oneself in public)

This *ayah* clearly denounces lewd or lascivious behaviour in public, and aims to avoid a sexualisation of public society.

As for 'staying at home', this is mainly for monastic reasons: prayer and charity are encouraged later in the *ayah*. A woman's prayer is traditionally regarded as being better at home (although Ibn Hazm famously disagreed), but so is a man's prayer, except for the congregational ones. In fact, the idea that 'a man's home is his monastery' is a common one in the Islamic tradition, since 'Islam is like a society of married monks and nuns'.

Conclusion

In much contemporary Muslim discourse, the issue of women's dress is blown out of all proportion to the far more fundamental and essential Qur'anic themes of faith, prayer, charity, spiritual purification and progress, and the constant remembrance of God.

The noble Qur'anic term of *hijab*, which in its highest sense refers to the veil between humanity and God that is lifted in the Hereafter for those who purify their souls sufficiently, has been reduced and incorrectly applied in modern discourse to a mere piece of clothing on a woman's head.

Traditionalist readings of the Qur'an tend to insist that women cover up in public, possibly including the face, hands and feet. These readings can be seen to be strongly influenced by culture and context, with many traditional views on the subject of veiling being problematic for even modern traditionalists, ranging from the extremely harsh to the extremely permissive.

A holistic reading of the relevant Qur'anic texts, balancing tradition with reason and law with spirit, would simply suggest the following: believing men and women are to dress and behave modestly in public; people should be careful when looking at the opposite sex, avoid lustful glances, lewd or lascivious behaviour, and guard their chastity; sexualisation of the public space is to be avoided; women, like men, have every right to participate in the public space in matters such as politics, education, commerce, healthcare, agriculture, leisure and worship.

Chapter 7

An Exploration of the Debates Pertaining to Head Covering and Face Veiling of Women in the British Muslim Context

Rabiha Hannan

The wearing of the head covering and/or face veil (this may or may not include the covering of the eyes) is often viewed as a prerequisite to being a 'good practising *Muslima*'. Dr Amina Wadud describes it as a perceived 'sixth pillar of Islam'.[211] So much importance is given to it, that without it many would not consider a Muslim woman to be pious. There may well be evidence to show its merits and importance, yet is such a judgement of internal piety justified, especially when there appears to be no precise parallel for men? Is there a possibility that the concept of the head covering and face veil has been misunderstood? Could it be that the Islamic texts say less than we have read into them with respect to the head covering and face veil, and it is actually cultural expression that has given form to many of today's practices?

This chapter aims to explore different perspectives in the interpretation of female dress in Islam, particularly with respect to the head covering and face veil. It seeks to understand where the principles of head and/or face covering are derived from, the purpose for which such coverings are worn, and their interpretation in modern life.

The chapter involves multiple methods of research, namely literature reviews, interviews with UK-based *ulama* (clerics) and data from focus groups of women living in Leicester, UK.[212] The British Scholars of Islam were selected for interview, primarily because of their very different opinions on the dress requirement of Muslim women in Islam.[213]

The focus groups were composed as follows:

- group a: women who cover all parts of their body including the face
- group b: women who cover all parts of their body except the face or hands
- group c: women who dress 'modestly',[214] but do not wear a head covering or face veil.

Exploring the discourse on the head cover and face veil

To begin to understand the issues around this area of research, it will be important initially to analyse what the references in the Qur'an actually say with respect to female covering. Appendix I at the end of the chapter lists the relevant verses of the Qur'an in full.

When women in the focus groups were asked what evidence they had based their interpretation of covering on, they all replied 'the Qu'ran and the *ahadith*';[215] when asked to specify where exactly in the Qur'an or which *hadith*, both groups 'a' and 'b' mentioned Sura an-Nur. In group 'a' some reference to Sura al-Ahzab was also made, but no specific language for head covering or face veil was identified. All groups articulated that, when clarity was not in the Qur'an, the *ahadith* were sought as back-up. But group 'a' failed to find a reference that clearly exhorted the covering of the face.[216] Group 'b' quoted the *hadith* about Asma[217] to clarify the requirement of covering everything except the hands and face. However when told that the Asma *hadith* had a 'weak' chain of narration[218] and asked if they knew any other, they could not think of one. Generally members of both groups felt that the underlying principles of covering were based on what scholars had understood from references in the Qur'an and *ahadith* and therefore it was not necessarily essential for them to be aware of specific references themselves.

One of the scholars, Momoniat, who felt it was better for women to cover their face, explained that although the Qur'an did not mention covering of the face there were some *ahadith* which demonstrated its practice. However, he felt the main understanding of dress requirements were derived through scholarly interpretation and discussion.

The initial understanding of a Muslim female's dress requirement is based upon early historical interpretation of verses in the Qur'an and *ahadith* by scholars. It becomes obvious to state that, as humans, they would have been influenced by their social context, the cultural and the political scene at the time.

What's in a word? An exploration of terminology used

Most of the literature available on female covering in Islam appears to rely upon the interpretation of particular verses in the Qur'an (see Appendix I). These 'translations' primarily form the basis upon which the female dress requirements have become established.

However, two issues are of paramount importance here. The first is that, when reviewing particular *ayat* in such a way, it becomes apparent that there are specific words for which the meaning and interpretation can vary quite significantly. Which interpretation is used impacts heavily on the perception of the dress/covering prescribed for women.

Second, the interpretation itself appears to be very much dependant on how the author/commentator of the *tafsir* (exegesis) regards the subject matter. This may be influenced by the author's social context, as well as their own understanding of what role Islam requires of a woman. The three scholars interviewed were asked about some of the terminology used in these verses and how their interpretation might impact on the dress of Muslim women.

In this section, I have tried to explain the words in the Qur'anic verses that appear to cause the greatest degree of controversy. I hope to demonstrate the diversity of translations, and the broad range of opinions that ensue as a result.

Hijab

Hijab is a term used by many to constitute the female dress in Islam. Its literal meaning in accordance with the Shorter Encyclopaedia of Islam is 'any partition which is used to separate two things'.[219] Many Muslims today, however, will attribute it to the body and head covering of a Muslim woman which may or may not include the covering of the face also.

During my focus group sessions I was very careful not to use the word *hijab* when enquiring about the requirements for female covering, yet all of the focus groups made some reference to it. For all of them, *hijab* meant the covering of the head and body (not including the face). Amongst group 'a' (those who covered the face), women drew a distinction between those like themselves who wore the *niqab*, and those that chose to wear *hijab* only (i.e. those who left only their hands and face exposed).

What is interesting to note is that, although the term *hijab* appears to be used frequently in modern terminology with respect to Muslim female dress code, it is not mentioned in this context in the Qur'an.[220] Perhaps this is why, when the question of *hijab* was deliberately posed to the scholars, al-Judai clarified[221] that the term in some way connotes its own specific impression of what Islamic dress should look like. As the Qur'an does not use it in this way, he prefers to use the term *satr* (covering) instead. He further explained that the reason that the Qur'an has not prescribed it in such a set format is to enable flexibility and thereby ease for one's own interpretation of it, in accordance with time and tradition. He further elaborated,

> ... if you ask any scholar to draw the exact *requirement* of what the female covering is, he will not be able to do so. (Interview)

It is not that his understanding of 'covering' does not have boundaries, but he limits those to what he believes the Qur'anic texts clearly specify.[222]

Regarding the mention of *hijab* in Sura al-Ahzab, Mernissi believes that this verse has been used incorrectly to enforce the concept of *hijab* as a separation of the woman from wider society. She says that on closer observation, however, and given an understanding of the historical context of the revelation, it actually reveals that this verse was not to provide a barrier between a man and a woman, but between two men. More specifically, between a man in the public sphere and a man in his more intimate and private sphere.[223]

Mernissi feels that the verse has been taken out of context. She quotes al-Suyuti: 'It is impossible to understand a verse without knowing the *qissa* [the story], and the causes that lead to its revelation' (Mernissi 1991: 93). She uses the *hadith* in Bukhari to back her perspective.[224] For Mernissi, the meaning of the verse should not only be assessed in the face of the *hadith*, though, but also in the historical and political context of the time:

> Islam went through a time of severe military crisis ... an epoch of doubts and military defeats that undermined the morale of the inhabitants of Medina ... a careful re-reading of the verse reveals that Allah's concerns in this verse are about tact. He wanted to intimate to the Companions certain niceties that they seem to lack – like not entering a dwelling without asking permission ...[225]

She explains further how the verse on *hijab* was specific for the Prophet and his family, and a symbol to 'a community that had become too invasive'.[226] The verse was meant to limit offensive behaviour and encourage treatment of the Prophet and his family with more respect. Mernissi is successful in adding another dimension to the debate, by contextualising it in this way. It challenges the notion that *hijab* is a means of confinement or separation of women (or at least the wives of the Prophet), instead interpreting it as a reprimand to the men at that time, to assess and control their behaviour, especially in respect of an individual's right to personal/private space, and more specifically the privacy of the Prophet and his wives.

Darsh further clarifies, saying that 'Most of Sura al-Ahzab deals with the household of the Messenger. The wives of the Prophet were pressing for a better life than the hard tough life they were facing.'[227] Hence the wives were given the option of staying with the Prophet and enduring the hardships and austerity that came with being the wife of a Prophet or being allowed to leave and have a better worldly life. They all chose to stay with the Prophet, and in turn were given a set of rules and regulations in exchange for double the reward for ordinary women, as well as the position of 'Mother of the Believers' (see Appendix I, verse 6).

Some believe that, if the wives of the Prophet are role models for all females, then they should be emulated in every way possible. This is reason enough for women to separate themselves physically from men, by using a complete covering, as did the wives of the Prophet.

It appears that a parallel has been drawn for men and women in respect to the Prophet and his wives. For men, the 'example' is the Prophet; for women, however, it should be his wives. This may seem logical at first; the wives were indeed great women worthy of respect. However, this logic does not hold, as Muslims believe the Prophet was the example for all of mankind (male and female). Also nothing exemplifies the difference between the wives of the Prophet and ordinary women more clearly than the aforementioned verse itself. In reference to the Prophet's wives, it states: 'You are not like other women.' And it gives the reason for their distinction: 'And Allah only wishes to remove all abomination from you, ye members of the Family, and to make you pure and spotless.'

How this verse is interpreted, then, can have a profound effect on how the interaction of the sexes is understood to occur in an Islamic society; on what the role of each of the sexes is, and how one should dress in front of the other.

Jilbab

Similar to reactions to the word *hijab*, when the word *jilbab* is used today, many Muslims will conjure up in their minds a very fixed dress requirement. This, as defined by Momoniat, is required to be: 'A long thick item of clothing which covers other clothes worn in the home. It either covers the complete top half of a lady or covers the chest down to the ankles and would therefore be worn with a *khimar*' (interview).

However, the dictionary definition of the *jilbab* (*jalabib*) is a 'garment, dress, gown, woman's dress'. Hence, according to the dictionary, it is not a specific type of clothing at all, or even an 'outer garment'. Thus it seems it could quite easily be adapted to different cultural norms; for instance as *shalwar kameez* in Pakistan, or as a blouse/shirt and trousers in the UK. Raza says:

> *Jilbab* [as viewed today] is one of the ways of fulfilling the institution of covering. It is not the only way, so if one chooses to conceal [...] in this way, it does fully fulfil the requirement. But I don't think it should be conceded as the only means of fulfilling the requirement of *hijab*. I don't think that any *ayah* [verse] in the Qur'an indicates one single design or shape, but anything that covers the *awra*, that is loose, not transparent, and does not disclose the shape of the body [will suffice]. (Interview)

Al-Judai agrees, but also clarifies how the head covering may also be a separate item of clothing from that which covers the chest: 'Provided the lower dress is covering the *jayb* (bosom) then there is no need to cover it with the *khimar* (head-cover) too' (interview). On being asked to explain why the Sura then says: 'draw your *khimar* over ...', he replied: 'The problem here is that [people have] the wrong understanding; we link this [verse] to the *khimar* itself, but it is not to the *khimar*, it is to this area that needs to be covered [i.e. it is] about covering the *jayb*' (Interview). In al-Judai's understanding, the verse has been misunderstood to mean that people must use their headscarf to cover their chests. However, the point is rather to ensure that the chest is covered; whether this is with a closed shirt/blouse or a *jilbab* is not the point.[228]

Khimar

This is the term used in Sura an-Nur, as well as various *ahadith* about dress. Its translation appears to take discussants off to even greater tangents than other words.

For some it means the covering of the face and head.[229] The dictionary describes it as a 'covering of the head/face.'[230] For others such as al-Judai it very clearly means 'the cover of the head, with no doubt in the use of the language.' Momoniat also felt that it was a head covering only. When asked if this was where he understood the covering of the face to be derived from, he replied that the *khimar* very definitely translates as the head cover, but the understanding of covering the face is not from the Qur'an itself, but from various *ahadith* and scholars' opinions (author's words).

Al-Judai further elaborated that the *khimar* did not have to be of a particular length or style:

What you are wearing now (a long scarf over the head, covering the chest area), and what your friend is wearing (a shorter scarf, only covering the hair), are both *khimar*; if someone wore a hat that too would be *khimar*. *Khimar*, constitutes a covering on the head. (Interview)

It was interesting to note that al-Judai did not feel that every hair on the head was necessarily to be covered, nor that it mattered if the earlobes or the neck were exposed. The baseline was for something to be on the head, and for the chest to be appropriately covered with something.[231] In contrast, Raza's understanding was that: 'As far as I understand it, the scholars have defined the word *khimar* as something for a woman for the covering of her head and the upper front part of her body.'

I probed further,and pointed out that, according to the English translation, the word *khimar* appears to be used incidentally in this verse and that the point of the verse is to actually draw attention to covering the chest region of a woman and not the head at all. That because the *khimar* was worn by most women at the time, often with part or the whole of their chest exposed, it was an item of clothing people were already familiar with and could use to cover their breasts. Raza replied:

Yes, you are quite right, the exact words in the Qur'an do not in any way expressly indicate the head covering at all in this verse. But the scholars of Qur'an and *tafsir* have consistently adopted this opinion that the Qur'an was revealed in the language of the people of that time, and in that time they were using the *khimar* as a head cover also. (Interview)[232]

'But does that not mean that, when you have a different culture, tradition and time, it would affect the way that the head covering is used today?', I asked.

Perhaps if someone insists that it is not prescribed strictly in *Sura an-Nur*. In that case we will go to the *hadith*, the sayings of the Prophet, as he is the most learned person of the Qur'an. And when he speaks about the concept of *hijab*, then he supports the head covering, and that will support the scholars' interpretation also. (Interview)[233]

Jayb

This word is found in *Sura an-Nur*, when women are asked to cover *juyubi-hinna*[234] with their *khimar*. On asking Raza the meaning of this word, he replied: 'It is the upper front part of the body, around the neck; this is what the word *jayb* means. I don't think there is any dispute of the translation of this word at all.'

It would appear that this definition would seem straightforward enough and not deserving of scrutiny in the same way as others. Ironically, though, the diversity in the translation of this word could not be more varied. Momoniat described it initially as the 'curve' (of the bosom), although he also felt the meaning extended to include the neck and ears also. Indeed in some translations of the Qur'an this would appear to be the definition.

However, al-Judai says:

> ... the Qur'an is clear that the *jayb* [he points to the chest area] needs to be covered. When this (neck slit) is opened it would show any movement of the body. Covering this makes very clear sense, if you go back and try to understand at the time when this *ayah* was revealed. (Interview)

Indeed, if we look at the history and context of this verse, it becomes apparent that the cultural practice of the time allowed women to cover the head and sometimes the face, but leave the chest exposed (either fully or partly).[235] The verse, then, was a direct command against this practice – in other words, 'use your *khimar* to cover your breasts'.

On closer examination of the Arabic language, the word translates as 'breast, bosom, cavity, heart'; it is even used for '(the mathematical sine) curve'.[236] Hence this demonstrates clearly which specific region of the body the term is referring to.[237]

Zeena

The term *zeena* is very intriguing, and is one of the terms that is most often disputed. Raza explains:

> Scholars have differed upon its interpretation since the early companions when Ibn Masud, who was a Sahabi, said the *zeena* included the outer garment, that is also the face and hands and every part of body, but in the opinion of Ibn Abbas, another Sahabi and, as far as I know, one of the first scholars of *tafsir*, he says it doesn't include the face and hands. (Interview)

So it is nothing new. Even in the basic translation there are differences; in Yusuf Ali it is described as 'beauty and ornaments'; however, Pickthall chooses to describe the word as meaning 'adornment' and not 'beauty'.

There is also discussion around whether *zeena* should include things like jewellery or make-up. Raza's approach to this is very rational, and, in accordance with many other traditional scholars, he feels: 'Anything on the face or hands is not included as part of the *zeena*, but anything other than that will be included. So if we exclude the face then we exclude anything on the face, like jewellery or make-up' (interview). Raza did, however, express some reservation about how the make-up was being used, and to assess the impact it may have.

Interestingly, this view is contrary to the thinking of the focus groups. Most women in group 'a' felt that any form of beautifying yourself other than in the home was wrong. Two of them used the concept of covering as a reason why the whole of the woman should ideally be covered (including the eyes and face), as she may cause 'attraction'.[238]

For ladies in focus group 'b' the idea of wearing make-up for some was acceptable (especially if necessary for work or when attending a wedding, so to fit in and not stand out). However, others who wore make-up saw it as a fault in themselves rather than something that was acceptable in Islam. One commented: 'I wear lipstick, but I do not see my *hijab* as ideal.'

Illa ma zahara minha

Much less emphasis appears to be put upon these words when trying to understand the female dress requirement, and yet they appear to hold the key to what (if any) are the precise requirements of covering.

In Muhammad Asad's *tafsir* (exegesis) of *Sura an-Nur*, he translates the verse as: 'And tell the believing women to lower their gaze and to be mindful of their chastity, and not to display their charms beyond *what may (decently) be apparent thereof ...*'[239] He says:

My interpolation of the word 'decently' reflects the interpretation of the words '*illa ma zahara minha*'.

He explains how the interpretation of these words is much broader than the 'restricted definition of a woman's face hands and feet (or even less)', and that 'the deliberate vagueness of this phrase is meant to allow for all the time bound changes that are necessary for man's moral and social growth'.[240]

Hence what may be 'decent' in one tradition, culture, or even time period may differ from that in another. The words appear to deliberately allow flexibility for change of circumstance, enabling the text to be not time-bound, and relevant for all.

In contrast, Maududi translates the same extract from *Sura an-Nur* as: 'And enjoin the believing women to restrain their gaze and guard their private parts and additionally not to reveal their adornment *except that which is revealed of itself*'.

Maududi explains how '*zeena*' (here, 'adornment') is anything that makes a woman look attractive: clothes, ornaments, cosmetics. He elaborates: 'Obviously the intent of this verse is that women should not intentionally show their charms and beauty.'

He therefore disagrees explicitly with the understanding that women may wear attractive clothing, jewellery or make-up. He interprets the face and hands of the woman as well as the rest of the body as something which it is 'customary to keep covered'. However, if, for example, a gust of wind blew away such a covering, and the woman was accidentally exposed, that would allow for '*illa ma zahara minha*' ('what is revealed of itself'). Maududi thus makes a distinction between what an individual chooses to reveal of themselves and what might reveal itself accidentally.

The late Sheikh Darsh felt that 'The *apparent* adornment (and therefore what can be shown) is that which is on the face and hands. For it is these which appear on the face and hands on *Hajj*, as an act of *Ibadah* [worship] and as a way of life they are customarily uncovered' (Darsh 1995: 23).

It is interesting that both Darsh and Maududi refer to the understanding of 'what is customarily uncovered'. They both come from societies which customarily would cover the hair. However, what if the society was one such as that in Britain, in which women don't customarily cover their hair – would the meaning of 'apparent adornment' then be different?[241]

All of the focus groups used the terms *hijab* and *jilbab*, some used the word *khimar*, but no one used the word *zeena* or the saying *illa ma zahara minha*.

Exploring the Practice and Purpose of the Head Cover and Face Veil

Differing interpretations of how much the Muslim woman should cover, and what type of dress or style should be worn, often depends upon the perception of what purpose that covering serves. So, for example, some Muslims believe that wearing a head cover and/or face veil enables a woman to participate fully in society, without being judged on her sexuality. Rather than separate or isolate her from society, it should allow her to engage actively in it, without the risk of being undermined or exploited because she is female. They feel this way of dressing demands respect.

For others a Muslim woman's main responsibility lies in the home, towards her husband and other family members. Leaving the home is only if really necessary. Thus she should be protected from the gaze of onlookers and prevented from being the cause of *fitna*,[242] by covering. Her dress for the 'outside world' then is quite different in extent and style.

Obviously, these are two very different views on the 'purpose of covering' and how that lends itself to the practice. It must be noted that women who choose to cover their faces do not necessarily feel this is an impediment to interacting in society. If anything the representatives in focus group 'a' – young, confident and articulate women, who all wore the face cover out of choice – clearly demonstrated otherwise.

In this next section I list the reasons why some women in Leicester (from each of the focus groups) felt it was necessary to dress/cover themselves in the way that they did.[243] I aim to draw a comparison between what they themselves believe to be the purpose of covering and what understanding the scholars derive from the Qu'ran, *ahadith*, and historical accounts.

Reasons for Covering

As an act of worship

Most women from all three focus groups felt their style of dress was overwhelmingly based on what they believed God had asked of them. For many it was through an increased religiosity and spiritual awareness (whether that came through a trip for *Umra/Hajj* or the death of a near relative) that triggered a desire to practise Islam more meticulously and had led to them covering themselves the way they do. Their understanding of the dress requirements was clearly based upon what they believed to be Islamic directives in the Qur'an, although it was not necessarily through reading the Qur'an that such meaning had been derived. For most, the understanding of what the dress requirement for a woman in Islam should be came from the example of other, more 'pious' women around them.

As protection

The idea of 'covering as a means of protection' comes from Sura al-Ahzab (33:59): '… so that they may be recognised and not molested'.

Some women in focus group 'a' (who covered the face) referred to this as one of the reasons that Islam requires them to dress as they do. However, not all women in the group felt that it did serve as a means of protection for them. In groups 'b' and 'c', it was only when asked whether protection could be viewed as a purpose that discussion began around it.

The verse appears to have been revealed at a time in which:

> ... the social structure of a slave-owning society in which sexual abuse (especially of slaves) was rampant ... In mandating the *jilbab* its purpose was to distinguish free believing women from the slaves, who were perceived by *Jahili*[244] men to be non-believers and thus fair game.[245]

It thus served for Muslim women as a means of protection from abuse, at a time when a woman had to look out for herself as there was no legal recourse in place for women who needed to go out, but did not want to be sexually harassed in the process. Raza, too, feels the verse has contextual significance:

> Historically there was a time it (head covering) was being used as protection definitely ... but it cannot be a general reason for all time, that if you are in a 'head covering' you are protected and safe. In certain circumstances it may be, but I would not see this as universal. (Interview)

Group 'a' was asked whether, after Jack Straw's comments, they felt less safe or less protected with a face covering. They agreed that it had further alienated people's perception of what the *niqab* (face covering with eyes visible) was about. However, when questioned as to whether they would take it off as a means of protecting themselves in certain areas of their city which may be less tolerant of ethnic minorities, they all vigorously agreed that they would not. One lady replied that she would just not go to such an area. Another felt that this sort of prejudice was similar to racial prejudice, and you could not defeat that by giving in. A third felt that she would go and trust that God would protect her – after all she was wearing it for Him. Raza commented:

> All the *fuqaha* agree on the law of necessity in *Sharia* law. If the life of a community is at risk, or if the security or safety of an individual is at risk, then this law is triggered. (Interview)

Hence in such circumstances it would be permissible to remove even the head covering. Momoniat also felt that such situations allowed for the removal of the face veil, but this should be left to the female's choice. Strikingly, although none of these women felt that the face covering was obligatory (only a recommended part of the *Sunna* – and therefore not a sin if they were to take it off), most of them would risk potential danger to stand up for the right to wear it.

This may be interpreted as devout piety or increased religiosity. But it does seem to run counter to the spirit of scholars' views, and to the 'ease' that Islam prescribes. This point is not to undermine the importance of standing up for your rights. However, the clarity sought here would be to distinguish between whether such practice is upheld for religious purposes (as a legal prescription) or for the principle of dressing as you choose. In an age when the right to dress as you choose is perceived to be a fundamental prerequisite of personal rights, it appears that the socio-political context of having that right was more important than one's own safety or what was actually an obligation to God. Was this position of covering, then, to somehow make a stand against the 'unjust' influences that said otherwise, more so than for the purpose of following religious injunctions?

Another interesting component of protection highlighted by Momoniat was the purpose of protecting the man. He felt that the covering of the woman, including the face, prevented much *fitna*. He described the woman as so beautiful that she was just like a pearl or a jewel that should be hidden away from greedy eyes. However, her dress was not just to protect her, but also to protect the chastity of man – because if he saw her it may induce in him incorrect feelings.

Barlas views this understanding to mean that women's bodies are perceived as 'pudendal, hence sexually corrupting to those who see them; it is thus necessary to shield Muslim men from viewing women's bodies by concealing them'.[246] However, Barlas feels that there is no evidence for this interpretation from Qur'anic teachings. Indeed it appears that the concept of protection has become somewhat inverted from that which protects and prevents a woman from being sexually harassed to protecting the male.

Barlas continues: 'the *jilbab* is not meant to hide free Muslim women from Muslim men, but to render them invisible to *Jahili* men as a way to protect the women'.[247]

For identity

For focus group 'b' (women who dressed modestly and covered the hair), this was one of the first reasons given for covering, and many of them viewed it as a key purpose of covering. This concept worked in three ways for most, if not all, of the group members:

1. because it clearly showed people that you were a Muslim (as distinct from other religions or none);[248]
2. because it made you an example of Islam to the public, in other words it was a means of showing people what Islam was about;
3. because it affected your own actions and behaviour, as you knew you had to present Islam in the best way.

The second and third points were particularly stressed by some members of the group. One commented: 'I went through a stage where I took it off (the head cover), and it affected my behaviour a lot.' Another woman who delayed wearing the head covering (even when she thought it was oblig-atory) commented: 'I didn't want to wear it and then be a bad example … I only wanted to wear it when I was being the best I could be.' A third commented: 'For me, I'm always aware that I'm giving an impression of a Muslim woman, so I'm always careful to behave in the best way, so that people get a good impression of Islam.'

Focus group 'a' also felt that identity played a part in the importance of covering the face, for similar reasons. The new Muslims in the group also agreed that: 'it's good *da'wah* (a call to Islam), as when people see that you are a Muslim, they can ask about Islam'. When asked if it was possible that covering the face could be a barrier to *da'wah*, as people might be scared of it, some did not acknowledge this. Those that did felt it was because of the way the media had depicted the image of the woman wearing the *niqab*, as opposed to its actual appearance.

Interestingly, however, two of the scholars interviewed felt that 'identity' should not be looked upon as a reason for Muslim women to dress as they do.

Al-Judai said:

I don't like the word 'identity' here. The female covering should be in the context of the culture. And therefore you have your identity as a British person (who covers),you're your identity as a 'Muslim'. I disagree with the concept of 'Islam as an identity', because Islam is a 'way of life'.

For al-Judai, the covering of the head is culturally dependant. In Pakistan it could be by way of a shawl or *dupatta*, and in Britain it could be a hat or a bandana. It is not dependant upon being 'recognised' or identified as a Muslim.[249]

Raza explains: 'Modesty or chastity should be the term used to reflect identity'. For him, too, it was not important for you to be seen as a Muslim, but that your dress reflected that you are a modest and chaste person. He continued:

> I'm sorry to say this, but there are examples of women in *hijab* (cover everything, but hands and face) that do things which are not Islamic, so how can *hijab* be used as a means of showing Islamic identity? (Interview)

For modesty

For members of all of the focus groups the concept of modesty appeared to be important, but how that modesty was defined varied significantly.

A group 'a' participant commented:

> At college, boys would sometimes come up and ask me to go out with them ... but as soon as I wore a headscarf that stopped. Even with the *abaya*,[250] the way that men dealt with and respected you was greater and with *niqab* it went up even more.

Another, in group 'b', said: 'Even non-Muslim boys in my class would respect me so much they would tell me if my hair was showing, etc. [so I could correct my headscarf].'

Women in group 'c' felt that, although they did not cover their head, they were still always very careful to wear loose clothing, so as not to emphasise parts of the body. They would also ensure the more private areas of the body were fully covered. Some of the ladies in this group also felt that some women who covered their head wore inappropriate clothing with their headscarf and that they had actually lost the concept of dressing modestly.[251]

For beauty/attractiveness

The women in focus groups 'a' and 'b' both felt that one of the purposes of covering was to 'hide' your beauty, and a few even felt it was to make you look less attractive. This, however, appeared to be in contrast to what was prescribed in the Qur'an: 'O children of Adam! Wear your beautiful apparel (*zeena*) at every place of worship, and eat and drink, but do not be wasteful ...' (7:31).

For Yusuf al-Qardawi the injunctions specified in these three verses must be adhered to: 'Whoever neglects these aspects, either "covering" or "adornment", has deviated from the way of Islam towards the path of

Satan. Allah accordingly warns people of nakedness and neglect of good appearance as these are snares of Satan.'[252]

Some in the focus groups felt that there was a difference between dressing smartly and dressing attractively. One commented: 'Attractiveness for me is deliberately going out of your way to attract attention; most women know if they are doing that.' For others, in group 'b', it was about not standing out. Interestingly, that could work two ways: by dressing up (wearing nicer clothing), or dressing down (by not wearing something that makes you stand out). As one participant stated:

> I think, provided it's loose, and not transparent, it could be anything. When I go to a wedding I will fit in, by dressing modestly but still wearing makeup etc. … but I don't believe I am attracting attention to myself because everyone else is dressed in the same way. But if I wore it like that to town I would stand out, so I feel in that context that would be wrong.

Most group 'a' members felt that any means of beautifying oneself in front of the opposite sex was forbidden. Hence the reason for covering of the *whole* body, ideally even the hands, face and eyes (although some disagreed about the eyes). For two women, the dress should be dull/dark-coloured, so as not to attract attention. 'If it's about covering beauty, then it makes sense to cover the hands and face, and any beauty attached to it, so even embroidery on a *jilbab* could be too attractive.'

Only one lady from group 'a' felt that there was flexibility. She explained that when she went to Jamaica she was attracting more attention by having her face covered, and was thought of as a 'tribal princess', so she chose to wear light pastel colours there instead, as this attracted less attention than the dark. She also chose to remove her face veil (though still kept her scarf closed in on her face). This indicated that the social environment made a difference to her style of dress.

Momoniat did not believe that the covering of the face was actually specified in the Qur'an. However, through interpretation of *hadith* and scholarly works on the subject, he felt that it was highly recommended for a woman to do so. He linked closely the idea of beauty with respect. I asked him whether this was an abdication of the man's responsibility to 'lower his gaze' and act respectfully towards a woman. He replied, 'Unfortunately that's what society has become, and that's why it is important for a woman to protect herself.' When I suggested that it was ironic that a woman would often feel more respected by men in a non-Muslim society than by men in a Muslim society, he agreed that this may be because the women were constantly being reminded how to dress, but the men were not told as much to keep their behaviour in check.[253]

Interestingly for Raza, the covering for the female was not actually about covering up her beauty, but more about preserving her dignity and being modest. He commented:

> ... as the face and the hands are not part of the *zeena*, what you choose to decorate them with is not part of the *zeena* also ... this is what is understood by ... 'what ordinarily appears thereof' – hence the use of jewellery, make-up etc. is thus allowed and not an issue. (Interview)[254]

However, what does appear to be an issue for Raza is when a woman knowingly dresses provocatively to draw attention to her body, and thus invites rude or improper behaviour, as this does not serve the purpose of preserving her chastity.

This particular rationale for the purpose of dress proved fascinating; what appeared clear was that beauty is not necessarily definable – perhaps, as the saying goes, 'beauty is in the eye of the beholder'.

To signify status

Mernisssi, Engineer and others regard the concept of covering the head and face as being, rather than a religious requirement, a means of identification of the status of a woman in society. Al-Judai would appear to agree with this, but only with respect to the covering of the face. He comments:

> There is a word from Imam Mujahid (the generation just after the Sahaba – he is the first imam in *tafsir* after the Sahaba). He says it is *Niqab ul-Muhdith*, which means its roots are *bid'a*.[255] He didn't mean that in Islam it is viewed as *bid'a*, it just means that it wasn't (started) at the time of the Prophet, but it came from Arab roots. It is known that some women used to cover their faces, even before Islam. (Interview)

So, although al-Judai feels that everyone has a right to dress as they choose, he doesn't feel that the covering of the face was actually prescribed by Islam at all, but is a dress style that was prevalent within Arab society even before Islam.[256]

Al-Albani further emphasises the attachment of dress to status, by referring to 'the *hadith* about a woman who came to speak to Umar. She was wearing a *jilbab*, with which she covered herself. The story ends by saying that 'Umar told her to remove the *jilbab* from her head as she was a slave and the *jilbab* was for free believing women to wear.'[257]

When I asked al-Judai about the verses of covering – did they apply to Muslim female slaves? – he answered in the negative. The reason he gave was that Islam didn't want to make things unnecessarily difficult for them: it was common for them to go out to work. This clearly shows that Muslim female slaves did not have the same requirement of dress as Muslim free women.[258] Al-Judai argued that, as she had a similar role to men and went about in all parts of society for work as did men, the slave had a similar dress requirement to men. For Islam to give them a more stringent way to carry themselves would amount to more *takleef* (extra burden) for them. This naturally begs the question, could one not apply the same principle to women today, when women in this society may 'go out to work'? Al-Judai's response was:

> Possibly, but I cannot give my opinion at this point, there are other factors to take into account. But when the woman needs to uncover some of the body out of necessity, then she is allowed to do that. Again I use the word '*takleef*', and to avoid this, as long as she is protected, it is possible ...'[259]

The diversity of reasons given in this chapter, and also the mismatch between the scholarly discourse and the beliefs and opinions of those who actually wear the head covering and face veil on a day-to-day basis, show that there is much ground for discussion and sharing of ideas. With so much contextual thinking these days among Muslim intellectuals, in the realm of politics, economics and other parts of life, the popular discourse on covering the female body seems remarkably conservative. Could the head covering be viewed as the cultural expression of what came from Arab roots? Indeed, in a sandy, desert climate the covering of the head (and at times the face) was very much prevalent for a man also. The Prophet wore a turban and recommended men to do so (especially in prayer). However, none of the scholars felt this to be a requirement for men today. Having acknowledged this, is there not a possibility that the female head covering could be viewed in the same way?

Conclusion

The purpose of this paper was to understand whether the Islamic texts say less than we have read into them with respect to the head covering and face veil, and to explore whether cultural expression has played a part in today's practice of the head and face covering.

Both the scholars al-Judai and Raza appeared to view the issue of dress in relation to one's situational context, and felt that the dress did not have to be of a specific colour or style as long as it covered what was required (as they understood it). Momoniatm however, had a more traditional interpretation: that it was necessary for all females to wear a *jilbab*, which he defined as a long and wide dress, made up of one or two pieces, to go over other clothing. Only al-Judai went to the extent of viewing the head covering in a British style, for example a hat or a bandana, as an acceptable form of covering. Although Raza would see such a covering as acceptable, it was not the ideal:

> ... we have to understand that people are trying, and Islam is not so hard on people.

It appears, then, that the interpretation of the female dress form today is also closely aligned with what is perceived to be the practice at the time of the Prophet, so that even when the covering requirements have been met, if the style is not the same then it will still be a little deficient for some.

The information derived from the focus groups demonstrated how some of the reasons identified by the participants for dressing as they do correlated with the scholars' interpretation of the purpose of covering – for modesty and protection, for example. Interestingly these are also the explanations which appear to be stated clearly in the Qur'an.

There were, however, 'purposes' of covering identified by the women in both focus groups 'a' and 'b' that did not resonate with at least two of the scholars. The first was 'identity'. What was ironic was the extent of importance members of group 'b' in particular attached to this. Yet both Raza and al-Judai did not just disagree, they also expressed a dislike for this interpretation by some Muslims.

The second was 'beauty'. Again, all the focus group members felt that part of the rationale for covering was based upon covering up one's beauty. Again both Raza and al-Judai accepted the wearing of cosmetics and jewellery (which would appear to be used to beautify). Al-Judai even expressed the requirement of dress to 'make you look good, according to the customs'.

What appears to be of greatest interest in the research findings is how little information with respect to the specifics of the female dress is actually found in the primary Islamic texts (the Qur'an and the *ahadith*). Although there is some reference to the attire of Muslim females there is little clarity as to what shape, form or extent of cover is required beyond that of covering the chest.

Traditionally, scholars have differed in their interpretation of specific words of the Qur'an, and some diversity of opinion with regard to the female dress requirement is derived from this premise. This becomes more evident when comparing translations of particular verses, demonstrating that there are divergent understandings of a woman's place in society; and hence a very different interpretation of the same words ensues as a result. Although such understandings and assumptions may carry noble intent, it is suggested that, as our social circumstances naturally change, and gender roles develop, there is a need for constant re-assessment of such interpretations.

What is apparent from this research, with three scholars holding diverse opinions with regard to the extent to which a woman should cover, is that it is not just the Qur'anic text which gives rise to dispute. All of them agreed that the word *khimar* meant 'a head cover'. They agreed also that the pertinent verse does not explicitly say 'put a head cover on', but rather to use it to cover other areas. Two of them felt that a *jilbab* was any garment used to cover the body. Momoniat felt it was a one- or two-piece covering that still allowed the face to be seen. All of them agreed that the *juyub* referred to the breast region (and more specifically 'the curve' or the neck slit which showed the curve).

The greatest discrepancy arose with the interpretation of the words *zeena* and *illa ma zahara minha*. Yet because the meaning of both is ambiguous, with no specificity in the Qur'an, it would appear that flexibility in its interpretation would be permitted. It could even be argued that flexibility is part of the rationale of the Qur'an, as Asad seems to suggest.

Furthermore, it appears that the understanding of the face covering has no definitive link to the primary sources of the Qur'an or *ahadith*. Although in texts some scholars have interpreted it as such, none of the scholars or focus groups I interviewed could give me a specific reference for its endorsement for all women. The only *hadith* that was provided – about the woman's face being *awra* – was found to be '*gharib*' (literally, 'strange', and often described as a 'weak tradition') and thus it was difficult to understand how a ruling could be based on it. Thus it becomes evident that the understanding of the face covering has been derived from historians and through traditional scholarly interpretations. Some of these scholars have extrapolated the direct commandments to the wives of the Prophet to be an instruction upon all women, but I do not feel that this is a strong argument, as the Qur'an clearly states that the wives of the Prophet are not the same as other women and requirements of them are different in a number of areas from those of ordinary women. Also, as these interpretations may well have been affected by the time and tradition, this might again infer that a renewed process of *ijtihad* (interpretation, reasoning) is required in this area.

That is not to say that there are no examples that show that Muslim women did cover the hair and/or face at the time of the Prophet. But there are a number of unanswered questions – how, for example, can this be strong enough evidence upon which to base such rulings as to what a woman is required to wear in Islam or not, when men too were dressed in turbans, robes and even face veils? Furthermore, if history is scrutinised more carefully, there will also be evidence to show that non-Muslim women too covered the head and face (some would even say this was a pre-Islamic practice), though they would at times leave their chests exposed. Does the social anthropology of a desert climate impact so much on Islamic practice that it dictates the dress of half of its adherents, even after a millennium?

Another interesting aspect to this debate is the understanding presented by Barlas and Wadud, that interpretations of the Qur'anic texts are not only influenced by the patriarchal agency of the commentator, but are also a realisation that the society that the Prophet came to was not the most perfect and fair of all societies – the often nostalgic view some hold of it – but instead was extremely patriarchal in origin itself. And although the Prophet was very fair in his treatment and encouragement of women, much of the rest of society was not so. This may be seen through the requests of Umar, who wanted Muhammad to screen his wives. Yet Muhammad was reluctant. It was not because Umar wanted to make life difficult for them, but because he acknowledged that not all men of the time were sincere and many were out to belittle or dishonour the respect and status of the Prophet and his household. The Prophet then appears to be the idealist and Umar the realist, and the verse of screening for the Prophet's wives is revealed in favour of this latter argument.

It makes some sense to assume, as Barlas advocates, that there is a general understanding that may be derived from these verses, but there are also some points that are very specific to the Prophet and his time, that can only be understood when contextualised in this way. Perhaps, then, there is a much greater need for female scholars to interpret such texts too, for a balanced argument to be obtained.

The research findings also indicate that there appears to be a need to re-assert Muslim identity, in which context critical debates become somewhat downplayed. Furthermore, the social and cultural contexts of the early commentators of the Qur'an and *ahadith* are an important starting point in framing the discourse. Another interesting observation came from both Maududi's and Darsh's understanding of adornment in the context of 'customary dress'. As they are both from societies where it is customary for the head to be covered (Pakistan and Egypt), it gives rise to the question of what to do in a country where the head covering is not a 'customary part of the dress'.

One final point of intrigue was related to the dress of female slaves. None of the scholars' interpretations of dress seemed to allow wholly for this apparent anomaly, though al-Judai made some very interesting remarks. Momoniat commented that, 'because she was a slave girl, her case is completely different'. This conclusion seems to be at odds with the notion that Islam came to show equality regardless of original status, colour or class. What it seems to demonstrate is that dress was a means of indicating the differentiation of one's status, but this again requires more investigation.

Unfortunately, I was unable to explore this and a number of other issues in a short chapter, including covering with respect to the Muslim woman at prayer, and the more relaxed covering of the elderly Muslim woman. These (and no doubt other areas) are all important topics of research, which need to be investigated further. What is clear is that the discussion around female dress in Islam is far from over, and many questions remain as to why current prescriptions of how a Muslim woman should dress remain so restrictive, when the evidence from the original sources does not appear to be specific.

Appendix I: Listing of Verses from the Qur'an

1. Say to the believing men that they should lower their gaze and guard their modesty; that will make for greater purity for them: and Allah is well-acquainted with all that they do. And say to the believing women that they should lower their gaze and guard their modesty; that they should not display their *zeena* except *illa ma zahara minha*; that they should draw their *khumur* over their *juyub* and not display their beauty except to their husbands, their fathers, their husbands' fathers, their sons, their husbands' sons, their brothers, or their brothers' sons, or their sisters' sons or their women, or the slaves whom their right hands possess, or male servants free of physical needs, or small children who have no sense of shame of sex, and that they should not strike their feet in order to draw attention to their hidden ornaments. And O you

Believers! Turn you all together towards Allah, that you may attain bliss. (24:30–1)

2. O Prophet, tell your wives and daughters, and the believing women that they should cast their *jalabib* over their persons (when abroad): that is most convenient, that they should be known (as such) and not molested: and Allah is Oft-Forgiving Most Merciful. (33:59).

3. O Children of Adam! Verily We have bestowed you clothing to cover your shame as well as to be an adornment to you ... (7:26)

4. O Children of Adam! Do not let Satan seduce you in the same manner as He expelled your parents (Adam and Eve) from the Garden, stripping them of their raiment in order to expose their shame ... (7:27)

5. O children of Adam! Wear your beautiful apparel (*zeena*) at every place of worship, and eat and drink, but do not be wasteful ... (7:31)

6. O Prophet! Say to thy Consorts: 'If it be that ye desire the life of this World, and its glitter – then come! I will provide for your enjoyment and set you free in a handsome manner. But if ye seek Allah and His Messenger, and the Home of the Hereafter, verily Allah has prepared for the well-doers amongst you a great reward. O Consorts of the Prophet! If any of you were guilty of evident unseemly conduct, the Punishment would be doubled to her, and that is easy for Allah. But any of you that is devout in the service of Allah and His Messenger, and works righteousness – to her shall We grant her reward twice: and We have prepared for her a generous Sustenance. O Consorts of the Prophet! Ye are not like any of the (other) women: if ye do fear (Allah), be not too complacent of speech, lest one in whose heart is a disease should be moved with desire: but speak ye a speech (that is) just. And stay quietly in your houses, and make not a dazzling display, like that of the former Times of Ignorance; and establish regular Prayer, and give regular Charity; and obey Allah and His Messenger. And Allah only wishes to remove all abomination from you, ye members of the Family, and to make you pure and spotless. And recite what is rehearsed to you in your homes, of the Signs of Allah and His Wisdom: for Allah understands the finest mysteries and is well-acquainted (with them).' (28-34)

Appendix II: Resumés of the Scholars Interviewed

Sheikh Abdullah al-Judai

Born in al-Basra, Iraq, al-Judai combines traditional method of studying with *mashayikh* (scholars) of Iraq in the fields of *Usul al-Fiqh*, *'Ulum al-Hadith*,

'Ulum al-Qur'an and many other fields of Islam. He has committed to memory the entire Qur'an and numerous classical Islamic texts. He published his first book at the age of 18, and he has been commended by the leaders of Islamic *Fiqh* and *Hadith* around the world including Sheikh Yusuf al-Qaradawi and the late Sheikh Nasir al-Din al-Albani. Sheikh Abdullah al-Judai has authored and produced *tahqiq* (verification) very widely on a plethora of topics, numbering nearly a hundred books. A founding member of the European Council for Fatwa and Research, he is currently the head of the al-Judai Centre for Research and Counselling and a teacher of *Usul al-Fiqh* at the European Institute of Human Sciences, Wales.

Sheikh Mohammad Shahid Raza

Raza is the Deputy Director of the Muslim College in London and is the President of the World Islamic Mission of Europe. Born in India, Maulana Raza earned a degree in Biology and Chemistry from the University of Agra in 1969. He then embarked upon postgraduate study at the University of Meerut in 1976. This was followed by an advanced degree in Islamic Studies from Jamia Na'imia Moradabad. Raza has been a board member, Executive Secretary and Registrar of the Muslim Law (Sharia) Council UK since 1988. More recently, in October 2004, he has become a founding trustee of the British Muslim Forum.

Sheikh Afzal Momoniat

Momoniat studied on the Alim Course – Higher Islamic Education and Islamic Law – at The Islamic Da'wah Academy in Leicester. He studied for a further 5 years to complete the course and training at Darul Uloom Zakariyya in Johannesburg. His research specialisation included various sciences of Arabic grammar, exegesis, Qur'an in depth, Islamic jurisprudence and *Hadith*. Some of the senior teachers among his many teachers include Sheikh ul-Hadith Maulana Radha ul-Haqq, Shaikh Shabir Salujee and Mufti Muhammad Ali.

Chapter 8

Norms of Gender Interaction

Javed Ahmad Ghamidi (translated from Urdu by Shehzad Saleem)

Believers! Enter not the houses other than your own until you have introduced yourselves and wished peace to those in them. That is best for you
that you may be heedful. If you find no one in the house, enter not until
permission is given to you. If you are asked to go back, go back, for it is
purer for you. God has knowledge of all which you do. It is no sin for you
to enter non-residential places in which there is benefit for you. And God
has knowledge of what you reveal and what you conceal. [O Prophet!]
Tell the believing men to restrain their eyes and guard their private parts
[if there are women present in these houses]. That is purer for them.
And God is well aware of what you do. And tell the believing women to
restrain their eyes and to guard their private parts and to display of their
ornaments only those [which are worn on limbs] which are normally
revealed and to draw their coverings over their bosoms. They should not
reveal their ornaments to anyone save their husbands or their fathers
or their husbands' fathers or their sons or their husbands' sons or their
brothers or their brothers' sons or their sisters' sons or other women of
acquaintance or their slaves or the subservient male servants who are not
attracted to women or children who have no awareness of the hidden
aspects of women. They should [also] not stamp their feet in order to
draw attention to their hidden ornaments. Believers turn to Allah in
repentance that you may prosper. (24:27–31)

In order to protect society from moral misconduct and to safeguard the
sanctity of personal relationships, the above-quoted verses outline the
norms and etiquette of gender interaction. They are stated in the *Sūrah
Nūr* with the warning that these norms of social interaction and communal
contact must be adhered to in order to maintain the purity of heart, and
are the most appropriate set of principles in this matter. If people follow
these norms, they will obtain the great blessings and favours they entail.
However, to obtain these, it is essential that they follow these norms while

regarding the Almighty to be all embracing in knowledge, and always remain aware of the fact that the Almighty is not only aware of their deeds but also the intentions and motives behind them.

These norms are:

1. If friends, relatives or acquaintances visit one another, they should follow a certain decorum. Suddenly barging into a house without introducing oneself is improper. The visitor should first of all properly introduce himself by paying salutations to the residents of a house. This will make the residents aware of the visitor, provide them with the opportunity to determine the purpose of his visit and whether it is appropriate for them to let him in. If the visitor hears a reply to his salutations and is given permission, only then should he enter. If there is no-one present in the house to give him permission, or if someone is present and the visitor is told that meeting him is not possible, he should withdraw without any feelings of ill-will.

   In this regard, while explaining this directive, the Prophet Muhammad (pbuh) has directed the visitor to seek permission to enter three times, and if he hears no reply even after his third call, he should turn back.

   Similarly, the Prophet is reported to have said that permission to enter must not be sought by standing right at the front door of the house and while peering in, because the very reason for seeking permission is that the visitor should not catch a glimpse of the residents.

2. In case the visited place is non-residential, no formal permission is required. The Qur'ān uses the words *buyu#tin@ ghayra masku#natin@* (houses which are not residential) for such places. They include hotels, rest houses, guest houses, shops, offices and meeting places. A person can enter such places because of some need without seeking permission as per the dictates of this verse.

3. In both types of visited places, if women are present then the divine directive is that both the men and the women present should restrain their gazes. The words used for this directive are *yaghud@du@ min abs@a#rihinna.* If there is modesty in the gazes, and men and women refrain from feasting their eyes on the physical attributes of one another and ogling each other, then no doubt the purport of the directive stands fulfilled. The expression *ghad@d@i bas@r* does not mean that men and women have to constantly stare at the floor while interacting with one another. It means to guard one's gaze from taking undue liberty and to refrain from staring at one another. If this vigil on the eyes is not kept, then in the words of the Prophet this would be tantamount to adultery

of the eyes. Once a person indulges in it, his sexual organ either fulfils the ultimate objective of what his eyes initiated or is unable to do so. It is regarding this first accidental gaze about which the Prophet has directed the believers to turn away.

Barīdah (a companion of the Prophet) reported that the Prophet said: 'Alī: 'O 'Ali! One must not follow up one's first glance by a second one because the first glance shall be forgiven while the second not.'

Jarīr Ibn 'Abdullāh (another companion) reported that he asked of the Prophet: 'What if such a glance takes place suddenly?' The Prophet replied: 'Immediately turn it away or lower it.'

In another incident during the Prophet's farewell pilgrimage, when a lady from the Khath'am tribe stopped the Prophet on his way, Fadl Ibn 'Abbās started to stare at her. When the Prophet saw him, he caught hold of his face and turned it to the other side.

4. One must properly cover one's sexual organs on such occasions of interaction. The expression employed by the Qur'ān is *h@ifz@ al-furu#j*. At various instances in the Qur'ān, this expression is used to connote inappropriate indulgence in sexual activity. However, it is evident from both the context in which it is used and the way it is used that, in the above quoted verses, this expression implies that men and women must properly cover their sexual organs. The purpose of the directive is that, on occasions of gender intermingling, body parts that need to be covered must be covered even more carefully. The primary way to achieve this end is to wear decent clothes. Men and women should wear such clothes which not only hide the ornaments worn but also the sexual organs. Moreover, on such occasions, care should be taken that a person does not expose his sexual organs. This is the very objective of *h@ifz@ al-furu#j*. The Qur'ān wants believing men and women, besides restraining their eyes, to also observe this norm of modesty.

5. It is necessary for women in particular not to display any of their ornaments except before their close relatives, attendants and people of acquaintance. However, exempted from this are ornaments which are generally never covered: in other words the ornaments worn on the hand, the face and the feet. In the opinion of this writer, the correct meaning of the Qur'ānic words *illa# ma# z@ahara minha#* used to indicate this meaning is the one pointed out by Zamakhsharī in the words:

Except limbs which a person does not cover generally and instinctively and they are always left bare.

Therefore, except for the ornaments worn in these places, women must hide the ones worn in all other places, so much so that they should not walk by striking their feet in a manner which draws attention to any hidden ornaments they may be wearing. On these very grounds, the Prophet bade women not to use strong perfumes when they go out.

Relatives and people of acquaintance before which the above-mentioned display of ornaments is not forbidden are:

    i. husband

    ii. father

    iii. father-in-law.

For the latter two relations, the word used by the Qur'ān is *āba*. This word not only implies the father but also the paternal and maternal uncles and grandfathers. Therefore, a lady can display her ornaments before adults of both her maternal and paternal family and those of her husband's, just as she can before her father and father-in-law.

    iv. sons

    v. sons of the husband

    vi. brothers

    vii. brothers' sons

    viii. sisters' sons.

The word 'son' implies the maternal grand- and great grandsons as well as the paternal ones. The same implies for the sons of brothers and sisters. In these relations also, the sons of real, step- and foster brothers and sisters is understood to be included.

    ix. women of acquaintance and maids.

It is evident from these words that unknown women should be treated the same way as men and a Muslim lady should be very careful in displaying her concealed ornaments before them. The reason is that this can result in both moral and financial afflictions, and in some cases a careless attitude in this regard may invite even graver dangers.

    x. slaves.

The institution of slavery existed in Arabia in the time of the Prophet Muhammad (sws). The words used in the above-quoted verse to refer to this institution are *ma# malakat ayma#nuhunna*. Some jurists have understood this expression only to mean 'slave-women'. However, there is no reason for this exception. As Imām Amān Ahsan Islāhī writes:

Had only slave-women been implied by this expression then the appropriate words would have been *aw ama#'ihinna*. A common expression that connotes both slave-men and slave-women would never have been used. Moreover, the verses already mention the category which, as has been explained, includes both women with whom one is generally acquainted as well as slave-women and maidservants. After a mention of this category, an independent mention of slave-women is needless.

xi. people who live in a house as dependents and, because of their subservience or owing to any other reason, are incapable of feeling any attraction towards women

xii. children who are as yet unaware of sexual matters.

6. Since the chest of a woman is a means of sexual attraction, and there also may be jewellery worn on the neck, women are directed to cover their chests with a cloak. In this way, the neckline shall also be covered as much as possible. If by some other means this objective is achieved, then this cannot be objected to either. The real purpose is that women must not reveal their chest and neckline before men; on the contrary, these should be concealed in a manner that they do not become prominent in any way.

The *sūrah* also mentions certain other clarifications regarding these norms.

First, slave-men[260] and women and sexually immature children who generally frequent a house are not required to ask permission every time they enter private rooms. They are just required to seek permission at three particular times of the day: before the *Fajr* prayer when the residents are generally in bed; during the afternoon nap when they may not be wearing proper clothes; and after the *'Ishā* prayer when they go off to bed for sleep. These three periods of time require privacy. If someone suddenly enters a private room in these times, he may see the residents in an inappropriate state. Except for these three times of the day, sexually immature children and slave-men and women can enter the private rooms and other areas of the house without asking any permission. This cannot be objected to. However, at the above-mentioned three times, they must seek permission when they want to enter a private room. Once children reach sexual maturity, they too need to seek permission at all times. The fact that they have been frequenting the house ever since their childhood is not reason enough for them to continue with the exception granted to them. Consequently, once they reach this age, they must follow the regulations that pertain to all:

Believers, let your slave-men and women and those who are under age ask your permission on three occasions when they come in to see you:

before the *Fajr* prayer, when you have put off your garments in the heat of noon and after the *Ishā* prayer. These are the three occasions when none may intrude upon your privacy. At other times, it shall be no offence for you, or them, [because you] go around visiting one another. Thus God explains to you His verses and God is all-knowing and wise. And when your children reach the age of puberty, let them still ask your permission as their elders do. Thus God explains to you His verses and God is all-knowing and wise. (24:58–9)

Second, the directive of covering the chest and neckline does not pertain to old women who are no longer of marriageable age, on the condition that their intention is not to display their ornaments. It is not necessary for a woman to cover her chest and neckline at the age at which she generally loses her sexual urge and at which a man feels no attraction for her. So old women can dispense with the cloth that covers the stipulated area. However, what is more pleasing in the sight of Allah is that even at this age they be careful and not dispense with this garment:

> It shall be no sin for aged women who have no hope of marriage to discard their cloaks on the condition that they do not display their ornaments. Better if they do not discard them. God hears all and knows all. (24:60)

Third, it is explained in these verses that there is absolutely no harm if people and their relatives who are disabled or impaired in any manner come and visit one another, and whether men and women among them eat together or separately in their own houses or houses of their children, of their fathers, mothers, brothers and sisters, of their paternal uncles and aunts, maternal uncles and aunts and of those people who are financially dependent on them. Indeed, when they enter such houses they must greet the residents in the prescribed way. The Muslim religious greeting *al-salāmu alaykum* is in fact a beautiful invocation to the Almighty to strengthen personal relationships. The norms of social interaction that are outlined in these verses are not meant to deprive people of mutual support or to curtail their social freedom. If people show prudence, they can maintain all these relationships even after following these norms. They must not think that these directives are meant to make difficulties for them. The Almighty does not intend to prohibit social interaction in any way:

There is no harm if the blind, the lame and the sick eat at your table, nor if you eat in the houses of your own children, your fathers, your mothers, your brothers and your sisters, your paternal uncles, your paternal aunts, your maternal uncles, your maternal aunts, or your friends; or of those who are [financially] dependent on you. There is no harm if men and women eat together or apart. [However, this much you should do that] when you enter a house, say 'peace to you' – an invocation fixed by God, and let your greeting be devout and kindly. Thus God explains to you His revelations, so that you may grow in wisdom. (24:61)

These are the norms of social interaction in general circumstances. However, in the age of the Prophet in Madīnah, when some miscreants started teasing and besmearing the character of Muslim women, then God revealed Sūrah Ahzāb, which bade the wives of the Prophet, his daughters and other Muslim women to draw their cloaks over them when they go out to places which were insecure. Such dressing-up would distinguish them from women of lewd character and they would not be teased on the pretext of being outwardly similar to such women. It is reported in various narratives that, when Muslim women in the dark of night or in the dim light of dawn would go out to relieve themselves, these miscreants would go after them and when they would be called to account they would say what they actually thought was that they were talking to slave-women. The Qur'ān says:

Those who harass believing men and believing women unjustifiably shall bear the guilt of slander and a grievous sin. O Prophet! Enjoin your wives, your daughters, and the wives of true believers to draw their cloaks over them [when they go out]. That is more proper, so that they may be distinguished [from slave women] and not be harassed. God is ever forgiving and merciful. If the hypocrites and those who have the ailment [of jealousy] in their hearts and the scandalmongers of Madīnah do not desist, We will rouse you against them, and their days in that city will be numbered. Cursed be they; wherever found, they would be seized and put to death. (33:58–61)

It is evident from the words *yu'rafan fala# yu'dhayn* and the context in which they are used that the directive mentioned in the preceding verses was not of a permanent nature. It was a temporary measure adopted to protect Muslim women from the evil of lecherous people. For similar reasons, the Prophet also forbade Muslim women from travelling alone on long journeys and from walking on pathways within a crowd of men. Consequently, if today Muslim women are faced with similar circumstances, they can adopt a similar measure to make themselves distinct from other women, but it should not otherwise be seen as the norm.

The *sūrah* also mentions certain directives that are specific to the Prophet Muhammad in his capacity of a Messenger of God. They bear no relation to other people; however, since certain scholars have extended their sphere of application to all Muslims, their explanation seems appropriate here.

A deliberation on the contents of the *sūrah* reveals the fact that, when the hypocrites and miscreants mentioned above embarked upon a campaign to scandalize the private lives of the wives of the Prophet to make the common man averse to them and to damage the moral repute of both Islam and the Muslims, God took certain measures to curb this evil. He gave the noble wives the choice to leave the Prophet and live the life of ordinary Muslim women enjoying its luxuries and comforts or to once again decide with full awareness to live forever as the wives of the Prophet in order to obtain the comforts and luxuries of the Hereafter. They are then informed that if they decided to stay with the Prophet they must realise that their status as his wives entails great responsibility. They are not like general women; they are the 'Mothers of the Believers'. Therefore, if they remain faithful to God and His Prophet and do righteous deeds with full sincerity, they will earn a two-fold reward. Likewise, they will be worthy of a two-fold punishment in relation to other women if they commit a sin. Their inner purification is beyond doubt; however, God also wanted to morally cleanse them in the eyes of the wider public so that no-one was given a chance to cast even slight aspersions on their characters. This is a requisite of their status and they must adopt certain things in their daily lives to achieve this purity.

First, if they are fearful of their Lord they should not be soft spoken and affectionate in speech to every person who enters their house. Though in normal circumstances, one must be gentle and kind when he speaks to others, in the circumstances they are facing, such an attitude would only embolden the miscreants and the hypocrites around them to take undue advantage of them. Such an attitude of kindness would create in them the expectation of success in their mission – the mission of whispering evil in people's hearts. So if ever they have to talk to such people they must speak in clear and simple tones so that those among their addressees who intend evil realise that they cannot achieve their objective. The Qur'ān says:

> Wives of the Prophet, you are not like other women. So, if you fear God, do not be too complaisant in your speech, lest the lecherous-hearted should lust after you. Talk with such people in plain and simple words. (33:32)

Second, they should remain in their homes in order to protect their rank and status. All their attitudes and mannerisms should be in accordance with the status that God has conferred them with. So if they have to go out to meet some compelling need, they must not go out displaying their ornaments and finery – something which was the way of women in the age of ignorance. Both their status and their responsibility entail that they remain in their houses and diligently pray and in the way of God as much as they can and with full sincerity spend their time in obedience to Him. However, if for some unavoidable reason they must leave their place, then they should do so in the most befitting of manners exemplifying the culture and tradition of Muslims and not allow any hypocrite even to cast an aspersion on them:

> Abide still in your homes and do not display your finery as women used to do in the days of ignorance. Attend to your prayers, give alms and obey God and His Messenger. O woman of this house, the Almighty wants to cleanse you from the filth [that these hypocrites want to besmear you with] and to fully purify you. (33:33)

Third, they should try to communicate the verses of the Qur'ān as well as the beliefs and moral teachings of Islam to people who come and visit them and refrain from other general gossip. It is for this very purpose that God has chosen them. Their objective in life now is the dissemination of the message of Islam and not indulgence in the luxuries of life:

> Communicate what is taught to you of the verses of God and the wisdom revealed by Him [to your visitors]. The Almighty is very discerning and all-knowing. (33:34)

It seems that, even after all these measures, the miscreants did not mend their ways. Consequently God gave some more directives to Muslims which were to be strictly followed. They were told that no one should enter the house of the Prophet unless they were invited. And if they are invited to eat at the house of the Prophet, then they should come right at the time of food (not too early), and they should also disperse immediately afterwards, and not linger behind talking for long hours.

The wives of the Prophet would be secluded from the Muslims and, except for near relatives and women of their acquaintance, no-one should come in front of them. Anyone who wants something from their private places must ask for it from behind a veil.

The wives of the Prophet are the 'Mothers of the Believers'. Those hypocrites who have the desire to marry them should know that, even after the death of the Prophet, they cannot marry them. They are eternally prohibited to marry after him. Consequently, every believer should honour and respect them the way he honours and respects his own mother. The Qur'ān explains how the Prophet is greatly distressed by the wrong attitudes of these miscreants. They must know that bothering the Prophet is not something trivial. A person may fashion an excuse for his misdemeanour in this world, but he would not be successful in justifying it before the Lord of the worlds who is aware of what is in the hearts:

> Believers, do not enter the houses of the Prophet for a meal without waiting for the proper time, unless you are given leave. But if you are invited, enter; and when you have eaten, disperse. Do not engage in familiar talk, for this would distress the Prophet and he would feel shy to bid you go; but of the truth God does not feel shy. If you ask his wives for anything, speak to them from behind a curtain. This is more chaste for your hearts and their hearts. You must not speak ill of God's Messenger, nor shall you ever wed his wives after him; this would surely be a grave offence in the sight of God. Whether you reveal or conceal them, God has knowledge of all things. It shall be no offence for the Prophet's wives to come before their fathers, their sons, their brothers, their brothers' sons, their sisters' sons, their women of acquaintance, or their slave-girls. [O] women [of the household of the Prophet!], have fear of God; surely God observes all things. (33:53–5)

Chapter 9

Hijab: a Symbol of Modesty or Seclusion?

Khola Hasan

The concept of the *hijab* clearly exists in the Qur'an, but not with this name. In the sacred text, *hijab* actually refers to a curtain or a screen to separate individuals, or to separate individuals from God.

Hijab as the Muslim woman's public dress is referred to twice in the Qur'an, but as *khimar* (head scarf) and *jilbab* (shawl or cloak). I see these particular verses as normative commandments, instructing women how to dress in public. But I also see these verses as providing implicit permission for women to enter the public sphere freely and confidently, and in the context of modest clothing, decency and prudent conduct in public. For traditional societies have usually placed huge emphasis on the personal reputation of individuals in general, and of women in particular. Reputations of chastity, decency, honour and veracity were prized, and losing such a reputation would easily ruin a person. This would be hard for a man to endure in a close-knit society, but even harder for a woman to endure. And it is within this context that the Qur'an ordains public lashing for a person who brings a charge of unchastity against a woman but is then unable to substantiate it in a court of law with four witnesses. Such a person is not only to be punished publicly but his testimony may never be accepted again in court. A person's honour and reputation are thus considered sacrosanct in Islam.

There has existed within traditional Islamic scholarship from its very infancy a tension between those who were happy to see women enjoy the freedom that the *hijab* gave them, and those who understood it to be a tool for the confinement of women. The *hijab* was often used to control and oppress women in many Islamic societies, but I believe this flew in the face of the Qur'anic *weltenschauung*, its general world-view. For there is no doubt the Qur'an sees women as equal members of the human race, with an equal spiritual presence, equal accountability before their Lord for their actions, equal free will and freedom of conscience, equal liability for their dealings with other human beings, and an equal responsibility to obey divine commandments. Tragically, not just for women but for Muslim society generally, this vision of women who stand tall with men had to jostle for position with a vision of women as temptresses, morally and spiritually weak, and incapable of contributing much to society except as mothers locked up within the four walls of their homes. Various Qur'anic verses were often interpreted narrowly to exclude women from the public sphere, to deny them any role in society except a very limited one, and to subject them to strict control by the men in their lives.

Lowering the Gaze

The Qur'an begins the discussion on the *hijab* with a command to lower the gaze and to protect one's chastity. It is interesting to note that this command is first addressed to men, and then repeated for women. Public morality and decency are therefore not just the concern of women (as is often the case in many Muslim societies) but men as well.

> Say to the believing men that they should lower their gaze and guard their modesty: that will make for greater purity for them: And Allah is well acquainted with all that they do.
> And say to the believing women that they should lower their gaze and guard their modesty; that they should not display their beauty and ornaments except what (must ordinarily) appear thereof; that they should draw their veils over their bosoms and not display their beauty except to their husbands, their fathers, their husband's fathers, their sons, their husbands' sons, their brothers or their brothers' sons, or their sisters' sons, or their women, or the slaves whom their right hands possess, or male servants free of physical needs, or small children who have no sense of the shame of sex; and that they should not strike their feet in order to draw attention to their hidden ornaments. And O ye Believers! turn ye all together towards Allah, that ye may attain Bliss.
> (*Surah An Nur* 24:30–1. Translation by Abdullah Yusuf Ali)

This verse clearly implies that there will be some temptation for men from some women in public, regardless of whether or not they are suitably attired, but the remedy given is to strengthen their own resolve, to look away from temptation, and to protect their own actions. A woman alone cannot be blamed if a man sins; he too must take the blame. Interestingly, the Qur'anic attitude towards temptation is not to lock women up and throw away the key, but to put the onus on men to protect themselves. And even more importantly, verse 31 shows that women too are subject to the same temptations as men, so they too are given the same advice as men.

The great scholar and ethical thinker of Islam, Imam al Ghazali (d. 1111) commented:

The 'fornication of the eye' is one of the major venial faults, and soon leads on to a mortal and obscene sin, which is the fornication of the flesh. The man who is unable to turn away his eyes will not be able to safeguard himself against unchastity.

Jesus (upon whom be peace) said: 'Beware of glances, for they sow desire in the heart, which is temptation enough.'[261]

The Andalusian theologian, scholar and poet Ibn Hazm (d. 1064) wrote one of his enduring masterpieces on the theme of courtly love. However, he cautions against 'love at first sight', as he explains that the gaze is fickle:

When a man falls in love at first sight, and forms a sudden attachment as the result of a fleeting glance, that proves him to be little steadfast, and proclaims that he will as suddenly forget his romantic adventure; it testifies to his fickleness and inconstancy. So it is with all things: the quicker they grow, the quicker they decay; while on the other hand slow produced is slow consumed.[262]

You should realise that the eye takes the place of a messenger, and that with its aid all the beloved's intention can be apprehended. The four senses besides are also gateways of the heart, and passages giving admission to the soul; the eye is however the most eloquent, the most expressive, and the most efficient of them all.[263]

The Headscarf

After the command to women to lower the gaze comes the injunction to extend the headscarf to cover the chest, and not to reveal their adornments except to females and to close male relatives. Al Qurtubi explains that verse 31 was revealed because of a custom among Arab women in that time to cover their heads with a scarf, but to leave their chests and necks uncovered.

The lesson from this verse is that a woman's beauty, both natural and artificial, is not for general public consumption. It implicitly accepts that women enjoy adorning their natural beauty, for example with make-up, jewellery and fine clothes. This finery is acceptably feminine, but needs to stay within closed, trusted circles. If it is not controlled, it can lead to terrible consequences for society. In our modern age, where magazines and television constantly carry images of beautiful but scantily-dressed female celebrities, we see many problems emerging as a result. An obsession with pornography, anorexia nervosa among young girls, obscenely provocative fashions sold to and worn by the masses, and rising rates of adultery are just a few of the issues that can be attributed directly to a deterioration of standards of public decency. Despite the growing number of women who use their intelligence and education to pursue rewarding careers, the female body is still ogled in magazines, displayed for public consumption, and used to enhance the appeal and market of other commodities.

The headscarf is thus not just about covering a woman's hair and upper body but about standards of public decency, modesty and propriety. That this verse was interpreted as a clear normative injunction is shown by the following narration in *Fath al Bari* from Safiyyah bint Shaybah.

> We were once with Aisha when we mentioned the women of Quraysh and their virtues. Aisha said, 'The women of Quraysh are good but, by Allah, I have never seen any better or more strict in their adherence to the Book of Allah than the women of the Ansar. When the verses of *Sura Al Nur* were revealed, their men went to them and recited to them the words Allah had revealed. Each man recited to his wife, his daughter, his sister and other female relatives. Each woman among them got up, took her decorated wrapper and wrapped herself up in it out of faith and belief in what Allah had revealed. They appeared behind the Messenger of Allah wrapped up, as if there were crows on their heads.[264]

What I find interesting is the use of Safiyyah's words 'decorated wrapper', as this implies that the scarves were not plain black but coloured and patterned. One wonders from whence emerged the modern obsession with wearing only black or very dull-coloured scarves and gowns.

Jilbab, the Outer Cloak

O Prophet! Tell thy wives and daughters, and the believing women, that they should cast their outer garments over their persons (when abroad):

that is most convenient, that they should be known (as such) and not molested. And Allah is Oft-Forgiving, Most Merciful.

(*Surah Al Ahzab* 33:59)

This verse commands all Muslim women, not just the family of the Prophet, to cover their ordinary clothes with a shawl or cloak when they are in public in order that they may be recognised and not molested. Ibn Kathir explains in his commentary that this concerned recognition of the women as free women and not slaves. He further explains that some evil young men in Madina would roam the streets at night looking for women to tease and annoy. If a woman was not covered with a cloak, she would be recognised as a slave-girl and so considered lawful game. The question then arises whether the *jilbab* is still mandatory, now that slavery has been abolished in most societies. Those who consider the *jilbab* to be a necessary requirement in the modern age explain that the Qur'an does not specify that the women should be recognised as free women; perhaps the recognition referred to is that they are believing women. In this case the injunction of this verse remains normative.

Modesty

My understanding is that the issue of *hijab* is less about headscarves and more about public modesty and propriety. A scarf that covers the hair but leaves the neck and chest exposed, or that is worn with figure-hugging outfits, or is accompanied with flirtatious behaviour, does nothing to promote modesty. My contention is that the verses on the *hijab* were instituted to protect women from the unwarranted attentions of some men when in public. This is in no way a negative observance on the male gender in general; it does not imply, as one feminist once said to me, that Islam considers all men to be potential rapists. It does not seek to segregate women from men, to lock women behind closed doors, or to deny them public space. Fatima Mernissi complains bitterly that the initial *hijab* was a curtain, a 'veil that descended from heaven was going to cover up women, separate them from men, from the Prophet, and so from God.'[265]

In fact, I see the *hijab* as implicit permission for women to be in the public sphere. If their presence in the public arena was not a normal occurrence, there would be no need for the *hijab*. What the Qur'an ordains is that women cover their bodies when in public. It does not suggest that all men are potential rapists or that all women are temptresses. But it does suggest that the free mixing of the sexes in an atmosphere where women are not modestly or becomingly attired can be a source of temptation, improper thoughts and improper conduct. The Islamic etiquettes of the interaction between the sexes are based on good manners, formal behaviour, decent and temperate language, and modest clothing. Men and women not closely related to each other may not hug each other or even shake hands. This may seem strange in our modern world in which there are few boundaries between the sexes, but was something that was clearly understood in traditional English society for centuries. High-class society, for example, would never have countenanced the fashion of women revealing their bodies apart from their faces and hands. Dresses were worn long, bonnets covered the head in public, a cape covered the clothes, and the sexes interacted with propriety. The English writer Emily Thornwell explained to her Victorian readers:

> ... to suppose that the great heat of the weather will authorise the disorder of the toilet, and permit us to go in slippers, or with our arms and legs bare, or to take nonchalant and improper attitudes, is an error of persons of low class, or destitute of education. [266]

On the issue of the interaction between men and women, she advised young women: 'Always seek to converse with gentlemen into whose society you may be introduced, with a dignified modesty and simplicity, which will effectually check on their part any attempt at familiarity ...'[267]

In the 1850s, women in the United States had begun to complain loudly about the tight corsets they wore which affected their health and posture, and about the long dresses that were impossible to keep clean. Interestingly, the solution they found to this problem was not in revealing their legs but in introducing the fashion of bloomers. These were baggy trousers copied from the Turks and worn with knee-length dresses. In fact the fashion was very reminiscent of traditional Turkish costume. In Britain it was considered unacceptable for women to show their legs in public as late as the 1920s. The slow change began when rationing during the Second World War was applied to fabric as well, so ladies were forced to make their dresses shorter and more practical. Dresses and skirts were, however, still worn below the knee. It was not until 1965, when Mary Quant invented the miniskirt, that women's fashion in Britain became so revealing that, soon, nothing was left uncovered.

The effect upon Muslim communities of changing women's fashion in Britain cannot be over-emphasised. Many Muslim countries emerged after the Second World War in the grip of colonialism, and so much of the discussion was focused on political weakness. The new, very revealing fashions in women's dress were anathema to Muslims and were a cause of serious worry. If Muslim women were to emulate European women in increasing rates of literacy, careers and political rights, would they also emulate them in standards of public modesty? This was a worrying issue indeed and led to many strict epistles being written on the importance of keeping women in the home.

The Concept of Seclusion and Purdah.

The verses on the *hijab* quoted earlier led to a tension during the earliest stages in the development of the Islamic understanding of the role of women in society. One strand of theological thought insisted that the *hijab* included the covering of the woman's face and hands, and that the verses on seclusion for the Prophet's wives applied to all Muslim women. Although the Qur'an does not mention the *niqab* (covering the face), some interpreters included the covering of the face under the rule of the headscarf. A second strand insisted that the *hijab* did not include the covering of the face and hands, and that women moved freely in public during the time of the Prophet. Maulana Mawdudi is a classic example of the first school of thought. His book entitled '*Purdah*'[268] gives dozens of examples of women attending congregational prayer during the era of the Prophet, coming out for Eid celebrations, travelling for Hajj and visiting graveyards. Despite the overwhelming evidence of the public role of women in the Prophetic era, his conclusion severely limits the role of women:

> Though he (the Prophet) allowed women to go out of the houses in view of the solemnity of the occasions, purity of the purpose and their delicate feelings, sometimes even took them along with him, imposed such restrictions of Purdah as would guard against the least probabilities of mischief. Then he ruled that, except for Hajj, it was better for women not to attend the other religious obligations.

I find this conclusion very strange, as the Prophet specifically made a pledge with women that they would attend the Eid prayers, even if they were in a state of ritual impurity and so could not pray.

Maulana Mawdudi was not unique in wishing to keep women locked up in the home. In fact, the move to keep women secluded began very soon after the death of the Prophet, when many interpreters merged verses of *hijab* with verses that specifically addressed the wives of the Prophet to create the tenet of seclusion.

> O Consorts of the Prophet! Ye are not like any of the (other) women: if ye do fear (Allah), be not too complacent of speech, lest one in whose heart is a disease should be moved with desire: but speak ye a speech (that is) just.
>
>   And stay quietly in your houses, and make not a dazzling display, like that of the former Times of Ignorance; and establish regular Prayer, and give regular Charity; and obey Allah and His Messenger. And Allah only wishes to remove all abomination from you, ye members of the Family, and to make you pure and spotless.
>
> (*Surah Al Ahzab*, 33: 32–3)

These verses clearly address the wives of the Prophet and advise them not to enter the public arena too freely. After the death of the Prophet, his wives were also not permitted to re-marry, as they had the exalted reputation of being among the best women on earth. But some interpreters extended these verses to apply to all Muslim women and, combined with the theory that the *hijab* included the covering of the face, devised the theory of veiling and seclusion. This tenet was used for centuries by male interpreters to control women and deny them access to the public sphere. Not only was a woman's body *awrah* (private) but so were her face, her hands and feet, and even her voice. For many scholars, the mere hint of a woman's voice in public was anathema: cursed, tempting and forbidden. Although these verses are clearly addressed to the female relatives of the Prophet, scholars of the seclusion theory believed that the *niqab* and seclusion were not simply for the wives of the Prophet but mandatory for all Muslim women. Their reasoning was that the family of the Prophet were role models for women, just as the Prophet was a role model for the whole community. If these women, the best women of the Prophet's generation, were instructed to cover their faces and stay in their homes, so too should all women. They often saw women only as a gender, never as intelligent, creative beings who could contribute to society just as men did.

Other scholars were deeply affected by the political situation of their day. Maulana Mawdudi, for example, was writing during the bloody struggle to rid India of its British colonial masters, at a time when the entire Muslim world felt itself besieged both physically and ideologically. A return to puritanical Islam seemed the only escape from the terrible humiliation the Muslim world was enduring at the hands of European colonialists, and controlling women became one of the rallying cries of the puritan movement. It was in this context that Mawdudi wrote:

> The Muslim woman cannot be compared with the European woman who came out of the house in view of the emergency created by the war, but even after the war was over, refused to return to her natural sphere.[269]

Maulana Mawdudi's worry, that if women freely entered the public sphere it would cause chaos in society, was not a new worry, and echoes of it can be heard in the writings of scholars throughout Islamic history. This is why Mawdudi says during his discussion on *hijab*:

> It is obvious that the law which has such trends cannot be expected to allow that the two sexes should freely mix in schools and colleges, offices and factories, parks and places of entertainment, theatres and cinemas, and cafes and ballrooms as and when they please.[270]

The late Sheikh Nasiruddin al Albani of Saudi Arabia would have fully agreed with Maulana Mawdudi that the free mixing of men and women in public, when there is no modest clothing or decent conduct, when music is raunchy and obscene, and when alcohol helps people push the boundaries of what is forbidden further and further away, is an evil to be avoided at all costs. But, despite this agreement, Sheikh Albani does not accept that the *niqab* and seclusion of women were the norm during the Prophetic era. The sub-heading of his book *Jilbab Mar'atul Muslimah*[271] is 'Evidence that the face of the woman is not *awrah*'. He thus dedicates his study to narrations from the time of the Prophet in which women were in the mosque, in battle, on the streets, and so forth with their faces uncovered. The fact that the Prophet did not reprimand them is proof enough that the *niqab* was not considered mandatory. He gives the example of Fadl bin Abbas, a handsome young man who was with the Prophet when a beautiful young woman came to ask the Prophet a religious question. Fadl turned round to stare at her face, so the Prophet took Fadl's chin and gently steered his face to a different direction. Fadl was thus encouraged to avert his gaze from a beauty that was obviously attractive to him. Similarly, Sheikh Albani gives the example of a beautiful woman who used to pray behind the Prophet regularly. Some of the men would deliberately pray in the last row of men so that they could turn round to stare at her. Although the Qur'an reprimanded them for staying in the back rows to look at her, there was no rule introduced to stop beautiful women from attending the mosque.

Another example he gives is that, during the pledge of allegiance taken with women by Umar on behalf of the Prophet, which came soon after the signing of the Treaty of Hudaybiyyah, he ordered them to go out to the two Eid prayers and to take with them women who were elderly or in a state of ritual impurity. He explains that this pledge was concluded after the revelation of the verses on *jilbab*, and so shows that seclusion was not the norm. Sheikh Albani finally concludes that the opinion that the face need not be covered was the opinion of the majority of the scholars, including Ibn Rushd, Abu Hanifah, Malik, Shafi'i, Ahmad and At Tahawi.

Women in Black

One of the issues one encounters is the modern obsession among women who wear the *hijab* of wearing black from head to toe. This may be part of inherited culture in the Gulf States, but makes no sense in modern Britain. Sheikh Albani is also critical of the fashion for white or black *hijabs* only, giving the example of the wives of the Prophet who wore *jilbabs* dyed with red or yellow colour.[272]

The style of *hijab* seen in many Gulf countries today shows a preference for long black gowns. This may be practical for women who do not have careers outside the home, do not have to run for a bus or train, do not walk on snow or icy paths, and do not have to carry heavy shopping. In Western countries, the climate, lifestyle and general dress are very different to those in the Gulf States and do not lend themselves easily to this *hijab*. So should Muslim women in Western countries confine themselves to Arabian styles, or can they adapt the style to suit their lifestyles?

I believe the Qur'an did not wish to mandate a uniform for men or women, any more than it mandates certain meals. For example, the Qur'an tells Muslims that pork and alcohol are forbidden, that the creatures of the sea are halal, and that animals must be slaughtered with the name of Allah before they can be consumed. But it does not concern itself with particular menus or styles of cooking, for that would have taken away from the universal message of Islam. In the same way, to dictate that Muslim women must wear a certain style of clothing would also limit the relevance of the Qur'an to a certain time and place. The Qur'an's injunctions are general and universally applicable. Women throughout the ages have adapted the concept of the *hijab* to their own situation. Muslim women in China wore traditional Chinese dress with wide-brimmed hats, as this was common culture in their time. Women in India wore the *sari* or the *burqa*. In Iran the *chador* has been the norm for generations. Women in East Africa wore traditional clothing, with a matching fabric wrapped around the head. In Morocco both men and women wore long gowns with a tassled hood on the head. In Britain today we see Muslim women wearing long skirts or trouser suits with headscarves. Their clothing is smart, practical, suited to the idiosyncracies of the British climate, and thoroughly at home in Britain.

I find it strange that many Muslim men are comfortable in Western-style suits and jeans, yet insist that their women must dress in a Middle-Eastern fashion. Yet other men insist on wearing Asian or Arab styles of clothing for Friday prayers, insisting that suits are not welcome in a mosque. And woe betide an imam who has the temerity to lead the prayer wearing a Western suit! He may well be thrown out of his office. I believe that if a man wishes to wear traditional clothing for Friday and Eid prayers, because it puts him in holiday mood, fair enough. But to insist that such a style is somehow more Islamic than a suit is nonsensical and contrary to the universal message of Islam. The reason often given for the insistence on foreign fashions is that they are according to the *Sunnah*. But we have seen that the women in the time of the Prophet wore patterned and coloured scarves and cloaks, and that they uncovered their faces. So why is this not considered *Sunnah*?

As far as emulating the Prophet (saws) in his dress is concerned, first, it is laudable but not mandatory. Second, the Prophet did not wear the *thawb* or *shalwar qameez* as worn by modern Arab and Asian men. He wore an *Izar* (waist-wrapper) and a shirt. Third, he made it clear that it was the duty of Muslims to obey him in religious or Qur'anic matters, but that they were free to follow their own customs in temporal matters. It is reported that, when the Prophet first came to Madina, he saw the farmers grafting their trees and advised them to stop the practice. As a result the date palms yielded less fruit than was usual. The Prophet then said the immortal words, 'I am a human being. When I command you on an issue pertaining to religion, accept it. But when I command you on an issue concerning my personal opinion, remember that I am human. You know better the affairs of your worldly life.'

Children in *Hijab*

Throughout the world one is increasingly seeing little girls wearing *hijab* in public. A minority will even wear the *niqab*. Given the importance attached to the innocence of childhood by the Prophet, I find the *hijab* on little girls to be an affront to their innocence. The *hijab* is enjoined for women; it concerns beauty, maturity and public sexual attraction. To dress a little girl in this style is to sexualise the innocent, and I find this just as unacceptable as dressing a little girl as a model or a prom queen. Given that many Muslim girls will wear the *hijab* from their teenage years until their death, why place such a heavy requirement on them when their young minds and bodies have no understanding of its significance? Why not let them enjoy their childhood as children, instead of treating them as mini-adults. To clothe a child in *hijab* shows a lack of understanding about the *raison d'être* behind the concept, and introduces sexual attraction to a space where it does not exist.

Those who dress their children in this manner argue that they are training the girl in her faith just as they would train boys and girls from the age of seven to pray or to fast. But when a child is being trained to pray or fast, the prayer or fasting is not considered obligatory. They will pray some prayers and miss others. They will fast some days, break the fast early on some days, and miss others completely. It is a slow journey of learning. The *hijab*, too, should be introduced slowly from the age of puberty. But to force a little girl to dress in a black scarf and gown from the age of seven, to separate her from her brothers and friends in their games, to make it physically impossible for her to ride a bike or climb a tree, is not training but an act of oppression.

Conclusion

The *hijab* remains the most potent symbol of Islam in the world today. It is worn by Muslim women for a variety of reasons, such as a desire to fulfil literally the commands of the Qur'an, by young women to convince their parents that they are pious and can be trusted alone out in the world, as a fashion accessory that makes the wearer stand out from the crowd, as a sign of confidence and pride among ethnic minority members, or to make a political statement of loyalty and affiliation in a world full of war and hatred. Some women are clearly coerced into wearing it by pressure from the legal system, general society or male relatives. Others choose to wear it for a variety of personal reasons. Many communities still use the *hijab* to control, intimidate and subjugate women. But more and more women are wearing it simply because they can and want to do so.

Part Three

Human Rights and Freedom of Expression

Chapter 10

Marginalisation or an Opportunity for Dialogue

Exploring the *Hijab* as a discursive symbol of the identity of young Muslim women

Sariya Contractor

Introduction: Why do we need a new Discourse on the *Hijab?*

The concept of *hijab*, which colloquially alludes to the headscarf worn by Muslim women is much debated and stereotyped in the annals of secular scholarship, feminist literature, Islamic theology, in Muslim communities and within the media. The nature of the debates varies from liberal feminist arguments about the *hijab's* perceived 'oppression' of women to the Muslim apologist's version of the argument that portrays the *hijab* as an emancipator of the women who wear it, as a hallmark of piety and virtuousness. This excessive focus on the *hijab* diverts attention from more important matters like education and healthcare for Muslim women.[273] Also, by excessively focusing on '*hijab* – the garment', these texts fail to convey to readers the deeper and more nuanced meanings that '*hijab* – the concept' holds for the women who wear it, and who consider it to be a divinely ordained framework which defines guidelines for both male and female modesty. Existing literature surrounding the *hijab* often treats it as a homogeneous practice, failing to contextualise the multifarious cultural, regional, theological and even linguistic understandings that influence the way it is practised and worn. These texts are often written by individuals who do not wear the *hijab*. They are written by:

- Muslim men who are modest, who are not required to wear the *hijab*, but who nevertheless seek to justify the practice and occasionally enforce it within Muslim communities; or by
- women who do not think it is a necessary part of the Islamic faith and

who may consider it to be a cultural anomaly that has become part of Islamic faith practices and that must hence be discouraged.

These texts rarely consult with, or voice the opinions, interpretations and narrations of, women who wear the *hijab*. Historically the *hijab* may have been manipulated for political gain, or to consolidate the male hegemony of religious doctrine; but only rarely a has female wearer (of the *hijab*) been asked her reasons for wearing it.

This chapter draws strongly upon the narrations and opinions of young British women with whom the author interacted as part of a larger doctoral research project. Semi-structured interviews were conducted with 45 young Muslim women who were studying or working at educational institutions. Participants were asked to speak about the *hijab* during interviews, contextualising it within their narrative about their lives, daily routines and the challenges they faced. The women's responses were coded using NVIVO 7,[274] and themes were identified in their comments about the *hijab*. These findings were taken back to the women, so that they could validate the findings as their voice – the *Muslima's* voice.

During interviews, participants' comments about the *hijab* were almost always underpinned by a desire to converse, to clarify and to demystify the *hijab* within the diverse pluralistic communities they inhabited. Identity and identification were another recurring theme within what the women were saying. This new generation of young *hijabis* seemed to have transformed a passive garment into an interactive tool that they use, often proactively, to create more understanding about their faith and hence to create semblances of cohesion in what some commentators describe as increasingly 'more polarised and segmented' societies.[275] This research will examine and contextualise this transition in constructs of the *hijab*.

Contextualisation: What is the *Hijab*?

The heterogeneity within the Muslim *Um'mah* is very apparent in the way that the *hijab* is understood and worn within various Muslim communities. The concept '*hijab*' can be defined as a broad set of modesty guidelines for men and women, including lowering the gaze, limiting unnecessary interaction with the opposite gender and subscribing to gender-specific dress codes,[276] as derived from the Qur'an,[277] the *Sun'nah*[278] and the *Ijmaa*[279] of Muslim scholars through history.[280] Of the Qur'anic injunctions[281] dealing with the *hijab*, one verse that is often quoted brings scriptural validity to arguments of identity and identification within *hijab* discourses:

> O Prophet! Tell thy wives and daughters, and the believing women, that they should cast their outer garments over their persons (when abroad): that is most convenient, that they should be known (as such) and not molested. And Allah is Oft-Forgiving, Most Merciful. (33: 59)

This verse contains an instruction for women to wear an outer garment so that they may be recognised as believing women. A woman who wears a *hijab* is intentionally and inherently recognisable as a Muslim; her 'Muslimness' is not hidden under her *hijab*, rather, the *hijab* is an affirmation of her faith. She is cognisant of the socio-religious implications that the *hijab* carries with it and she carries this with her whatever role she plays in society.[282] It ceases to remain the piece of cloth that Aisha Bewley[283] says should not define the identity of a woman. Rather, it becomes an expression and communication of the meaning that the woman gives to it.

An earlier trend to move away from the *hijab* is seamlessly dissolving into another trend – of young educated Muslim women, particularly in the West, going back to wearing the *hijab* as a religious practice.[284] This resurgence of the veil challenges views expressed in certain genres of literature that described the *hijab* as a symbol of the backwardness of Muslim women, which would gradually become less prevalent as education levels and development increased in Muslim societies.[285] Daughters are reclaiming what their mothers sometimes discarded. This is described by some social commentators as the emergence of 'political Islam'. But it can also be understood as a culmination of various quests that young British Muslims must undertake to structure an identity position which is harmonious with their Islamic and secular selves. 'These women use the *hijab* to carve out public space for themselves and see it as a symbol of their transition to Modernity.'[286]

The *Hijab*: Historical Contexts

Much of what was written about Muslim women focused on the institution of the veil, with anthropologists and historians alike relating the practice to social organisation in a given society.[287] Lady Mary Worthley Montagu[288] was one of the earliest Western women to write about Muslim women and the veil in the 18th century. She wrote that she disagreed that the veil was oppressive and argued instead that, in her own experience, while it was uncomfortable wearing it for the first time, it gave women the freedom to create their own realm that was separate from male authority. She was impressed with the liberties of Turkish Mohammedan (sic) women and intended to use this as a stick with which to beat English society!

Unfortunately not all interactions between 'secular' feminist thought and discourses about Muslim women have led to Muslim systems being used to influence Western society. Edward Said[289] in his critique of Orientalism describes how the Orientalists in their exploration of Islam as the 'other' recognised the *hijab* as a symbol of the Islamic degradation of women. It was this practice, according to imperialist ideology, that stood in the way of the 'progress' and 'civilisation' of Muslim societies.[290]. *Hijabs*, veils, head coverings of various sorts were labelled in one sweeping gesture as a personification of misogynist culture, of backwardness and of the need for external intervention leading to emancipation. These harbingers of emancipation did not reflect upon the significance of this garment to the women who wore it, nor did they actually ask the women. The fact that they themselves understood it as regressive and uncultured was enough to demand unveiling and persuasion to imbibe 'the true spirit of Western civilisation'.[291] The feminists were quick to grasp this idea of the subjugated and unheard Muslim woman, who was desperately hoping for her voice to be heard. The mind conjured up images of exotic locales, barred, prison-like harems and beautiful women. The media then, and still today, speaks about the invisible women, unheard of and unseen in society, with but a limited role outside the walls of the gilded cage in which they live.

The colonial Western woman empathised with the Muslim woman's struggles, but her opinions and voicing of the latter's problems were often coloured by notions of Western superiority.[292] The Western feminist 'heard' Muslim women and began busying herself in removing the most obvious expression of these women's 'oppression' – the *hijab*! The Islamic modernists, who were educated to respect and admire the culture of their colonisers, were easily influenced by these new-fangled ideas of freedom, emancipation and no more headscarves. There was a wave of feminist action – public unveilings, lifting of veils and one Egyptian girl, a young feminist, was so agitated by her grandmother's refusal to unveil that she threw all the older woman's headgear into the Nile![293] It proclaimed itself to be a movement for and by Muslim women, but was in fact initiated by Western male colonisers for political gain. It was propagated by their elitist Muslim male servants and workers of the colonisers and was practised by their wives and daughters – a small minority of elitist women who admired

Western culture, and who did not represent the voice of practising, believing women who wore the *hijab* out of their own choice and Islamic faith.

The *Hijab*: Two Discourses

Clarke[294] asserts that it is interesting in the context of women's studies that, in the majority of cases, when a *hadīth* mentions *hijab* it normally refers to modesty or dress code guidelines *for men*, whereas only a few discuss or present evidence of *hijab* guidelines for women. This seems to be indicative of an attitude of relative openness and flexibility towards the *hijab* of women in classical Islamic texts. In more recent 'Islamic' literature this attitude seems to have dissipated, especially in certain 'modern' texts that are considered to be sources of authentic religious guidance for Muslim women. *Bahishti Zewar* (*Heavenly Ornaments*) is a book written 'exclusively for women', by the early 19th-century scholar Ashraf Ali Thanvi,[295] to address the lack of Islamic knowledge among them. While this book usefully discusses many aspects of Islam relevant to the daily routines of women, it endorses an understanding of the *hijab* that includes covering of the face and strict segregation. Abua'la Maududi, a 20th-century Pakistani scholar, presents in his book *Purdah and the Status of Woman in Islam*[296] an understanding of the *hijab* which uses modesty as a pretext to limit a woman's role to her home, what he calls 'her own natural sphere'. More recently Maulana Wahiuddin Khan[297] has echoed similar opinions.

At the other end of the *hijab* discourse there are opinions by writers, mostly women, who use what they perceive as ambiguity in the Qur'an to justify an opinion that the *hijab* or headscarf is not a necessary aspect of the dress code of a woman.[298] Clarke,[299] for example, argues that 'women's covering for the sake of modesty and sexual peace, including the covering [of] the hair, really owns no field of hadīths of its own'. Asma Barlas,[300] in her brief discussion about the *hijab*, concludes that while the Qur'an does mandate 'that both men and women comport themselves modestly ... there is absolutely nothing in these values that supports the conservative Muslim position on ... the practice of veiling'. Nawal El Saadawi[301] is also assertive in her opposition of the *hijab*, associating it with suppressed Muslim women, while Fatima Mernissi[302] argues that it is an unjust symbol of the male oppression of women that must not be encouraged.

Initiating a New Discourse: What are the Women Saying about the *Hijab*?

The young British Muslim women I spoke to for this research feel that the *hijab* is an important and integral aspect of their lives. Most participants were aware of the different meanings that the *hijab* can hold for the cultures they live in. These young women are proud to be British and Muslim, and seem to be living through a process of cultural evolution. They no longer try to bridge two cultures, one British and one from 'back home' – wherever that might be. Rather, it is Britain that is home. This may not necessarily be true for the older generation, who often subscribe to social systems that are still deeply rooted 'back home'. This original multiplicity of cultural affiliations within the social constructs of the Muslim diaspora, when confronted by the youthful desire and ability to be 'British and Muslim', creates tensions in many aspects of Islamic practice for youth, and more so for young women.

The religious 'differences of opinion' which might permeate the same family unit and causes stress lines within it is exemplified in the experiences of Maryam,[303] a young Irish woman who coverted to Islam. When Maryam converted, she slowly realised that her faith and a desire to be 'recognised as a Muslim' made her *want* to wear the *hijab*. She had to be careful how she introduced the practice to her family, especially her mother, because the *hijab* did not fit into the culture of her secular family who considered religiosity to be 'meaningless'.

> I started off like wearing it because firstly people were telling me that as a Muslim you have to wear it. But I wasn't ready because I was struggling to learn the prayer and stuff. But then I felt like when I was in the street I wanted to be recognised as a Muslim, I wanted to say 'Assalam alaikum',[304] and I tried to say 'Assalam alaikum' to people, but because I looked like a normal British young woman they would just pass by. They would just look at me and walk off because they always thought that I am not Muslim. So I wanted people to see that I am Muslim. So that's when I started to wear the scarf out. I did it gradually – (I wear it) when I get far away from my house and then walk around and then I took it off near my home so that my mother didn't see because she didn't like me wearing it in the beginning.
>
> (Maryam, London, January 2009)

Some would argue that a convert's experiences are not representative of the experiences of an individual born and brought up in a Muslim family or community. This may be true. Some 'born Muslim' participants mention that they were initiated to wearing the *hijab* at the age of nine, or when they first 'grew up', and how they felt 'it was the right thing to do'. Others speak about wearing the *hijab* because everybody in the family, including highly-admired aunts and older cousins wore the *hijab*. A few even mentioned being 'cool' among their peers because they were the first in their class-rooms in Muslim-dominated schools to wear the *hijab*. They fitted in!

However, for many participants the choice to wear the *hijab*, or to continue to wear it, was a decision they often took independently and occasionally without the support of parents who subscribed to cultural understandings of the *hijab*. Some elders felt that the *hijab* was something to wear within the community and not in multicultural settings; other more 'modern' parents felt that it was not required at all – their Western-educated daughters did not need to wear the *hijab*; while more 'culturally traditional' parents did not appreciate the fact that the *hijab* gave strength and emancipation to the young women who wore it. And it is in this context that Maryam's tensions with her mother regarding the *hijab* become relevant to many other young women. When Samina, a 'born Muslim', decided to wear the *hijab* she had the support of her immediate family, but her extended family was not as supportive:

> But at the same time within the social community of people whom we used to meet as a family, I didn't get such positive support. They were like 'Why are you wearing it?' and 'Do you need to wear it?' And that was the challenging part. At weddings people would be like 'Oh! just take it off.
> (Samina, Markfield, August 2008)

Not only do young women use the *hijab* to assert their religiosity to their families, they also use it as a symbol of authority to gain Islamic rights that may be denied to them for cultural reasons. When families whose origin lay primarily in the Indian sub-continent first moved to the UK, external symbols of religion were sometimes cast off in an effort to be assimilated into the Western culture. This waning of external symbols was often inversely proportional to the strength that private/personal practices gained, and occasionally these were not always Islamic practices. So while *hijabs* were occasionally abandoned, young girls and women needed to be protected from the corrupting influences of Western education. It is practices like these that young women can challenge when empowered by the *hijab*. The *hijab* is invariably perceived in many Islamic communities, including the most 'moderate', as an unassailable symbol of piety, which hence gives the wearer religious authority. Hence the *Muhajjabah* or the *hijabī*[305] brings 'religious' or 'theological' validity to any argument that she makes, including those that may be 'classified' by some as inherently feminist. Many young women realise this strength invested in them by the *hijab* and use it, along with their knowledge of the Qur'an and the *Sun'nah*, to articulate and demand their rights. In their quest for rights, Islam seems to be women's most effective tool. It is definitely not an easy struggle, as it involves challenging and sometimes rejecting certain aspects of their family's and community's ethnic culture. Alvi *et al.*[306] discuss a similar phenomenon where Canadian Muslim women use the veil as an 'adaptive strategy' to articulate their religious, social and cultural standpoints by choosing to practise or not practise the veil.

Hence for participants in this research the veil signified the various life-choices they make, and during interviews they almost invariably discussed the reasons that informed these choices. It is understandably difficult for a young woman to decide that she is going to cover all herself in a society that glorifies physical beauty, and so the decision to wear the *hijab* was often made after much reflection. The participants' reasons to wear the *hijab* were many – faith, identity, modesty, spiritual strength, security, comfort, protection being some of the key themes. However, faith and identity stand out as the two core reasons for almost all the young women I spoke to, which is in agreement with the Qur'an's injunction – 'so that they may be recognised as believing women'. When asked what was more important to them as a group, faith or identity, women found it difficult to decide. The ensuing discussions were long and animated, as the women took sides. However, gradually an understanding of faith and identity as two overlapping and complementary reasons began to emerge – 'We assert our identity through our *hijabs*, but our identity is our faith.'

It is these two concepts, faith and identity, that I think are central to the new *hijab* discourse that this chapter aims to unravel and perpetuate. Katherine Bullock, a Canadian academic convert to Islam, says in the conclusion of her book *Rethinking Muslim Women and the Veil* that 'the *hijab* acts as an empowering tool of resistance to the consumer capitalist culture's beauty game … it is a religiously endorsed dress, and its link to tradition makes it the wearer's gateway to faith'.[307]

All 45 young women who collaborated in this research, including those who did not wear the *hijab*, agreed that modesty was part of a Muslim's life – male or female; and 44 of the 45 agreed that covering all your hair was an integral and obligatory part of the modesty guidelines for Muslim women. The participant who disagreed that covering your hair was obligatory still wore the *hijab* and felt that it was a part of Islam and had a function to play in the life of a woman. However, she disagreed with the fact that in certain Muslim communities the '*hijab* has become too prescriptive'. The three women who did not wear a *hijab* also agreed that it was an essential aspect of Islamic guidelines for Muslim women; wearing it or not wearing it was a choice that they would consider making in the future, based on personal and social circumstance – the *hijab* became almost an ideal that these young women *aspired* to achieve. Two participants, a French woman and a Turkish woman, had immigrated to Britain simply so that they could escape the *hijab* ban in the countries of their origin; they could practise the *hijab* freely in Britain and also get an education.

During group discussions I discussed some of the liberal opinions with participants who deemed the *hijab* to be an unnecessary cultural innovation within Islamic communities. Participants overwhelmingly disagreed with these opinions; they recognised the *hijab* as an integral requirement of their faith which they intended to conform to. These young women all wear the *hijab* out of deep religious conviction and faith. At the same time they do not subscribe to conservative understandings of the *hijab* that limit a woman's role. They each articulate their own varied and at the same time balanced understandings of the Islamic principles of modesty, which may require them to cover their hair, but which do not impede educational or professional achievement. And while proactively choosing to talk about their *hijabs*, participants often refer to the comfort, protection and confidence they derive from the *hijab*.

Identity

Identification is an iterative process of evolution, change, adaptation and transfer. Far from being all-inclusive, the resultant identity is in constant negotiation with the history, language, culture, class, society and caste of the individual.[308] It arises from the narrativisation of the self within external representations – the discursive construction of a 'we', of which the 'I' becomes a loyal and, perhaps, a contributing part irrespective of any differences or divisions.[309] This is the 'we' that discerning Muslim women have been able to represent in their donning of the *hijab* and which should not be confused with any political process. This 'appropriation of the Islamic garb' as an expression of identity is very apparent in the narratives of the British women I spoke to, as well as in research with American women.[310]

I wear the *hijab* because it's me.

(Shamsia,[311] Birmingham, March 2008)

Shamsia wears the *hijab* because she feels it epitomises who she is. Maryam, the convert to Islam who was quoted earlier, narrates how she *wanted* to be recognised as a Muslim woman. Young women derive their identity positions from their Islamic faith as well as from their social positions living and working in a multicultural society which respects the standpoints of the individual. Identity implies a degree of 'sameness' yet it is constructed out of 'difference'. It is relational with 'another'[312] which is 'different' – the personal and the external. In Islam the religious/personal life is not different from the social/public life. It is, rather, a smooth progression of one into the other. Identity is created at the intersection of the public and private lives, it is the reflection of the social on the individual, but for a Muslim this difference between the two realms is blurred to the extent that there *is* no difference, and this poses a problem that is difficult to resolve in societies where religion is considered external to social spheres. Hence the identity of a Muslim woman – as expressed in the *hijab* – may seem to be in conflict with her secular environs but is simply an articulation of her self and her individuality which she defines within her inherent religious framework.

And whether or not the Muslim woman approves, the *hijab* – a piece of cloth – can make her symbolic of her faith, a badge that categorises her as Muslim and which defines how she is perceived in society. The *hijab* has become representative of the Muslim woman and a part of her identity. It is a construct that she derives, in part, from her faith, and in part from the role that society assigns to her and that she in turn accepts. More than being a mere piece of cloth, it is an articulation of her belief system, her milieu, her values, her ethics, her limits, and also of her responsibilities as a representative of her community.

Personally I didn't really have much of a perception of me as a Muslim woman. I was trying to find me as me! But because I had the *hijab* on it made me aware that I was representing a group of people and it made me aware of what I was doing.

Zeba,[313] Birmingham, March 2008

Hijab as Dialogical Tool

Stuart Hall[314] describes identity as 'the meeting point, the point of suture, between on the one hand the discourses and practices which attempt to "interpellate", speak to us or hail us into place as the social subjects of particular discourses, and on the other hand, the processes which produce the subjectivities, which construct us as subjects which can be "spoken".' It is in many ways therefore a reflection of society on the individual, but it must be understood that the individual consciously engages with this reflection and invests in it. Therefore identity does not simply *identify*; rather, it *articulates*. This is perhaps the Muslimahs' construct of the meaning of the *hijab* – to articulate their faith:

> I started wearing *hijab*, previously it was faith. But when I came over here I felt a dual responsibility – I must wear it myself and I must also wear it to present a correct understanding of Islam as well.
>
> (Roohi, Loughborough, August 2008)

While talking about the *hijab*, participants seem to attribute to it qualities that are way beyond the scope of a passive piece of cloth. The *hijab* has the potential to label an individual, and wearing it makes them a representative of their faith. This was a common theme that underpinned the women's stories as they described their initial decisions to wear the *hijab*; their experiences while wearing it; and how wearing the *hijab* influenced their behaviour in society. Participants describe being very aware that wearing the *hijab* made them identifiable as Muslims, and hence, as representatives of the Islamic faith, they made extra efforts to ensure that they did not portray Islam negatively through any of their actions.

> But I wear it (the *hijab*) due to faith and I also feel that it helps me improve myself because I know that the way I dress, people will know that I am a Muslim, people will not have to ask me what religion I follow, they will know from what I wear.
>
> (Somaiya, Warwick, August 2008)

Participants also describe the *hijab* as being instrumental in initiating dialogue with people from other faith backgrounds. Stray encounters on trains, on buses, at university, often evolve into discussions about faith and the beliefs of Muslims as represented by a young woman who wears her *hijab*. Basariya, a student at Warwick University, describes how her roommates were shocked that 'a Muslim girl wearing the Hijab watched TV and had fun', but that led her to have 'a big talk' with them in which she discussed the basics of the Islamic faith. Another participant mentions a conversation with a co-passenger on a bus who wanted to know what Ramadan and fasting meant to Muslims. These impromptu intercommunity dialogue sessions seem to be a direct implication of participants wearing the *hijab*. And the young women seem to be keen to talk about their faith and eager to answer legitimate questions that individuals may have. They often say that if they did not wear the *hijab* people would not recognise them to be Muslims and that, while they are honoured to be representatives of their faith, they understand that it comes with a massive responsibility which they are happy to shoulder. Hence understandings of the *hijab* evolve – from being a passive piece of garment to become a religious standpoint that describes a theological truth; then an identity position which articulates a one-sided story; and now the *hijab* seems to have been extrapolated by the women who wear it into a dialogical tool which can stimulate exchange of information between more than one individual.

Conclusions

Through this research I hope to have initiated a new discourse on the *hijab* that is informed by the opinions of the women who wear it and who respect it as a religious obligation. While acknowledging that, in certain patriarchal societies, extreme interpretations of the *hijab* continue to hamper women's freedoms and rights, I argue that in the British context women who wear the *hijab* have often chosen to do so because of religious conviction and faith. Rather than being impeded by it in any way, young women describe being strengthened by the *hijab*, both spiritually and pragmatically – it empowers them to justify and achieve their aspirations in societies that are occasionally still culturally backward.

These women are passionate about the Islamic ideology that informs not just their *hijab* but also other aspects of their life, including their careers, family life and everyday routine. They are cognisant of the stereotypes of the *hijab*, both within the Muslim community and in multicultural society. This research, however, seems to indicate a paradigm shift in the signification that the *hijab* holds for young British Muslim women, and indeed British society as a whole. Rather than being an ostentatious and visible religious symbol that highlights difference and separates communities,[315] the *hijab* of these women seems to be actively challenging traditional stereotypes. It has evolved into a dialogical tool which acts as a catalyst for initiating discussion and dialogue – a part of the Cultural Revolution where the margins come into representation, or rather where marginality becomes a powerful space – an opportunity in itself for the marginalised to find their own voices.[316] And the debate about dealing with difference is hence iteratively pushed forward through the actions, words and conduct of the young women who wear the *hijab*. It will be apt to end this chapter with an opinion expressed by a participant:

There is so much meaning that the *hijab* can give. I think that in this day and age it is important that I be identified as a Muslim woman.

(Basariya, Warwick, November 2008)

Chapter 11

The Islamic Veil
A focal point for social and political debate

Malika Ghamidi (translated from French by Nicholas Farelly)

The issue of the so-called 'Islamic' veil represents a major international challenge in this 21st century. For instance, it poses the question of the relationship between Islam and the West, two worlds that are sometimes said to be diametrically opposed. The French concept of *laïcité* (sometimes translated as 'secularity'), which is the basis for the country's principle of separation between religion and the State, is debated throughout Western countries as well as in the Arab and Muslim world. Though the veil represents the symbol of Islam's visibility in the public arena, it is considered a major obstacle to women's emancipation, a threat against secularity and against one of the foundational values of European societies: the equality of men and women.

Thus, for several years, we have experienced in France and elsewhere in Europe impassioned debates about this particular religious symbol and its prohibition in schools and other state-owned institutions. Beyond the fact that these debates have created an Islamic veil 'problem', our conceptions and representations of democracy, secularity, and also of feminism and Islam, are being challenged.

Today, how should we assess these debates? Are not the spirit of tolerance and the principle of secularity exploited to foster an 'exclusive secularity'? Is the scarf really a symbol of discrimination against women, or could it be considered a symbol of emancipation? Why do so much passion and fear surround this religious symbol? Does focusing on this divert us from the real social and political problems? Is there an unspoken fear of the 'Green Peril'? Can we really speak of women's emancipation if we decide not to listen to the voice of the Muslim women in the decision process that involves her?

The following pages are intended for those who wonder about the meaning of the so-called Islamic veil and the true issues at stake in this recurrent polemical debate. At the same time, this chapter is an attempt to take the heat out of this debate and reject any demagogical manipulation.

The Many Faces of the So-Called Islamic Veil

In the collective subconscience, the veil does not have any other function than to lock the Muslim woman into the private sphere. It is seen as synonymous with oppression and is accused of totalitarianism. Yet, today, the truth is that women of faith do not hesitate to be present in the public sphere.

> From stigmatisation and a sign of inferiority, it is about to become the symbol of power-conquest and prestige. This metamorphosis constitutes a double declaration of war: on the one hand against the secularist conception of feminine emancipation, and on the other hand against the representation of Muslim men, for whom the veil embodies women's submission.[317]

Most women do now consider it as a source of liberation, not of oppression.

Although the veil was at one time synonymous with 'cover', today it crosses over social classes. The meaning that one gives to the veil can also vary from one woman to another: while some wear it out of 'tradition', others wear it as a sign of cultural identity or even as a politico-religious banner, according to several commentators.

In any case, the veil is so loaded with biases and stereotypes that it continually raises questions and frustrations: It is the symbol *par excellence* of women's submission to men. Furthermore, it is used to aggravate an opposition between the 'modern enlightened' West and the 'barbaric and obscurantist' East, as the debates surrounding the Islamic veil have shown in France and Belgium, where political and feminist circles have been quite confused. In France, in order to fight against the symbol of women's oppression, a law was voted to ban the *hijab*, and in Belgium, a school Principal can now include a ban on the veil in the school's regulation handbook. Yet, those who supposedly fight in favour of women's emancipation have supported a regulation that, ironically, sends schoolgirls back into the domestic sphere – the very sphere that political and feminist circles consider to be oppressive. Some feminist movements should have fought for freedom against all forms of domination, not against this 'symbol'. We will come back to this issue later in the chapter.

From this standpoint, it is important to note that the 'covering' or 'uncovering' of women is nothing new – it has a history. Already during the colonial era, in Algeria, women were caught in the crossfire of colonialist and nationalist struggles. They were the 'guardians of the nation' in the eyes of both the colonised and the colonisers. Starting in the early 20th century, several governments in the Arab Muslim world considered the 'uncovering' of women to be a step towards a Western model of modernity, their only model of emancipation. For instance, in Turkey and in Iran, Mustapha Kemal Atatürk and the Shah adopted the 'Western' dress code, imposing the 'uncovering' in order to go further in terms of modernity. In Morocco, King Mohammed V, Hassan II's father, used his daughter as a symbol of Moroccan women's emancipation, requesting that she took off her veil in public. Finally, in Tunisia, President Bourguiba officially forbade those hired in public service from wearing the veil. To attain 'modernity' and 'civilisation', women had to 'uncover' in their own countries.

What about Europe?

In the European Union, the attitude towards the veil is far from homogenous. In 2007 in Copenhagen, a symbolic catastrophe occurred: the Little Mermaid, nakedly enthroned on her rock since 1913, was found wearing a black scarf! (This is the main character of the famous story by Hans Christian Andersen of a mermaid willing to give up her identity to gain a human soul.) After having endured much aggravation over the years, now she was veiled. Meanwhile a debate was underway on the place of the veil, in reaction to the declaration of Asmaâ Abdoul-Amid that she would keep wearing her veil if she was elected to the Danish parliament. The Danish People's Party considered this to be an affront to French values and sought to get a ban on the veil.

In Germany, the constitutional court decided to clear an Afghan teacher after she had been forbidden to wear her veil in a public school of the Baden-Wurtenberg region. German regional parliaments urged schools to 'find an acceptable regulation for all'. Yet, on 19 March 2008, after a long legal dispute, an administrative court forbade a teacher who had converted to Islam from wearing her Islamic veil during classes in the public school. The decision taken by the Baden-Wurtemberg administrative tribunal endorses the ban on teaching while veiled, adopted in 2004 by the Stuttgart school where this Muslim woman taught for over 30 years. This ruling, however, goes against a decision of the administrative tribunal of the city which, two years earlier, had proven the school wrong, in the name of equality of treatment between religions. As argued by the Stuttgart tribunal, Catholic sisters can teach with their veil in the district's public schools.

In Spain, the veil is rarely at the centre of public debate. In case of conflicts, ultimate decisions are taken by the autonomous regions. In Greece, students wear veils in the schools of the large Turkish Muslim minority without it being a problem.

Finally, in Belgium, where since 2004 the question of the veil is a divisive issue amongst political leaders, two francophone senators, the socialist Anne-Marie Lizin and the Liberal Alain Destexhe, requested a veil law '*à la French*'. For them, Belgium should have adopted dispositions that were 90 per cent similar to those expected in France, even though the term *laïcité* or 'secularity' was replaced by 'neutralist', a term more appropriate to Belgian traditions. They evoked the equality between men and women (also affirmed in the Belgian constitution), the role of the school 'as a place where individual autonomy and political consciousness are learned', and the necessary protection of children. 'To my colleagues who state that the veil emancipates certain young girls or that it pertains to their freedom, I say that it is especially important to protect them against those who wish to maintain them in an inferior status,' explains Alain Destexhe. 'It is profoundly abnormal that each school solves as it is able a problem which, at times, is submitted to a degree of proselytising and force from a nearby Muslim community,' adds Anne-Marie Lizin.[318] There is no legislation in Belgium forbidding the veil being worn in school. However, the principals of public schools are able to insert this ban into their schools' regulations handbook. About 15 Muslim organisations have voiced their disagreement with the proposal of these two elected officials, judging that 'to forbid the veil in schools, in hospitals, and in administrations is equivalent to depriving the Muslim citizen of the enjoyment of civil rights.'[319]

In this debate, it is of utmost importance to say a few words on the case of Turkey, where the veil has entered the presidential palace in the person of Hayrünnisa Gül (President Abdullah Gül's wife). Moreover, Turkish deputies have introduced a controversial bill allowing women to wear the veil on campuses, a bill which most secular thinkers believe is another step towards the 'Islamising' of society. This reform, supported by Prime Minister Tayyip Erdogan, was approved by 411 votes against 103 in parliament, where Erdogan's majority party 'Justice and Development' (AKP) was supported by members of the Nationalist Movement (MHP). Defenders of secularity denounced the regression of Turkey to archaic values, and the attacks against secularity, a sacrosanct concept in the country of Mustapha Kemal Atatürk.

The French Debate: Secularity Unveiled ...

According to Article 2 in the law of 9 December 1905, 'the Republic neither recognises, pays, or subsidises any religious group. France is an undividable, secular, democratic, and social Republic. It ensures equality before the law for all of its citizens, without distinction of origin, race, or religion. It respects all beliefs.' France is the only country in the European Union that establishes a total judicial separation between Church and State.

Since the early 1990s, the debate over the Islamic veil has been at the forefront in France, and to a disproportionate extent. The question was taken up again when two young girls, Alma and Lila, refused to take off their veils in school. A law, over which social and political movements were divided, was then passed by the French parliament in March 2004, forbidding any 'ostensible' religious signs in schools. 'The division that exists in France between those who want to utilise the power of the State to eradicate religion and those who seek to allow the pluralist confrontation of beliefs and ideas has persisted until today.'[320]

The objective of the 1905 law was to legislate regarding the conditions of religious groups' practice within the Republic. Nothing anti-clerical or negative is mentioned regarding religion, which must play its proper role in the democratic sphere. The principles are oriented towards a protection of religions as expressions of freedom of conscience and of belief, a position promoted by Socialist leader Jean Jaurès. Catherine Samary argues that freedom of conscience must not be transformed into 'official thought', an 'atheistic State religion'.

Let us not be naïve, the law of March 2004 is a direct hit against the visibility of the veil in the public sphere. Yet, in 1989, when the first 'veil cases' emerged, the French Council of State judged that to wear the veil was perfectly compatible with the law of 1905.

Thus, a number of specialists argue that this debate was unfairly exploited and that it has been truncated. According to Françoise Lorcerie, young French Muslim girls have been the first victims. Even more, they have suffered the costs of the dispute. According to the president of the Human Rights League, Jean-Pierre Dubois, the veil law is 'an additional humiliation, and to speak of success in this regard is greatly cynical. In attacking a symbol, the law eradicated the visibility of the integration problem, but it has not solved the problem itself. What does this France of fear do to help its youth find their place? These young girls aspire, in a great majority, to study, to work, and to be emancipated. Yet, once more, we have stigmatised them.'[321] If the choice to wear the veil is devoid of any social or family pressures, it does not contravene the law of secularity. But in 2004, the voices of those who disagreed were inaudible. For instance, the declarations of 2003 Nobel Peace Prize winner Shirin Ebadi (contrary to those of Taslima Nasreen) concerning the veil were completely ignored by the media. Ebadi argued for the right to wear the veil just as she denounced its imposition ...

Is the 'Red Peril' Going ... Green?

What if the problem was Islam, in its representation as a barbaric obscurantist religion, and a threat of the 21st century? In *The West and the Others, the story of a supremacy*, Sophie Bessis notes that:

> It has become a habit in the West to consider Islam to be responsible for all the archaisms of the societies in which it is established. Thus, the words of the Bengali Taslima Nasreem have been abundantly used. As she faced fundamentalists in her own country, she credited Islam with just about all of the evils of which Bengali women suffer, without making distinctions between that which comes from religion and that which originates with tradition, and without realising that the terrible conditions for women in all of India's sub-continent transcend any religious affiliation.[322]

Since the fall of the so-called 'communist' bloc, we are witnessing the elaboration of a dominant discourse that spreads a binary worldview, opposing West and East, the civilised world and its obscurantist counterpart. Two worlds are supposedly confronting each other: the Judeo-Christian world and its antithesis, the Arab-Muslim world. This presentation of the world is an intellectual regression, which puts into the background social identities.

Islam is analysed from the perspective of a politico-religious phenomenon which is dangerous for the Western world and which is incompatible with reason, the founding values of Western societies, just as several self-proclaimed specialists of 'Islamic' movements present Islam as a religion which is unable to evolve, to reform itself from within, and to adapt to modernity ... Thus shortcuts are used and abused: Islam = Islamic militantism = Arab = Terrorism. We have gone full circle!

The media and political parties continue to feed this collective paranoia, seeking to convince citizens that a confrontation of civilisations is necessary in order to counter the famous 'Green Peril'. Debates surrounding this religious symbol, the veil, are but the symptom of a fear influenced by clichés linked to violence and the submission of women, along with the fear of seeing European societies being Islamised by this 'push for the Islamic veil' in the public sphere. The veil is supposedly hurting the European identity ...

To conclude, the true threat comes from those who, in the guise of defending freedom, actually limit it. Those who present themselves as representatives of civilised society, pro-democracy and pro-freedom, whilst in reality they curtail it. In its relation with secularity, it is urgent to promote a re-reading, a new definition of this concept in the wake of a new reality, of a society constantly changing, the presence of the 'new' Muslim community, though it has been around for a long time!

Chapter 12

Muslim Women, the Veil and Activism

Rajnaara C. Akhtar

The Muslim woman's *hijab* as witnessed today is the result of a complex historical manifestation evolving with changing social, legal and cultural norms within Muslim communities all around the world. The *hijab* observed by the women living at the time of the Prophet Muhammad (peace be upon him) is perhaps vastly different to what we witness in European societies today. However, despite revolutionising fashion trends and cultural norms, the basic essence of modesty encouraged by the Islamic religion remains the underpinning philosophy behind observing the *hijab*.[323] If media discourse is to be believed, the single most pertinent issue effecting Muslim women in Europe would be the *hijab*, *niqab* (face veil) and general issues of dress. However far from reality this may be, it is evident that most media and academic focus is on this issue.

The *hijab* is a term that holds a variety of meanings that extend in scope beyond a simple head covering. For the purposes of this discussion, the *hijab* is the cloth that is used by Muslim women to cover their hair, neck and upper torso, and is intended to fulfil the requirement of modest attire required by the Islam.[324] However, it should be noted that Muslim women extend the *hijab* to include behaviour that is modest, as the *hijab* is intended to form part of Muslim women's character, behaviour and identity.

Historically, even within majority Muslim populated countries, the observance of the *hijab* has risen and fallen. Many studies have been conducted into the phenomenon from a social perspective[325] and all have established varying reasons for its observance by Muslim women, including basic religious conviction,[326] political statements and symbols,[327] expressing a personal identity, customary practices, and legal requirements.[328] In countries where Muslims are a minority, it can be argued that this spectrum of rationale for the *hijab* still exists.

The issue of the *hijab* has been contentious since the 1990s when various jurisdictions around the world moved to ban it on ideological grounds. France, Turkey and Tunisia are oft-quoted examples of states intolerant to such an outward manifestation of traditional Islamic views. Following the events of 9/11 in New York, the Muslim community felt under siege[329] and, in the backlash against Muslims across Europe and North America, a strange phenomenon appeared to take shape. Rather than distance themselves from Islam, thousands of young Muslim women began observing the *hijab* in what some have termed an expression of their Muslim faith. This rise occurred at a time when intolerance towards Muslims was on the increase,[330] and vulnerable Muslim women became the targets of assaults and attacks. Following the July 7 bombings in London, the backlash against Muslims in Britain was swift and strong, and the subsequent fear was so great that it gave rise to the head of the Muslim College in London, the late Professor Zaki Badawi, advising Muslim women who feared attack to remove their *hijab*s to protect themselves.[331] This advice was not well received by many Muslim women in Britain, who viewed it as a vital front on which compromise was not an option. While the removal of the piece of clothing that forms the external manifestation of the *hijab* would not change a Muslim woman's character or personality where modesty is concerned, the issue was of infringement of the rights of these women to cover themselves as they personally deemed fit and considered a religious obligation.

The 'Muslim Woman'

The focus of most discussion around Muslim women seems to presuppose that they form one collective group with a single identity. Miriam Cooke[332] propounded the notion of a collective identity of the 'Muslim woman' developed from the extreme concern around the world about what is right for Muslim women. They are no longer viewed as individuals with personal needs, views and convictions, but rather as a collective with a singular identity. This religion/gender-centric identity overcomes all 'national, ethnic, cultural, historical, and even philosophical diversity.'[333] Perhaps such a collective identity can explain why such a cross-section of Muslim women was galvanised into protesting so vocally against the French *hijab* ban in 2004, as it was a shared right and belief that was being challenged. However, this compartmentalisation fails to explain the reality of the widely divergent approaches taken by women fighting for this same cause. The diversity of responses ranged from street protests and demonstrations to the quiet intellectual discussions intended to change opinions on an individual basis.

As part of that very movement against the *hijab* ban, this writer can confirm that the steps taken in response to the French ban on religious 'symbols' which would impact on the *hijab* were bold and confrontational, but were spurred on by a feeling of being wronged and wanting to ensure that rights guaranteed by the secular laws that governed Europe were upheld. The international mobilisation between Muslim women which occurred following the French ban took place with great speed. Existing organisations connected via a common language of asserting their rights.

Cooke makes the significant observation that 'While women from the tropical societies of Southeast Asia may seem to have little in common with women in the Arabian deserts or in cooler climes of Europe, some are realising that the Muslim woman cage might provide a paradoxical platform for action.'[334] An experience which supports this assertion is one in which this writer attended a meeting of Muslim women activists from across Europe which took place in Germany in 2005, where there was no common language and yet a feeling of solidarity permeated and a uniform action plan was set out. There were no need for introductions, and a shared belief in the common goal fostered trust, respect and open communication.

However, there are obvious limitations and fallacies of this view of a collective identity for all Muslim women. Primarily, its failure to take account of the vast differences between Muslim women derived from differing ethnicities, cultures, languages, personal histories and life experiences means that it is viewing Muslim women via a narrow optic. Empirical research focusing on the individual and differing views of Muslims challenges this notional collective Identity. An example is the qualitative study led by Dr Sara Silvestri into the opinions of Muslim women across Europe on a diversity of matters, including the main issues of concern to them in their daily lives and how Muslim women mobilise between themselves on issues affecting them collectively.[335] This study aimed to look beyond the issue of the veil, which seems to be the focus of most issues pertaining to Muslim women in general.

Although the sample of Muslim women was relatively small (49 Muslim women across Europe), the findings showed a diversity of views and attitudes which reflected complex and multifaceted opinions which cannot be divided strictly into the 'feminist/modern' and 'conservative/backward' categories.[336] This research crucially found that, despite the very vocal opposition to the treatment of women under Islamic laws widely spread across Europe,

... all the respondents ... affirmed to love and follow their religion freely. Islamic principles and practices were seen not as blind impositions but as a rational source of personal morality that the individual is free to follow. They were adamant in explaining that they were not submitted by their faith. On the other hand, they rejected the cultural approach of those communities and religious leaders that often exploit Islam to impose ethnic rather than faith-based beliefs and un-necessarily strict norms of conduct.[337]

Crucially, on the issue of diversity and integration, the study found that:

... none of the respondents said that they wished to live under ... Sharia law in Europe, not even those who wore the full *jilbab* (full length robe, covering the body from top to toe). Instead, they felt privileged for living in democratic European countries where the rule of law is in place that protects gender equality, diversity, and fundamental freedoms. Benefiting from these rights and freedoms and being well integrated were also the two key things that the Muslim women wished for their children and the future Muslim generations.[338]

Quite simply, this finding reflects the identification with Europe of European Muslim women who believe that their religious identity does not and should not come at the cost of their European identities. Both exist in parallel to, if not synonymous with, each other.

Silvestri concluded the following:

In the face of these aspirations and dreams of European Muslim women, it became clear – thus confirming previous research – that wearing the *hijab* and fighting for their right to do so is not an assertion of a 'primitive and backward' belief about female subjugation that originated in tribal or rural societies that embraced Islam. Although there are several Muslim women who are fiercely battling themselves against the veil, which they consider an imposition, many others defend this practice, which they consider to be full of a modern meaning. Even when it is not instrumentalised politically, putting on the scarf is nevertheless perceived as a path to emancipation, whereby Muslim women assert their right to free choice and stand up for and articulate their own human rights within a secular context. Simultaneously, though, as it emerged also in side conversations before and after the interviews, veiling can also be adopted tactfully as a strategy for marriage, which both embodies an assertion of modern individualism and independence and conforms to a traditional image of feminine piety, modesty, and motherhood.[339]

The resurgence of the veil and the resultant debate has become tiresome for some who feel the 'focus of energy … could be better used elsewhere.'[340]

The *Hijab* Ban

The French ban on conspicuous religious symbols in public schools in March 2004 was a turning point for many Muslim women in Europe and in particular in Britain. Although political activism from British Muslims had been a rising trend for a few years before this,[341] the activism of Muslim women specifically was motivated by this perceived threat to their liberty from just across the English Channel. For the first time, young Muslim women were galvanised into publicly speaking out on their own behalf, no longer relying on Muslim men to voice their opinions. In reality, the male-dominated public face of Islam across the globe has inadvertently substantiated the view that Muslim women are oppressed and in need of 'saving'. The confidence, independence and strong mindedness of Muslim women in *hijab* within Europe were witnessed in mainstream media for the first time.

The women across Europe involved in Project-Hijab were a diverse collective of Muslim women with only one binding rope – Islam and conviction in their right to wear a head covering. The network of women produced virtual relationships made possible by modern technology, and thus the campaigns were unified in their aim, yet vastly different in their methodology. The women in France were astonished by the bold British moves to protest vocally outside the French embassy in London. Such behaviour in France would be deemed unacceptably confrontational. Certainly, Cooke's suggestion that 'transnational, transmodern connections are daily forged and reinforced as Muslim women become integrated into the fabric of public life across the globe'[342] has a ring of truth.

The move towards the politicisation of Muslim communities in Britain was a gradual process that witnessed them move from the pre-1970s participation in the public sphere which was very much dictated by foreign cultural identification,[343] towards becoming firmly established British citizens who live, work, contribute and believe in Britain and demand their rights as British citizens. The events of September 11 had a worldwide impact on Muslims, and in Britain a community on the defensive was established and the siege mentality can be considered as one of the contributing factors leading to increased political activism as a means of defence.[344]

The mapping of the Muslim community in Britain became a possibility when the 2001 census included a question on religion, following lobbying by Muslims. This allowed wide statistics relating to Muslims in Britain to be compiled accurately and in a way that would reveal a great deal about the community and its presence in the UK.[345] The political activism of this community became more significant when a figure of 1.6 million Muslims was revealed (thought to have risen to over 2 million by 2008).

The move towards secularisation in Western Europe has not been mirrored by sizeable proportions of its Muslim citizens who do not believe religion can be compartmentalised and separated from their public life, and practices such as the *hijab*, which is an open and outward symbol of their faith, are a reflection of this.

The historic context of the ban on the *hijab* lies in the view of the *hijab* as a tool for the oppression of Muslim women, which has roots in the patriarchal cultures under which women have historically been oppressed. Such cultures span the globe and continue to exist today, but are by no means limited to societies where people follow the Islamic faith. Akbar Ahmed suggests that the treatment of women in Islamic societies reflects the stability or otherwise of the state: 'When Muslim society is confident and in a state of balance, it treats women with fairness and respect. When Muslim society is threatened and feels vulnerable, it treats women with indifference and even harshness.'[346] He views the current malaise as the result of two centuries of European colonisations and the aftermath which resulted in severely fractured Muslim communities, a loss of confidence and a need within Muslim men to 'protect' the women, which had a drastically adverse impact on the status of women.[347] Ahmed contrasts the treatment and role of Muslim women over the last two centuries with the historic role played by Muslim women from the time of the Prophet Muhammad (peace be upon him) as leaders of armies, business women and leading figures of great nations. It is these roles that young Muslim women in Europe are trying to reprise in defiance of some of the limitations placed on them by cultural norms with dubious religious roots.

The misconceptions about the status, position and role of Muslim women are not an exclusively external perception. The stereotypes have been formed based on widely reported practices within Muslim communities. Anouar Majid suggests that 'To conduct dialogues and expand the spaces of freedom in the Islamic world today, it is necessary to critically redefine and thoroughly reassess Islamic traditions, including entrenched but Islamically questionable assumptions about women.'[348]

Contemporary discourse of Muslim women's rights and the veil or *hijab* has moved away from opposing the traditional arguments about oppression and subjugation towards a rights-based discourse where women themselves are spearheading very public campaigns to assert their human rights in Western Europe and demand that secular laws which guarantee them freedoms are upheld. A young generation of European Muslim women, who have chosen to adopt the *hijab*, form the backbone of organisations such as Project-Hijab and have taken to the national and international stage in order to challenge the stereotypes that engulf the issue of Muslim women's dress.

The questions that arise are what changes have taken place in society to bring about this movement, and what does the *hijab* now represent for those wearing it, their religious communities and the wider British and European societies in which they live.

Progression of Muslim Communities

The Muslim community in Europe is aging and progressing as it becomes entrenched within European cultures. Younger generations cannot be distinguished from the rest of society as easily as earlier generations. A cultural fusion has allowed young Muslims to practise Islamic beliefs while maintaining a Eurocentric identity. While many would argue that the *hijab* is a visible sign of separation, it is adopted by many young girls (especially teenagers) as a fashion accessory, accompanied by designer jeans and accessories. This is a clear sign of an infusion of cultural practices and religious doctrine. However, in this scenario, it is easy to argue that the *hijab* has metamorphosed into a symbol of Islamic identity and away from being modest attire.

As well as the Islamic traditionalists, there is a growing movement of 'progressive Muslims' who undertake 'relentless striving towards a universal notion of justice in which no single community's prosperity, righteousness, and dignity comes at the expense of another.'[349] This wider view of the role of Muslims in Britain is increasing in popularity and is perhaps the result of increasing numbers of Muslims identifying strongly with European cultures. The movement against the *hijab* ban has goals that mirror this ethos, and their philosophy reflects European laws that protect freedom of religion.

Muslim women in Europe are expanding their roles so that the traditional function within the home is supplemented by outward contributions to society, whether through charitable works or otherwise engaging with the communities in which they live. The generation of young Muslim women born and bred in Europe are viewing the *hijab* not as a barrier to integration, but as a means of integrating, as it provides them with modesty and a sense of identity both for themselves and for others. The competence of these women is leading to a greater acceptance of their roles and contributions by the predominantly patriarchal leadership within Muslim communities. Although a great deal of work is yet to be done within Muslim communities in order to change the conventional mindset relating to the role of a woman, these young communities are still in their infancy and the fusion between Islamic beliefs and European cultures is still evolving for older generations.

There are numerous young Muslim women in Britain who are taking religious learning and understanding seriously in order to empower themselves with knowledge of Islam that does not originate from the male-centric classical opinions. This search for knowledge is being aided by the increasing numbers of Arabic texts and writings being translated into English, which reflects the contributions made by women in Islamic history – something that is often missing from the library shelves in Britain.[350] Such texts challenge the notion that Muslim women's lives should exist behind closed doors, and instead provide a clear picture of Islamic history scattered with examples of religiously pious and knowledgeable women who received and imparted knowledge at public events amongst some of the most renowned male Muslim scholars in history. These women were not deemed as outsiders trying to transgress Islamic bounds but, rather, they provided the perfect example of Muslim women observing *hijab* and engaging in a respectable public life as a consequence. Thus, these women from historic eras are actually role models for young Muslim women living in Muslim communities which have forgotten the contributions made by Muslim women in their history.

The *Hijab* and Human Rights

The issue of freedom of religion was by no means a nascent concept of the 20th century. For centuries before, laws relating to religious freedom were being formulated to protect rights which were often oppressed.[351] Freedom of religion is incorporated into numerous universal and regional treaties, and each one seeks to safeguard similar rights. While not identical, the wording of each provision is very similar in nature, with some treaties offering wider and others more restricted rights.

Challenges to *hijab* bans were brought before the national courts of Switzerland, Turkey and Germany, and in each of these states, the courts decided that the ban adhered to the state constitution. A woman seeking to challenge a ban on the *hijab* within Europe can do so under the following treaties: the European Convention on Human Rights 1950,[352] the First Optional Protocol to the International Convention on Civil and Political Rights 1966, and the Optional Protocol to the United Nations Convention on the Elimination of All Forms of Discrimination Against Women 1979.

Article 9 of the European Convention on Human Rights provides for freedom of thought, conscience and religion:

1. Everyone has the right to freedom of thought, conscience and religion; this right includes freedom to change his religion or belief and freedom, either alone or in community with others and in public or private, to manifest his religion or belief, in worship, teaching, practice and observance.
2. Freedom to manifest one's religion or beliefs shall be subject only to such limitations as are prescribed by law and are necessary in a democratic society in the interests of public safety, for the protection of public order, health or morals, or for the protection of the rights and freedoms of others.

Where the *hijab* is concerned, some have argued that there is no conclusive evidence that it is unequivocally required by Islamic laws, while others consider that it is a positive obligation. In either case, human rights provisions for freedom of religion operate in a way that gives religious communities the right to interpret their faith themselves and follow those interpretations.[353]

Numerous cases have been brought before the European Court of Human Rights (ECHR), challenging the right of a state to curb the wearing of the *hijab*. In 2004, the ECHR heard the case of *Leyla Sahin v Turkey*[354] where Sahin, a Turkish student, challenged the ban on the *hijab*. Sahin was a university student who suffered discrimination when she continued wearing the *hijab* and was denied entry into lectures and exams at her university. The arguments put forward by Sahin included that her rights and freedoms enshrined in Articles 8, 9, 10 and 14 of the European Convention on Human Rights were infringed by the ban.

The ECHR ruled in favour of the state of Turkey in its judgement on 29 June 2004. The Turkish government had argued that there was a difference between what could be termed a religious duty and the notion of freedom of religion, and the two were not necessarily synonymous. The apparent different interpretations for the veil across the Muslim world were cited to reflect a lack of uniformity in dress derived from the same religious doctrine, which they concluded could not be reconciled with the secular principle of neutrality within state education. This writer feels compelled to question this reasoning, on the grounds that religious principles of a universal religion such as Islam will by their very nature draw differing interpretations according to cultural norms in different parts of the world. This fluidity is a defining characteristic of some principles of Islamic practice, and for it to be cited as the very reason to place a curb on that religious practice lacks conviction.

A more convincing argument belying the real fears of the Turkish government was covered in the Court's judgement when it stated that 'the reasoning of the Turkish Courts showed that the Islamic headscarf had become a sign that was regularly appropriated by religious fundamentalist movements for political ends ...'[355] McGoldrick argues that this dual use of the *hijab*, by some women as an expression of their religious beliefs and by others as a political symbol, means that the issue for discussion here becomes whether the misuse of the *hijab* by some can be used as grounds for restricting its legitimate practice.[356] Katherine Bullock[357] sets out a multitude of 'meanings of *hijab*' in her text on the veil and recognises that political symbolism may be one of the facets for its observation. However, she does not suggest that any of the motivations behind observing the *hijab* are exclusive. Thus, one is forced to question to what degree the Turkish argument is based on factual analysis and data, and to what extent political concerns have played a part in the formulation of these arguments. The Court did reiterate that national decision-making bodies are to be given special importance in such hearings so as to strike a balance between the various interests in need of balance, especially where public order was an issue.

The matter did not end there, and Sahin applied for the case to be referred to the Grand Chamber, in accordance with rights under Article 43 of the European Convention. The Grand Chamber took the assumed position that the ban on the *hijab* did constitute an 'interference with the applicant's right to manifest her religion.'[358] However, the Court found that in, imposing the ban, Turkey was pursuing a legitimate aim in protecting 'the rights and freedoms of others and of protecting public order.'[359] The rationale for this decision was that the interference with the right was a necessity for the sake of secularism and equality. The ECHR referred to the case law of the Turkish Constitutional Court which had established that freedom of dress was not absolute within higher education institutes in Turkey.

The summary judgement further states:

> As to whether the interference was necessary, the Court noted that it was based in particular on the principles of secularism and equality. According to the case-law of the Constitutional Court, secularism, as the guarantor of democratic values, was the meeting point of liberty and equality. The principle prevented the State from manifesting a preference for a particular religion or belief; it thereby guided the State in its role of impartial arbiter, and necessarily entailed freedom of religion and conscience. It also served to protect the individual not only against arbitrary interference by the State but from external pressure from extremist movements. The Constitutional Court added that freedom to manifest one's religion could be restricted in order to defend those values and principles.

A further statement of the court which one may consider as inflammatory and imposing value judgements is the following:

> As had already been noted, the issues at stake included the protection of the 'rights and freedoms of others' and the 'maintenance of public order' in a country in which the majority of the population, while professing a strong attachment to the rights of women and a secular way of life, adhered to the Islamic faith. Imposing limitations on the freedom to wear the headscarf could, therefore, be regarded as meeting a pressing social need by seeking to achieve those two legitimate aims, especially since that religious symbol had taken on political significance in Turkey in recent years.[360]

In effect, the court has placed its own value judgement on the *hijab* and promoted the interests of women who do not observe it, over those who do.

Where human rights are concerned, clearly a balance needs to be struck between what can be termed selfish individualism and the wider needs of a society. However, where the harm emanating from an individual's actions on society is not readily observable, or the harm is subjectively established, problems begin to arise. Who chooses to put the rights of a society above the rights of an individual? If it is an organ of the state or general state policy, how would citizens fare under undemocratic or repressive regimes? Where the *hijab vis à vis* the state of Turkey is concerned in particular, the political turmoil between Islamists and secularists within the state is intense and laws are clearly dictated by the ideology of whichever party is in power, which reflects to some degree the legal and religious pluralism that exists there. Each can argue for a Public Order defence to infringing human rights which would contradict the other. However, the political reality is that both would have public support in measureable degrees from Turkish citizens.

The Future for Muslim Women and the Hijab in Europe

Following the ban on religious symbols in France, French schoolgirl Cennet Doganay sought and found refuge in the UK following her public protest against the French legislation. Doganay shaved her head in order to draw attention to the fact that she believed that, while she respected France, the state did not respect her rights. Upon reaching the UK, Doganay continued her studies unimpeded by the ban. Such seemingly extreme measures are a reflection of the conviction of this young French citizen, and of many young Muslim women like her across Europe.

In Britain, where the *hijab* is more acceptable attire, cases before the courts have focused on the *jilbab* and the *niqab* (face veil). The most publicised case relating to the right to wear the *jilbab* involved schoolgirl Shabana Begum,[361] who took her case against Denbigh High School to the House of Lords where the Law Lords held that the right to wear the *jilbab* was not protected by Article 9 of the European Convention on Human Rights. In this case, much of the discussion surrounded the subjective nature of ascertaining religious obligations.

Within Europe, the *hijab* has not been protected as a human right for Muslim women. The ECHR has placed European ideals of secularism beyond the right to freedom of religious expression on a number of dubious grounds. However, this reality is reflected by the increase in bans on the *hijab* being witnessed across Europe. As the European Muslim community grows beyond the estimated 15 million citizens present today, this issue is set to re-emerge repeatedly.

Chapter 13

Hijab and Belonging
Canadian Muslim women

Katherine Bullock

In 2005, France denied citizenship to a woman in *niqab* (face veil), arguing that her dress showed 'behaviour in society incompatible with the fundamental values of the French community, specifically regarding the equality of the sexes.'[362] And yet many contemporary Muslim women embrace the headscarf (or face veil) and find in it a connection to a meaningful fourteen-hundred-year-old religious tradition, a spiritual centredness, an answer to the hollowness of modernity, and the objectification of women in consumer capitalist culture.[363] Given the alarmingly growing number of state laws, in Europe and less so in North America, that restrict or ban the wearing of *hijab/niqab* by Muslim residents, it is necessary to ask ourselves, is this kind of dress really such a threat to modern Western secular values?

I intend to answer this question by asking Muslim women themselves. While a great deal is said about Muslim women and their relationship to covering, equality, modernity and life as Western citizens, there are few spaces that allow Muslim women themselves to speak to these issues. In the French debates that led up to a ban on headscarves in French schools, the government-commissioned report did not consult the *hijabi* schoolgirls, nor the French sociologists who studied them.[364] Overall, Muslim women are marginalised in policy and public debates, and seem to be powerless to stop these state attacks on their dress. I believe that it is important to provide sociologically-grounded data in a hope, perhaps naïve, that the presence of such data will eventually have a bearing on policy, so that policy is formed out of the real-life experiences of Muslim women, rather than on externally-generated discourse about them. I believe that questions of compatibility (Islam and the West) are actually best dealt with by those living at the boundaries of the issues, rather than by outsiders, especially xenophobic outsiders, who are motivated by fear and are unable to see the creative possibilities in merging Muslim identities with Western secular identities. My research demonstrates that Muslim women in Canada are proud to be Muslim, to wear the *hijab*, and to be Canadian. There is no conflict for them in this regard. If they can join these two great entities in their persona, why should others make an issue of it, complicate it, and try to sunder it? Why push them out of the West, since they feel themselves to be proud Westerners who are Muslim?[365]

I focus on Canadian Muslim women. I know that the socio-political context in Canada is vastly different from that of European states, so, while Canada provides a sculpting context to Canadian Muslim women's experiences, I believe that, nevertheless, their experiences offer visions and possibilities that transcend the particular place of Canada, and suggest solutions to these issues faced by Muslim women and Western states. This chapter contains interview data from four Muslim women in Canada. Their stories originally appeared in my thesis/book, and have been updated for this chapter.[366] Two are immigrants, and two were born in Canada. By accident, three of them are converts, as these are the ones who responded to email queries for follow-up interviews (which were already limited, as contact was lost with many of the initial interviewees).

Two things need to be said clearly before I proceed. First, the image of the 'veiled woman' in the West functions to erase the identities of real Muslim women. For the *hijabis*, the symbol of 'the veil' erases them as subjects, because they become reduced to the 'passive victims of oppression'; for non-*hijabis*, because their identities are left out in the representation, they are not the 'veiled victim' but they are not really Muslims either.[367] Scholars in the 'women and Islam' field have been working for at least 40 years to ensure that the real identities of Muslim women as subjects are known. It is time that popular culture is broadened to recognise this.

Second, because of the erasing nature of this widespread stereotype of 'the veiled woman', I rely on the qualitative interview method because it is the best way to sketch in the details of real Muslim women. Qualitative interview data does not claim to be a representative sample, nor to capture the experience of all Muslim women. It gives us nuance, context and humanity at a micro level. It reveals the unique identity of some Muslim women, and hence turns them into subjects. Identity construction is always a work in progress, and interview data is but a snapshot in time, but it provides a window into the lives of real women, and hence illuminates the debates that go on above and around them. The voices of the women I am about to present, Raneem, Bassima, Halima and Yasmeen, are thus theirs alone, though I would argue that they evoke the experiences and ideas held by other Muslim women.

So, in this chapter, I privilege the voices of *hijabi* women. More than that, I privilege the voices of Muslim women who have chosen to wear the *hijab* in a country that allows them such a choice. This is not because I wish to deny the experiences of non-*hijabi* women, nor to erase the tragedy that many Muslim women cover or have experienced covering through violence and coercion. One can only do so much in a single chapter. Here, I want to speak to the negative politicisation of the veil in Western public policy: the state's attempts to control, limit or banish the public expression of Muslim identity via a headscarf or veil. This is best done by consulting *hijabi* women who are convinced in their choice. I believe that the interview material I look at in this chapter provides answers to the supposed compatibility issues raised by Western states: can a *hijabi* be a good citizen of the West; does her lifestyle choice threaten 'Western values'?

I first interviewed these women in 1994 for my PhD thesis, at long sessions (sometimes 2½ hours), and in 2008 I asked them five follow-up questions via email for this chapter. I have gone back to the original transcripts and found a wealth of data not exploited fully for the thesis, so some of the material is being published here for the first time. Their names and ascriptive aspects of their identity have been changed in order to preserve anonymity.

There are many aspects to wearing the *hijab*. As I seek to address the politicisation of the veil, I present data from the interviews that address certain key assumptions behind state policies to ban veils. In the first section I introduce the women, and focus on what the *hijab* means to them; the second section explores issues of 'false consciousness' and 'submission to patriarchy', and the third discusses their perception of the relationship between being Muslim and 'Canadian values'.

I will begin by sharing these women's initial responses to the question 'why do you wear *hijab*?' (taken from the original transcript, not from the book), and then give their follow-up responses.

Raneem, a Francophone, converted to Islam in 1988 when she was 26. As a graduate student at a university in Ontario, she met Muslims who piqued her interest in learning about Islam. She liked what she was learning: 'I was really pleased to find an actual belief that fits me and suits me ... and I can see it's the truth – so that's why I became Muslim.' A few years later, she married a Muslim, had three children, and decided to leave her career as an engineer to home-school them.

When asked why she wears the *hijab*, Raneem provides an answer with at least two important dimensions – spiritual and gender-related. First she believes that the Qur'an mandates women to cover their hair. She is aware of feminist arguments that suggest covering is not in the Qur'an, but she disagrees. She believes the Qur'an has very clear verses on the topic. But she adds, and here is where the gender dimension comes in: 'even if it was just culture it's a good thing to do. It is a command of Allah in the Qur'an, but it's a command I do understand very well and fully, it's not something I do just blindly. I do understand it fully, all the implications, not all, but the basic implications and how the problems resolved, the problems it might create ...'

Raneem talks about how in her career she was often a lone woman in a male-dominated office. She was constantly fighting off unwanted sexual advances from men at work, and, before she had even heard of Islam, she had decided that the best solution was to alter her appearance, degrading her feminine side:

> I used to work with men most of the time so I used to get a lot of attention from them – unwanted attention. So I was thinking what should I do; this is a problem? What should I do? This is what I was thinking, so my solution after a long time of thinking was to first of all dress differently. I would wear more conservative clothes and I would look like a professional lady and I will have shoes like my potential husband. I will cut my hair. I will never grow it again and that will be it. – I was looking for a solution. So that's what was my solution.

When she discovered Islam and the *hijab*, she felt that she had stumbled upon a solution that was better than hers, because it allowed her to cover her femininity while at work, but still keep it in the privacy of her home – she could keep her long hair:

> I was living the problem in my everyday life so later on I came to Islam and I found the *hijab* ... before Islam I was seeing the problem and after Islam I found a better solution than the one I thought of.

In spite of having already converted, Raneem, like most Westerners, had negative stereotypes of Muslims and Arabs, so it took her about six months to feel comfortable wearing *hijab* full-time, and to transcend the fear of being associated with 'Muslims' or 'Arabs'. A move to Toronto helped crystallise her decision; as she planned to wear *hijab* in the future, why not appear at the interview as she planned to be? So she began to wear it full-time, and now, about 20 years later, nearly at the age of 50, she is still convinced in its benefits for her, as we shall see later on.

Bassima's story is somewhat similar to Raneem's. She was an under-graduate at a European university, studying Arabic, and became attracted to Islam. She converted in 1983 at age 18, and later married a Muslim, had three children, and decided to work from home as a translator, so she could be with the kids while they were little. They emigrated to Canada after experiences with racism, both from the larger European society and from Muslims with regard to her 'whiteness', in the belief that Canada would provide a better home for Muslims. Why does she wear the *hijab*?

I believe it is important for a Muslim woman to cover and it's actually become part of my identity now, and I don't think I could go out without a *hijab* on, I'd feel naked. I guess I've kind of internalised it. [*Why is it important?*] Well I think the main reason is because it's the commandment of Allah, so if Allah is telling us to do this, then we should be doing it.

Like Raneem, Bassima draws on religious as well as gender-related reasons to explain her decision to cover:

It's liberating. We grow up in the West with a pressure to follow fashion and be thin ... *Hijab* is a liberation from the tyranny of fashion. It is humanising, because it takes away the sex-appeal nonsense. You're not a sexual object, just a face. It may be disconcerting for those on the other end.

Bassima, like Raneem, transitioned over a few months into wearing the *hijab* full-time:

I did it gradually. I started off with like just tying a scarf behind my neck and calf-length dresses and things, and I didn't wear that full-time even in the early days. But I felt kind of hypocritical taking it off and putting it on if I went to the mosque or something, I felt that wasn't right, so ... that first summer that I was Muslim, I was a student, I had quite a bit of free time and I was able to spend a lot of time with Muslims and I just kinda got into it ... And I'd already had the tendency to dress modestly anyway, so it didn't take a lot of effort to convince me ... so there was something already in my heart I think.

Halima, an Anglo-Ontarian, married a Muslim man she had met at work, and converted six months later in 1991, at age 24. She had gone from Christianity to agnosticism to a kind of atheism by the time she met him, and although she had always told him she would never convert, she found by being married to him and learning about Islam that she was very attracted to the religion. They had four children and, like Raneem, she decided to home-school them.

Her decision to wear the *hijab* came out of a belief that it was a religious commandment. Like Raneem, she began wearing it sometimes, but fear of Canadian reactions held her back from wearing it all the time. She remembered how she herself used to look upon covered Muslim women, and hesitated to embrace that image for herself:

I thought it was really drastic and strange like because when I worked at Disney we would see women who came who were covered and I thought it was like so unfair, why is the women dressed that way and the men dressed basically like an American or Canadian, and ah ... I had the same reaction as many people. [*Did you remember knowing Muslims when you were younger, or was that at Disney your first time you saw women in* hijab?] I lived in (Northern Ontario) when I was younger, there's no Muslims who cover there, but ah the first time I saw them was in university but I didn't really recognise them, I didn't know who they were, there were three sisters who were always together and they were covered, they wore *jilbab* and long *hijab*s and I didn't know what they were (laughing). I guess I lived a fairly sheltered life and I didn't watch TV a lot. I knew of Muslims but I didn't know what they looked like, how they dressed.

She transitioned, like the other converts, slowly to full-time *hijab*:

I had been covering sort of part-time when I first accepted Islam in non-threatening situations, where I won't know people, like going to the grocery store or going to the park, or something, just sort of getting used to it. And when my husband's friends came over I would cover too. Then I started feeling like some sort of hypocrite because, doing it half the time, so then I just, I would do it all the time. [*Was it a difficult step?*] It was, thinking about it. But not actually doing it. It wasn't as hard as thinking about it. Like I didn't get, I was expecting a big reaction but I didn't get it, maybe they had them behind my back, but they didn't say anything to my face.

Like the other women, Halima draws on gender-related issues to talk about what the *hijab* symbolises to her:

That's a very big question. I think it does symbolise submission to Allah, I think it symbolises the woman herself, her power, because the view is here that the man is somehow forcing his wife to wear it, but if she didn't really want to wear it she probably wouldn't, I mean you could take it off at work or whatever and unless your husband was really sort of spying on you and talking to people 'what's my wife doing?' If you have that kind of husband there's bigger problems anyway, but I ... it's a rejection of the society and their values and the sexual, I mean everything in this society goes to sex, if you watch the sitcoms that's what they're based on the humour is all sexually oriented, 90% per cent of it anyway, it's a rejection of all that so I think in a way it's the woman's power to take back her own dignity and her own sexuality, it's not public.

Yasmeen had a slightly different trajectory from the converts, though her story echoes aspects of Raneem's, Bassima's and Halima's stories. She grew up in the Middle East and emigrated to Canada after her marriage in 1978 at age 20, where she had six children and stayed home to be with them, while completing by correspondence her BA with Arabic Language as her major. Although having been raised in a Muslim country, Yasmeen talks about how in her youth the *hijab* was quite rare, and in fact was actively discouraged. She remembers being in middle school, and a girl once came to school wearing a *hijab*, and the Principal took her outside, after morning assembly, and punished her, by making her stand alone against the wall while all the classes went out. She had to bring her parents in to discuss this at the school, and they did this to her every morning until she eventually took it off. It is not only Western states for whom the *hijab* symbolises something threatening that must be sanctioned and curtailed.

Yasmeen's decision to wear the *hijab*, based on the belief that it was a religious commandment, occurred as an undergraduate at university, when she was nearly 17:

Since I started to go to the university, I felt it's really compete [sic] environment every sex look to each other in a desire way, so I didn't like that and ah ... I felt the *hijab* can protect me, you know direct my way, like ah – and a felt I really need to know my background, my Islam and the Qur'an. At that time *hijab* was not ah ... very famous [*Common, you mean?*] ... yeah common, no.

Because her entire family (parents, aunts, uncles, cousins) opposed her, out of a fear that she would not be able to get married and that she was too young, she waited a year between deciding to wear it and actually wearing it, when she felt she had the strength to resist their disapproval.

Yasmeen also draws on gender issues when discussing her decision to wear the *hijab* and what it means to her:

> I feel in peace, and ah ... I feel I respect myself more, I am not concentrated about my beauty and ah ... the fashion and this stuff ah ... I think it's a peace of mind.

Hijab, then, for these women, contains a two-fold dimension: (i) a religious one, symbolising piety, a commitment to adhering to God's commandments, as they understand them; and (ii) a positive gender-related dimension, in which *hijab* becomes a healthy way of desexualising women in public space, a move for them that is liberating, as it frees women from being slaves to the fashion industry, the Western cultural beauty ideal, and from being commodified sex-objects, returning to women personhood, dignity and respect.

State policymakers ought to take into more serious account what the *hijab* means to these women. It is such an integral part of their identity as women and as Muslims that state policies to restrict or ban the *hijab* represent a devastating attack on their identity.

In popular Western culture Muslim women are usually portrayed as docile creatures who submit to strictures, including the *hijab*, laid upon them by patriarchal males. The French ruling that denied a *niqabi* woman citizenship cited her apparent total 'submission to the men in her life' as a reason for the denial.[368] This was in contrast to how the applicant herself understood her choice to wear *niqab*. 'They say I wear the *niqab* because my husband told me so. [...] I want to tell them: It is my choice. I take care of my children, and I leave the house when I please. I have my own car. I do the shopping on my own. Yes, I am a practising Muslim, I am orthodox. But is that not my right?'[369]

This woman's claim, like that of my interviewees, is often met with a sceptical reception, and the concept of 'false consciousness' is usually mobilised as the explanation. Even some feminist literature, which is supposed to rely on women's experience for developing feminist theory, has treated *hijabi* women as victims of 'false consciousness' – 'I know you've chosen this, but if you really knew what it meant, you wouldn't.'[370]

The 'false consciousness' assumption does violence to *hijabi* women's agency and intelligence. A recent trend in scholarship on Muslim women has been to recognise this, and treat Muslim women as independent human beings – as agents who make, in the same way as do men, indeed as do all human beings, decisions based on their ideology as well as social, political and economic contexts. This trend is laudable and must continue.

It needs, though, some fine tuning, as there remains at least one significant methodological problem in qualitative data on covering – in spite of emphasising women's agency, this agency is often framed by the researcher's own convictions with respect to covering: that is, that the commandment to cover *per se* is not really in the Qur'an. So what we get is this: the commandment to cover is not really in the Qur'an, but these women think it is, and we should understand their perspective.[371] What this overarching framing by the researcher does is to call into question *hijabi* women's ability to interpret the Qur'an, so ultimately to question their own intelligence. They may have some kind of agency – that is, they have freely chosen as a subjective human being to cover – but they are not smart enough to know that they are choosing something as a religious act that is not really one.

This way of framing covering has a serious and negative impact for *hijabi/ niqabi* Muslim women, because it reduces the necessity for Western states to make religious accommodation for those women convinced of the mandatory nature of covering. To say that *hijab* is not in the Qur'an is to say, as these states wish to, that *hijab* represents a backward view of women, incompatible with the modern state, and that since it is not in the Qur'an it cannot be claimed as a religious identity for modern women. It is not a necessary aspect of modernity for Muslim women, indeed, the French Urban Affairs Minister, Fadela Amara, herself a Muslim, came out blazingly in support of the ruling, as did the mass of French public opinion: The *niqab*, she said, 'is not a religious insignia but the insignia of a totalitarian political project that advocates inequality between the sexes and which is totally devoid of democracy.'[372]

If we agree that the Qur'an is a fungible text, capable of being interpreted in multiple ways, depending on the social, political and economic context of the interpreter, then it must be recognised that the interpretation that the Qur'an mandates covering is an extremely plausible reading of the key texts. I do not have space to go into this and make these arguments here, but the practice of the first community, the classical *tafseer* on the relevant verses, and the traditional jurisprudence on the topic have all agreed upon, at the minimum, a head-cover for Muslim women as obligation, and face-cover as laudable, with a minority conclusion that the face-veil is the minimum. Medieval European women, Catholic women and nuns until 1965, and many contemporary Jewish and Christian groups (Amish) all consider/ed the covering of women's hair as religiously mandated.[373] The uncovering of women's hair even in religious settings in Western states is a late 20th-century phenomenon. It is providing the backdrop for new Qur'anic interpretations about the meaning of verses said traditionally to oblige covering – either that 'modest' dress for women no longer means covering the hair, or that verses ordaining head-covering are no longer applicable.[374] Yet the existence of these modern interpretations does not negate the continued validity for some of the classical interpretations.

Given the high political stakes now over this issue of 'to wear or not to wear a *hijab* in Western societies', academic research must frame *hijabi* voices within a paradigm that accepts religiously mandated covering as a plausible and reasonable interpretation of the Qur'anic texts. This will undo the violence done, not to a *hijabi*'s agency so much, as to a woman's intelligence and ability to read the text for herself. And reduce, I hope, some of the hostility to it in Western political circles.

All four of my interviewees have engaged intellectually with alternate perspectives on covering, and have chosen to follow the one that most accorded with their own understanding of the Qur'an and the *Sunnah.* Since they all told me they covered because it was in the Qur'an, I pressed each of them on this issue. Bassima's response is typical:

> [*Some people think the Qur'an doesn't command women to cover. Where is it the commandment of Allah?*] Oh gosh, chapter and verse, you've got me! There is the verse about um, I think, pulling the headcover over the bosom or something so that you're covered and that you be known as a religious or righteous woman and not be molested. There are also, I mean you have to look at the Qur'an and the *hadith* together and there are several *ahadith* that say when a woman reaches puberty you should see nothing but the face and hands ... well that's just the way that I've understood it from my earliest introduction to Islam. I'm aware that there are people who don't see it that way and I guess everything is open to interpretation, but ... um ... that's just the way that I've understood it. [1994]

Halima also talks of the importance of understanding the Qur'an via the practice of the first community, as contained in the *hadith*:

> There are some people who read the Qur'an, and they do not believe that it orders women to cover. They think it's a traditional or cultural explanation. [*What do they believe that it tells them?*] That it just tells women to dress modestly and that the way it is now is like a traditional

explanation which isn't necessarily contained in the verses themselves. This is why we need the *Sunnah*, that's how we explain the Qur'an, according that Prophet and his Companions' explanations, because we can make our interpretations, but with the *Sunnah* ... I mean people can still take their own interpretations, that's why you need the Companions, so that it's not left up to each individual. [*How do you know that you're not receiving just an interpretation which tells you to cover?*] The *hadiths* ... the debate among the scholars is whether or not you can cover the face, not whether or not you have to cover your hair, it's understood that you have to, I mean there's the famous *hadith* Asma, Aisha's younger sister, the Prophet said to her that the believing woman does not show anything but her face and hands. [*That's a good enough explanation for you?*] Well I mean, that's not the only one, but the only one off the top of my head, and that's not even the best one, there are more authentic *hadiths*, but I don't know them off the top of my head. [1994]

Yasmeen's narrative offers a particularly compelling confirmation of women's agency, even when it comes to religious matters. I asked my interviewees (1994) to define 'a Muslim'. Yasmeen said: 'to follow what Gods wants from us, what's it called submission. [*How do you know what God wants from you?*] From the Qur'an and the Prophet's sayings, *hadith*. I don't take the opinion of scholars, of sheikhs, unless it comes from the Qur'an and *Sunnah*.'

This last aspect is crucial, because it shows that Yasmeen weighs the opinions of scholars against her own independently arrived-at understandings. I am not saying that she is acting as a scholar, because I am sure she would dislike that imputation, considering herself lacking the proper Islamic scholarly credentials, but what she does is check scholarly opinions against the Qur'an and *hadith* collections that she reads herself in Arabic, and chooses to follow the scholars' opinions that are most reasonably supported by the indications of the Qur'an and *Sunnah*. She will then filter another scholar's interpretations through that of one she feels to be a trustworthy scholar. If a scholar does not back up his argument with specific verses from the Qur'an or *Sunnah*, Yasmeen will not take that scholar's opinion.

Yasmeen feels that 'the calamity of Islam these days, they take the interpretation about Islam from the mouths of people, not from the source, it doesn't explain Islam, and even the act of Muslims it doesn't explain Islam, because unfortunately in many ways, they act very bad, they act against Islam, and they say this is Islam.' And so we spent quite some time discussing different interpretations of women's status in Islam. Yasmeen is convinced the Qur'an treats men and women equally, so when I asked her about certain restrictive interpretations of the Qur'an that seek to keep women indoors, she said she always says 'give me your evidence from the Qur'an and from *Sunnah*'. She asked me if I, as a new Muslim, was affected by 'bad ideas' from books, and I told her that sometimes I was, and it made me question having converted. Her reply, still on this theme of agency again, is instructive:

> I have the same feeling like if I read the bad book, sometimes I feel I want to throw it in the garbage, but *Al hamdulillah* I never thought about I should be a Muslim, because I feel I am really lucky and fortunate to be a Muslim, when I see the corruption here, like how they treat women, you know even the cartoon for the children, they put a woman in bikini, and just to attract people or ah if someone think a cartoon Bugs Bunny or Woody Woodpecker if he think just to enjoy himself, they put woman in bikini, ah see they are advertising, how they put women you know, how they treat women so *Al hamdulillah*, Islam is really what God want for the human being is wonderful, *Al hamdulillah*, but sometimes I feel all this is just in my mind, like especially when I read book and I find ah bad garbage, I feel I want to throw it ...

Is the veil men's way of controlling women's movements? All interviewees disagreed, sometimes with impatience. Yasmeen and Halima both pointed out that the commandments to cover come 'not from men, it's from Allah' [Halima].

Since I first conducted my interviews in 1994 a growing number of Muslim women have become convinced, by the new readings referred to above, that the Qur'an does not in fact mandate covering. Many of them are taking off their scarves, some after as long as ten years, having previously been convinced of its obligation. I asked my interviewees in 2008 about this phenomenon, and if anything had changed for them as far as the 'why they wear the *hijab*' question was concerned since the first interview. Again, their answers are very instructive, because they demonstrate how much thought goes into their continued wearing of the *hijab*. They continue to consider the interpretations of Qur'anic verses by various scholars, and choose the ones that seem most true, reasonable or compelling to them.

Raneem:

> The *hijab* had never been imposed on me. I was looking for a solution before I accepted Islam to really too much male attention and bold

sexual invitations. Whether the Qur'an mandates it or not, (which I believe it does) it is a really good idea to dress modestly and intelligently. I did eventually figure out on my own, when I was young (no one told me), that wearing dress suits seemed smarter than sexy clothes when what you want is respect and intelligence.

Wearing the *hijab* has never been a negative experience for me, it has all been extremely positive. I just don't understand why other Muslim women would want to unveil themselves.

Bassima:

I wear the *hijab* because I am a Muslim, for all the reasons of modesty and identity that are so often mentioned, and because I do it for God, pure and simple (*in sha Allah*). I don't think much has changed since our first interview, except that I wear *jilbab* less these days, for several reasons ... I am really rather distressed by the 'unveiling' and the notions that *hijab*/covering the head is not obligatory. This is partly because it makes it that much harder for those of us who are still persevering, because a lot of these women seem to be in positions where they are representing Islam in the wider culture. If I am utterly honest, I would say that I resent them saying such things in such positions, because it then makes those of us who believe it to be obligatory look like fanatics to outsiders. And it is also worrying because they are on theologically shaky ground. It is one thing to struggle with a concept and say it's hard to do or you're not ready for it yet, but when you deny that something is obligatory that Islam says is obligatory, that is a serious matter which carries major implications in terms of faith and belief.

And if I hear 'when in Rome' or comments about the *hijab* being outmoded and irrelevant in the modern world one more time, I may just snap and write something very outspoken myself!

Halima:

I actually do not know anyone who has completely unveiled – I know several women who took off the *niqab* but still cover their hair. If people are taking off their *hijabs* I think that's sad. I ask Allah to guide them. I believe the Qur'an does order women to cover – it is still applicable in the modern world – Islam is for all times – it could be argued that it is even more important now because of the lack of respect given to women and the sexual exploitation of women.

Yasmeen:

[*Why do you still wear the hijab?*] Because it is me! I am a Muslimah, I'll try my best to please Allah. I can see it clearly it purify the society if everyone applies it. I have to start by my own self. There always trials, but with the help of Allah I am still what I was and will be *insha'a Allah*. They [women who unveil] are free to think what they want. The guidance only from Allah. I believe they are wrong, but there is no force in religion. They are free and they have to answer their Creator later. I treat them nicely and with a good manners.

As students of social science seeking to understand humanity, we want theories that best explain what our research finds. Interpreting these women's answers can stumble if a secular paradigm that 'Muhammad wrote the Qur'an himself' is applied to these questions. I am well aware of the scepticism that will have greeted the idea that covering is 'not from men, but from God'. It surely looks like these women have fallen victim to male strictures. But if we move the paradigm into a spiritual realm, secular researches can none the less understand that spiritual encounters are real to those who experience them. So even if the interaction between their intelligence and their spiritual experience cannot be completely fathomed, it is hard to apply a 'victim' or 'false consciousness' paradigm to such thoughtful and self-reflective women.

In addition to demonstrating contemplation and agency, my interviews also reveal that social and political context influences the way Muslim women make their decisions with respect to how they choose to cover. Raneem points out that she wears basically Western dress (skirt and top), with only the addition of a headscarf, which she tries to match. In our original interview (1994) she told me that in her experience she gets more negative reactions dressed in non-Western clothing, like a *jilbab*, so she has made a point of wearing Western dress, with the addition of a headscarf. The irony of this decision is that she has faced the issue ever since of people not knowing that she is a Muslim, in spite of the headscarf:

I happen to be white, French, and I dress well, with my scarf. I wear Canadian clothes that follow the Islamic dress code with the addition of my matching colour scarf. Even the week after 9/11 in my class, one of my classmates, in graduate school, was thinking that I was wearing my scarf, the only reason being because of fashion. I told him that I was

Muslim. It was not the first time that people told me that they thought I was wearing a scarf for fashion purposes. [2008]

In the follow-up interview, Bassima noted that she has also switched from *jilbab* to Western dress, for several reasons, ranging from practical ('I tend to stumble more easily over the long hems these days') to socio-political ('I get personal and invasive comments and questions when I wear it') to religious ('most of the available *jilbab* styles these days do not cover properly as *hijab* is meant to do') to feminine:

> ... and [are] more flattering (because I am only human). I often wear long tops over loose pants too, especially when out and about with the kids. I try to wear the same or similar colours of clothes so that the monochromatic effect of the *jilbab* is still there (and the monochrome look is supposed to be more flattering too. Vanity of vanities ...). My long tops always come to or below the knee, though, unlike many.

Halima, who opted early on to wear *jilbab*, finds herself feeling awkward in her own country. In the initial interview (1994), she talked about how the expectation of negative reactions would deter her from going out. She connected her ability to withstand negative comments to the strength of her faith:

> Like your *iman* [faith] goes up and down, sometimes when you feel strong you feel good about it [*hijab*], feel proud of yourself and proud of Islam, and other times, I'm feeling weak, I guess I feel like it's a ... I don't want to go outside because I don't feel like putting on my *hijab*, I don't feel like getting dressed up, so I'll just stay home. [laughs] So it varies I guess, like there's a lot of things to it, like when you are wearing [*hijab*] you're not going do things that maybe you would otherwise. In my earlier days I was very tempted to go to McDonalds [laughs] because I loved McDonalds food, but I just would never go in *hijab*, even though some people buy ice-cream, or french fries and stuff, I just can't go in McDonalds, I just feel like everybody's going to see me, so I don't. But ah, stuff like that I guess. [laughs]

Yasmeen, after having successfully married in spite of her *hijab*, decided that she wanted to wear the face-veil. As they were about to emigrate to Canada, her husband told her to wait until then, and to decide later, but she insisted on wearing it before they emigrated. Her husband acquiesced, so she arrived in Canada wearing a *niqab*. She found the negative reactions from people off-putting (staring, being yelled at by passers-by), and became worried that she was giving 'a bad impression about Islam' to Canadian society, as she understood that they thought that 'the people who cover are a people from backward or they are not civilised and or terrorists, or they are not sure if this is man or woman'. Her husband also felt embarrassed to go out with her, so after six months she took off the face-veil (while continuing to wear *hijab*).

So my interview data shows that the social and political anti-Muslim context affects their sense of self and how they choose to instantiate the *hijab*. It also shows the women's flexibility in implementing their under-standing of religious requirements.

The question of freedom of conscience arises here when Western states are considering banning *hijab/niqab*. Because Yasmeen had never considered the face-veil to be religiously mandated she was able to take it off in the face of racism. But there is a minority of women who are convinced that not only the *hijab*, but also the *niqab* is religiously mandated by the Qur'an. What would have befallen Yasmeen if she felt she was religiously obligated to wear the *niqab* in Canadian society? It seems better for a state to educate the public about the meanings of the Muslim covering from women's own point of view, to reduce the negative reactions to them, rather than to feed the xenophobic flames of anti-Muslim prejudice.

I turn finally to consider my interviewees' reflections on 'being *hijabi*' and 'being Canadian'.

Just after I began my research in 1994, a young girl was sent home from school in Québec because she refused to remove her *hijab*.[375] This was the opening volley in what has become a growing number of state attacks against Muslim women's dress rights across Europe, and less so in North America. The assumptions mobilised in support of such bans are that the veil is a symbol of inequality between men and women and is incompatible with modern secular nation states, which prioritise women's equality. Leaving aside the remarkable assumption that most Western women, excepting Muslim women in headscarves or veils, have achieved equality, let's consider what my interviewees' opinions are with respect to the relationship between the *hijab* and equality, and the *hijab* and 'belonging'.

All four women expressed a strong commitment to the notion of women's equality in Islam. For them, men and women are equal in the eyes of God. But they believe that men and women are physiologically and psychologically different (but not that men are more rational), and that the differential rules with respect to dress stem from such differences.

Raneem's opinion is illustrative:

Well there are – men and women are brothers and sisters to each other
... I do have a very caring relationship with my husband and like it says
in the Qur'an we're like clothes to each other. That's the way it is in my
family and my relationship. So we have a very, very close relationship,
like my husband is my best friend. They [men and women] are equal in
the eyes of Allah, but they are different, like the equality doesn't mean
the same. We are equal in the eyes of Allah, but are different, we have
roles we are complementary to each other ... Men are stronger, they are
bigger, they are stronger ah ... biologically we are the ones that carry
babies, we are the ones that nurse them, so like when the time – having
children biologically is very, very important. [*Are men more intelligent then
or more rational less emotional?*] No, I think it depends on the people,
on different people, like some men are very emotional, some women
are very rational. I don't take that for granted like women are more
emotional than men are less or more rational. Like I think men tend to
hide their emotions, it doesn't mean they don't have any. I think they are
as intelligent as the other one, like men are as intelligent as women and
women are as intelligent as men ... I don't think that at all.

This idea of 'equal but different' comes under a lot of attack from liberal
and Muslim feminists,[376] but it does have echoes in other feminisms,
such as radical French feminism (ironically). The point is, whatever one
thinks about the 'equal but different' argument, it is important to note
that these women believe in and feel themselves to be equal to men. They
are committed to women's equality, which problematises their exclusion
from modern Western secular societies for their dress which is allegedly
a symbol of inequality. Once the state is in the business of defining what
kind of 'equality' its citizens should believe in, we have moved away from
secular liberalism and into a kind of authoritarianism that dictates what
beliefs citizens should hold. Will Orthodox Jewish women who also believe
that women should cover their heads be denied French citizenship? Or
Orthodox Jewish men because part of their morning prayer is 'Blessed
are you, Lord, our God, ruler the universe who has not created me a
woman ...'[377] What of Catholics who will not allow women to become
priests?

Just after the incident in Québec mentioned above, the CBC did a
documentary on the *hijab*, and asked the question: can the *hijab* pass the
test of being Canadian?[378] We discussed this in the initial interviews, and all

my interviewees expressed a strong commitment to Canada, as well as to their interpretation of their faith.

Halima's answer captures the themes nicely:

> Yes I think so [*hijab* passes the litmus test] because I mean if Canada boasts you can practise your religion, freedom of thought and beliefs, if a woman believes she should wear her *hijab* why shouldn't she, 'she's not hurting anybody' [laugh'] I mean if people can go down Yonge street almost naked, why should her putting a scarf on her head bother people, even for that matter wearing a veil on her face, why should that upset somebody?

In the follow-up interview, I pursued these questions, asking the women if they still feel they belong to Canada, and what Canada means for them. Raneem:

> I have always lived here. I go everywhere without problems. I work here. With my education and my work, I have more economic and social advantages than most people. I am as Canadian as anyone else. I sometimes have to explain details about Islam to my employers but it is done respectfully … Canada is the land where I live and the people I live with.

Bassima:

> Yes. I chose Canada and Canada welcomed me and my family. This is my home now … Canada is all the usual things like snow, hockey, maple leaf, beaver, mountains, prairies, arctic tundra, wolves, polar bears … and it is all the precious intangibles like freedom, respect, decency, kindness, the Charter of Rights and Freedoms, official bilingualism, multiculturalism with all its pros and cons. It's not Britain and it is definitely not America – which is a good thing when I look at what Britain and America have become, especially since the dawn of the 21st century. It's not perfect – we need to do more about the environment, and the First Nations have suffered so many wrongs that need to be righted. But I wouldn't want to live in any other country on earth.

Halima's answer was slightly more equivocal, perhaps not surprisingly given her sense of awkwardness going out of the house in her *hijab*. But this is not because she doesn't believe ultimately that she can live here and be Canadian; her answer expresses more the sense of alienation and being 'pushed out':

> [*Do you feel like you belong to Canada?*] Yes and no. I am Canadian. I have no other nationality, but I feel very different from the average Canadian – I feel my beliefs separate me from the mainstream. [*What is 'Canada' for you?*] Canada is my birth place, I grew up here – I had a good childhood with many blessings. I feel I was blessed to grow up here in a safe, healthy environment – but that seems to be slowly dwindling for our own children – the level of violence in public schools is frightening, our healthcare system is crumbling, etc.

Yasmeen's answer was different, as she expressed through it her religious understanding of human beings and their ultimate relationship to God:

> [*Do you feel like you belong to Canada?*] I don't understand the question! I am belong to Allah. When I die I'll return to him and leave the land behind. All Canadian will leave the Canadian land behind, because it is belong to Allah. The earth belong to Allah. But if you mean that I am Canadian citizen. Yes, I feel that strongly. [*What is 'Canada' for you?*] Canada is home to me and my family, I have all the rights like the other Canadian. I am really content that Allah made me live in Canada.

In the 21st century, Muslims face rising anti-Muslim prejudice which is weaving its way into Western public policy, and yet it is consistently the case that committed Muslims profess commitment to their secular Western state. As I said in my thesis/book, it is not the Muslims who have a problem with 'being Canadian and being Muslim' – it is the non-Muslims that wish to push them to conform or to push them out.[379]

Conclusion

After Raneem converted to Islam, her brother did not speak to her for six months; Bassima left her country of birth to avoid being called a 'f ... ing race traitor'; Halima feels out of sync with a Canada that cannot seem to understand her choice; and Yasmeen fought her family for over a year to wear the *hijab*. Why would these women continue to wear the *hijab* in the face of such negative surroundings, if they were not convinced of it, and did not experience benefits from it?

I have shown that for these women the *hijab* is a symbol of piety, with feminist overtones of giving back to women control over the sexualis-ation of their bodies. I looked at questions of choice to show that they intelligently interact with their religious text and its interpretation, and choose to follow that which is most persuasive to them. And I showed their strong attachments to Canada and to Canadian values such as equality and freedom.

An ill wind is blowing through the globe that seeks to alter Muslims' lifestyle choices. Secular liberal Western states are betraying their founda-tional principles by selectively denying membership in their communities to Muslims. While scholars are investigating the country-specific reasons for such legislation (that is, that particular country's historical state–church relationship, multiculturalism and pluralism discourse, experience of immigration, and so on),[380] in general terms it can be said that Muslims are being singled out and forced to conform. Excuses such as 'the veil is a symbol of women's inequality' cannot hide the targeted nature of these kinds of public policies.

The Muslim women's veil has come under attack not so much because of its existence as a piece of cloth, but for the lifestyle it is supposed to stand for – one in which women are subordinated to men. Since the 19th-century colonial campaigns to unveil Muslim women, this has always been the Western symbol of the veil, as a metonym for the backwardness of the Muslim world.[381] Without reducing the reality that some women the world over, Muslim or not, are oppressed by men and by customs, this is not the appropriate paradigm in which to explore veiling in modern secular states. In 2006, Amnesty International reported that '[every] four days a woman dies of domestic violence in France'.[382] Are these women's male partners to be denied citizenship for not exhibiting the 'French' value of equality of the sexes?

My interview data demonstrate that Muslim women can be intelligent, religiously committed, convinced of the equality of men and women, and committed to their Canadian country. They actually appreciate the Canadian values such as religious freedom, as they are prime beneficiaries of it. It is not they who are a threat to such values – they have a vested interest in maintaining them. It is those who are trying to protect their societies from women such as Raneem, Bassima, Halima and Yasmeen, who are more of a threat to cherished Western secular liberal values.

Notes

[1] 'It will not be welcome on French soil,' he said. 'We cannot accept, in our country, women imprisoned behind a mesh, cut off from society, deprived of all identity. That is not the French republic's idea of women's dignity.' news.bbc.co.uk/1/hi/world/europe/8113778.stm

[2] Romain 1988, p. 130.

[3] See Braybrooke 1992, and Swider 1999.

[4] Gombrich 1987.

[5] *Ibid.*

[6] El Guindi 1999, p. 10.

[7] Bullock 2002, p. xvi.

[8] El Guindi, *op. cit.*, p. 153

[9] Bullock, *op. cit.*, p. xvii.

[10] The regulation that two people of opposite sex who are not *mahram* (cannot be married to each other) should not be alone in a secluded space.

[11] *Hadith* from at Tabari and al Muslim quoted in J. Badawi (2006), *The Muslim Woman's and Muslim Man's Dress according to the Qur'an and Sunnah*. London, Ta-HA Publishers; p. 12.

[12] A tradition from Wasa'il. See Mutahhari 1992, p. 61.

[13] Quoted in Bullock, *op. cit.*, p. 96.

[14] El Guindi, *op. cit.*, p. 11.

[15] *Ibid.*, p. 17.

[16] *Ibid.*, p. 15.

[17] Quoted in Bullock, *op. cit.*, p. 108.

[18] Malti-Douglas 2001, p. 38.

[19] *Ibid.*, p. 12.

[20] Mernissi 1997, p. 94.

[21] Ahmed 1992, p. 154.

[22] From the *Wasai'sl al shi'ah*, quoted in Mutahhari, *op. cit.*, p. 23.

[23] *Ibid.*

[24] Said 1978.

[25] Ricoeur 1974, pp. 182–3.

[26] S. Cavell (2003), *Disowning Knowledge in Seven Plays of Shakespeare*. Cambridge: Cambridge University Press; pp. 9–10, 143–4.

[27] The Greater London Authority commissioned Insted's (2007) survey of treatment of Muslims in the media: the team of Insted researchers who analysed English newspapers in a typical week, 8–14 May 2006, found 97 per cent of tabloid coverage and 89 per cent of broadsheet coverage to be negative towards Islam. The Islamic Republic News Agency (2008) reports the distress caused by Islamophobia.

[28] Contractor, S. and Scott-Baumann, A., *Women under pressure*. In preparation.

[29] www.minab.org.uk

[30] See, for more detail, Scott-Baumann, A. (2009), *Ricoeur and the hermeneutics of suspicion*. London: Continuum; pp. 22–39.

[31] *Ibid.*, p. 70. Ricoeur discusses this in terms of Mannheim's analysis of Marx.

[32] Security concerns can take strange forms: I was denied an invitation to the Siddiqui Report launch because I was considered to be a security risk, even though I was on the advisory committee for the Siddiqui Report.

[33] Contractor and Scott-Baumann, *op. cit.*

[34] This will be Ricoeur's linguistic turn, and it happens at a time when Saussure's linguistics and then Lévi-Strauss's development of Saussure's work into anthropology are offering French academics an opportunity to break free of classical traditions. Saussure saw both signifier and signified as purely psychological forms, not substance.

[35] Ricouer 1992, p. 387.

[36] Bunting, M. (2008), 'Secularists have nothing to fear from women wearing headscarves', *Guardian*, 25.02.2008.

[37] Contractor and Scott-Baumann, *op. cit.*

[38] Modood, T. (1994) 'Establishment, multiculturalism and British citizenship', *Political Quarterly*, 65.1, 71.

[39] Contractor and Scott-Baumann, *op. cit.*

[40] Ricoeur 1987, p. 255.

[41] Halstead 1986, p. 18.

[42] Contractor 2010.

[43] HPA (2008), 'All new episodes seen at GUM clinics: 1998–2007'. UK and country-specific tables. Health Protection Agency, July 2008. Available online at www.avert.org/stdstatisticuk.htm

[44] Halstead 1986, pp. 7, 25.

[45] Scott-Baumann, *op. cit.*, p. 184.

[46] Ruthven 2000, p. 328. The next sentence of this quote reads: 'The strength of his system is that particular aspects (such as his insistence on traditional *purdah* for women) can be discarded without damage to the structure as a whole.' Whilst I can agree with this sentiment, it is unfortunate that this particular aspect is not so readily discarded by Sunni activists.

[47] Whilst Mawdudi was in prison, the members of *Jamaat* had to decide whether to support the candidacy of a woman, Fatimah Jinnah, to be President of Pakistan. The idea of a woman participating in politics went against Mawdudi's teachings, but as he had been put in prison by Ayub Khan, the candidate opposing Jinnah, he saw the support of a woman in this case to be the lesser of two evils.

[48] For more on the life and thought of Mawdudi, see Jackson 2009.

[49] For example: 24:31; 33:58, 59; 33:32, 33; and 33:53.

[50] Mawdudi 1947, pp. 1–8.

[51] *Ibid.* pp. 29–30.

[52] Mawdudi 1971, p. 16.

[53] Mawdudi 1986, p. 83.

[54] *Ibid.*, p. 91.

[55] The term Mawdudi uses is 'theo-democracy', but in reality the democratic element would be non-existent.

[56] Mawdudi 1986, p. 12.

[57] *Ibid.*

[58] *Ibid.*, p. 14.

[59] *Ibid.*

[60] *Ibid.*, p. 59.

[61] *Ibid.*, p. 60.

[62] *Ibid.*, p. 61.

[63] *Ibid.*, p. 62.

[64] *Ibid.*, p. 63.

[65] *Ibid.*, p. 111.

[66] *Ibid.*, p. 112.

[67] *Ibid.*, p. 113.

[68] *Ibid.*, p. 115.

[69] *Ibid.*

[70] All quotes in this paragraph, *ibid.*, p. 116.

[71] *Ibid.*, p. 118.

[72] *Ibid.*, p.1 19.

[73] All quotes in this paragraph, *ibid.*, p. 119.

[74] *Ibid.*

[75] *Ibid.*, p. 120.

[76] *Ibid.*, p. 121.

[77] *Ibid.*, pp. 121–2.

[78] *Ibid.*, p. 122.

[79] *Ibid.*, p. 202.

[80] Mawdudi 1980, p. 262.

[81] Fatima Mernissi's excellent study traces the unreliability of this particular *hadith* as, basically, a product of convenience on the part of Abu-Bakr. Mernissi 1991, pp. 49–61.

[82] Mawdudi 1980, p. 322.

[83] *Ibid.*

[84] *Ibid.*, p. 323.

[85] Sayyid-Vali Reza Nasr (1992), *Islamization of Knowledge*, Islamabad: International Institute of Islamic Thought; pp. 10–11.

[86] Rahman 1982, p. 20.

[87] Wadud-Muhsin, Amina (1992), 'Understanding the Implicit Qur'anic Parameters to the Role of Women in the Modern Context', *The Islamic Quarterly*, 34.2, 128.

[88] For all Imami Shi'is, among whom are the Isma'ilis, the imam is the spiritual and political leader of the community and a direct descendant of the Prophet Muhammad. While the majority Twelver Shi'is follow a line of twelve imams as legitimate successors of the Prophet (for most, 'Ali being the first and Muhammad al-Muntazar, who went into occultation in 874 CE, the last), Nizari Isma'ilis hold that the genealogical line of imams continues to the present day with the imam Karim Aga Khan IV, whom they believe to be the 49th imam. The political authority of the imam ceased for Twelver Shi'is with the occultation of

the twelfth imam, while, for Nizari Isma'ilis, it stopped with the demise of the last imam-caliph of the Fatimid dynasty (909–1173 CE).

[89] On the issue of seclusion, see Wadud 1999, p. 98; for women in seclusion (*dhat al-khudúr*), see for instance the *hadith* collection by Abuú Da'ud, al-Sijistani, *Sunan abuDa'ud*, ed. al-Da 'as, ÿumß: Nashr wa tawzi' Muhammad 'Ali al-Sayyid, vol 1, 1969, pp. 675–6.

[90] Referring to a 1953 message in Sultan Muhammad Shah (1977), *Message to the world of Islam*, 4th edn. Karachi: Isma'ilia Association for Pakistan; pp. 58–9.

[91] *Ibid.*, pp. 60–1.

[92] *Ibid.*, p. 61.

[93] Fifty years on, the issue of women's attendance at Friday prayer in mosques is far from being resolved. To this day there are mosques in Britain which do not allow women to enter to pray. The elimination of this practice is implied in the 2007 Draft Constitution by the MINAB (Mosques and Imams National Advisory Board), art. 2, objective c: 'advice on improved access and involvement of women and youth to mosques', in MINAB (2007), *Draft Constitution, Draft Standards*; for the final revised Draft Consitution of 11 October 2007, see online at www.mcb.org.uk/uploads/MINABConstitution.pdf

[94] Aziz 1998, p. 210.

[95] *Ibid.*, p. 211.

[96] *Ibid.*, p. 602.

[97] *Ibid.*, pp. 646, 668.

[98] For the website of the Aligarh Muslim University see online at www.amu. ac.in. The vision of its founder, Sayyid Ahmad Khan (d. 1898), who 'reached the conclusion that education was the main cause of the backwardness of the community', comprising his embrace of modernist ideas and his ideal of balancing Western knowledge with 'oriental learning', is advertised in several pages of the university's website, particularly under his biography and on the admission pages.

[99] *Kalam-e imam-e mubin, Holy firmans*, quoted in Kjellberg 1967, p. 37.

[100] *Rahebari-e-Imam Sultan Muhammad Shah* (1960), vol. 2, 2nd edn. Bombay: Isma'ilia Association for India; p. 40.

[101] *Ibid.*, p. 19.

[102] *Firman* or *farman* generally means a 'command' or an 'edict' and, during the Ottoman empire, the term was used to indicate the edict of the sultan or, in Mughal India, the royal orders issued by the padshah. For Isma'ilis it is a written directive by the imam, usually read in the local places of worship (*jama'at khana*).

[103] Sherali Alidina Kassim Ali (1961), *Firman Mubarak (Precious Pearls)*. Karachi: Isma'iliyya Association of Pakistan; quoted in Boivin, Michel (2003), *La rénovation du Shî'isme Ismaélien en Inde et au Pakistan*. London and New York: Routledge; p. 280.

[104] Like *firman*, *ta'liqa* is a term from the Mughal period, and has the meaning of executive order, originally indicating an abridgment of an order or of a memorandum of orders, and can be used to indicate a marginal note.

[105] Boivin, *op. cit.*, p. 281.

[106] Shah, *op. cit.*, pp. 50–1.

[107] Quoted in Lambert-Hurley 2007, p. 100. In fact Sultan Jahan Begam aimed to

maintain the *pardah* system and, if women were to have activities beyond the domestic realm, they could do so only by full observance of the veil, including the covering of the face. As noted by a number of scholars, to wear the veil as a symbolic shelter allowed women to enter domains such as the Zenana madrasa which, in turn, led to the necessity for female teachers and hence to job opportunities for educated women.

[108] See *ibid.*, p. 10; for the Aga Khan's endorsement of petitions in favour of women's suffrage – and Sultan Jahan Begum's negative response to them – see *ibid.*, pp. 168–70.

[109] See, for instance, the educational and women's rights work by Rokeya Sakhawat Husain (d. 1932), the author of the well-known work of fiction *Sultana's dream* (1905).

[110] Mawdudi 1986, p. 252.

[111] Mawdudi classified Muslims according to their positions *vis-à-vis* modernity. In his view the Aga Khan would probably have been an example of those he called 'Oriental Occidentals', those who adopted Western values and for whom a woman's education results in her being able to earn a living and contributing to the family's budget; see *ibid.*, pp. 100–1.

[112] *Ibid.*, p. 252; for his response to the Muslim modernist historical argument of veiling as a pre-Islamic custom, which was adopted by Muslims long after the prophet's time, see *ibid.*, pp. 254-5.

[113] *Ibid.*

[114] *Mubarak Taalika and messages*, in Kjellberg 1967, p. 69.

[115] Shah, *op. cit.*, p. 273; this *firman* was pronounced during the Aga Khan's second visit to Zanzibar, on 17 August 1905.

[116] For marriage reforms and legislation in East Africa, see Asani, Ali S. (1994) 'The impact of modernization on the marriage rites of the Khojah Isma'ilis of East Africa', *Journal of Turkish Studies*, 18, 23–4.

[117] See Adatia, A. K. and King, N. Q. (1969), 'Some East African *firmans* of H. H. Aga Khan III', *Journal of Religion in Africa*, 2.3, particularly 179–80.

[118] With reference to the adoption of European dress fashion and to learning English or French, see *ibid.*, particularly p. 190.

[119] *The Constitution, Rules and Regulations of His Highness the Agakhan Isma'ilia Councils of Africa*, Mombasa: His Highness the Agakhan Isma'ilia Supreme Council for Africa, 1946, p. 61, ruling 16.(a).

[120] 'European Dress', *East African Standard*, 2 August 1952, and 'European Dress for Isma'ili women', *Goan Voice*, 8 August 1952, both quoted in Walji, Shirin Remtulla (1974), *A history of the Isma'ili community in Tanzania*. Ph.D thesis, University of Winsconsin, p. 218. Walji explains that to don simple Western dress for the Isma'ilis of East Africa would facilitate blending with the indigenous population and dilute the 'image of an economic gap between richer Indian and poorer African', *ibid.*, p. 219.

[121] Nanji, A. (1974), 'Modernization and change in the Nizari Isma'ili community in East Africa: a Perspective', *Journal of Religion in Africa*, 6.2, 134.

[122] Kjellberg, *op. cit.*, p. 31. For some visual evidence of the changing attire of Isma'ili women over time, compare some pictures of Count Fatehali Dhalla's photographic collection of the Noorani family taken in Mombasa, Kenya, in

1940 and in 1945, online at www.Isma'ili.net/gallery/dhalla_album/1930-1950/
index.html as well as some group pictures of Aga Khan III jubilees online at
www.Isma'ili.net/sultan/jubileeph.html. For contemporary images of Isma'ili
communities during the visits of Aga Khan IV, see online at www.Isma'ili.net/
gal.html

123 Kjellberg, *op. cit.*, p. 64.

124 De Souza 2004, p. xv.

125 See for example the data on Karachi in 1959 (45 per cent) and the 1955 data for
Isma'ilis (92 per cent) in Papanek 1962, p. 28.

126 See Nanji, A. (1974), 'Modernization and change in the Nizari Isma'ili
community in East Africa: a Perspective', *Journal of Religion in Africa*, 6.2, 129–30.

127 For a pragmatic view of the economic and financial bases of the Aga Khan's
reform policies in Tanzania, see Amiji, M. (1982), 'Islam and socio-economic
development: a case study of a Muslim minority in Tanzania', *Journal of Institute
of Muslim Minority Affairs*, 4.1–2, 175–87.

128 For Ataturk's 1925 'Hat Reform' and his argument set within the context of
forging a national Turkish identity as opposed to the former Ottoman identity,
see Göle 1996, especially pp. 60–2.

129 Aga Khan 1954, pp. 187–8.

130 In a 1965 interview, the present imam Karim Aga Khan IV referred to his grandfather's directive for Isma'ili women not to wear the veil as a change of tradition
rather than a change in the faith or religion. Available online at www.Isma'ili.
net/intervue/651212.html

131 Bullock, *op. cit.*, p. 46.

132 See, for example, the various opinions expressed online (under Current Issues:
dresses) at www.Isma'ili.net/html/modules.php?op=modload&name=phpBB2&
file=viewtopic and note the reference to Aga Khan III's *firman* on dress for the
community in East Africa (but not specifically for that of Pakistan).

133 See in this regard the various rulings and the Bohora practice in Ghadially, R.
(1996), 'The campaign for women's emancipation in an Isma'ili Shia (Daudi
Bohra) sect of Indian Muslims: 1929–1945', *Women Living Under Muslim Laws,
Dossier 14-15 September 1996*, especially pp. 8-11; available online at www.wluml.
org/english/pubsfulltxt.shtml?cmd%5B87%5D=i-87-2634

134 Blank 2001, pp. 184–8.

135 *Ibid.*, pp. 184-6.

136 An expression of this priority is expressed by Noha, a Canadian Isma'ili interviewed by Katherine Bullock; among a group of Muslim interviewees, she was
the only one to define herself as Canadian first, then Isma'ili, then Muslim: see
Bullock, *op. cit.*, p. 81.

137 The issues of identities and of representation through the veil are directly voiced
by Salima Bhimani, an Isma'ili South Asian Muslim (as well as Canadian) woman
who states in her book 'the image of a Muslim woman wearing the *hijab* ... does
not represent me ... This is not an issue of rights or choices. It is an issue of one
image being used to represent all Muslim women, and that is highly problematic
... [The *hijab*] cannot be the sole representation of Islam and of women as
followers of faith. This representation dismisses the many identities of Muslim
women.' Bhimani 2003, p. 102.

138 Cf. Qur'an, *Surah al-Mutaffifin* (The Fraudsters), 83:15; 'God's veil is Light', as stated in a *hadith* of *Sahih Muslim*, '… were it to be removed, the emanations from His Countenance would destroy everything upon which the Divine Gaze fell.'

139 Qur'an, *Surah al-Nur* (The Light), 24:30–1. All translations are taken from Abdullah 2004.

140 *Ibid.*, 24:31.

141 Qadi Abu Bakr ibn al-'Arabi (468-543 H), *Ahkam al-Qur'an* (*Legal Rulings of the Qur'an*), ed. 'Abd al-Razzaq al-Mahdi, Dar al-Kitab al-'Arabi, Beirut, 1421/2000, vol. 3, p. 285.

142 Al-Tabari, *Tafsir*, Dar al-Kutub al-'Ilmiyyah, Beirut, 1412/1992, vol. 9, pp. 303–7.

143 Ibn 'Abbas says, in one of the narrations transmitted by Tabari, that such 'apparent adornment' may also be displayed at home to men who enter the woman's house. It is also known from numerous *ahadith* that male and female Companions would visit each other with their spouses. Ibn al-'Arabi mentions the *hadith* that proves that many of the male Companions used to visit the elderly female Companion Umm Shurayk. Thus it is not an Islamic requirement to have gender segregation at home, but a matter of culture and tradition.

144 Ibn al-'Arabi, *ibid.*

145 *Ibid.*, where he states that 'Aishah and Mujahid, the student of Ibn 'Abbas, disagreed respectively as to whether bangles were apparent or hidden adornment, based on whether they were worn on the hands (that is, the wrists) or the forearms.

146 Qur'an, *ibid.*

147 Abu Bakr al-Jassas, *Ahkam al-Qur'an* (*Legal Rulings of the Qur'an*), Dar al-Kutub al-'Arabi, vol. 3, p. 316.

148 al-Qurtubi 1965, vol. 12, p. 227.

149 al-Jassas, *op. cit.*, p. 290.

150 *Ibid.*, p. 311.

151 *Ibid.*, p. 312.

152 Qur'an, *op. cit.*, 33:59–60.

153 al-Tabari, *op. cit.*, vol. 10, pp. 331–2.

154 al-Qurtubi, *op. cit.*, vol. 14, p. 243. The word '*qina*' can refer to any of these three possibilities.

155 al-Jassas, *op. cit.*, p. 496.

156 *Ibid.*, p. 569.

157 *Ibid.*, p. 570.

158 al-Qurtubi, *op. cit.*, p. 244.

159 al-Jassas, *op. cit.*, p. 451

160 *Ibid.*, pp. 496-7

161 Quoted in Al Albani, p. 44.

162 *Ibid.*, p. 45.

163 *Ibid.*

164 Qur'an, *Surah al-Ahzab* (The Combined Forces), 33:53.

165 For a fascinating discussion of this *ayah* and related issues from a feminist, social-science perspective, see Mernissi 1997.

166 Cf. Qur'an, *Surah Maryam* (Mary), 19:17, where the Virgin Mary uses a screen (*hijab*) to isolate herself from others.

[167] al-Jassas, *op. cit.*, p. 284. The authenticity of the latter *hadith* is disputed.

[168] Qur'an, *Surah al-Ahzab* (The Combined Forces), 33:32–3.

[169] al-Jassas, *op. cit.*, pp. 450–2.

[170] Traditional commentary on Qur'an, *Surah al-Qasas* (The Story), 28:26, has Moses' eventual wife and her sister walking behind him, throwing pebbles to inform him of the way to their father's house.

[171] al-Jassas, *op. cit.*, p. 531.

[172] *Ibid.*, p. 312; al-Albani (1385), *Hijab al-Mar'ah al-Muslimah* (The Muslim Woman's Veil), 2nd edn. Beirut/Damascus: al-Maktab al-Islami, p. 24.

[173] al-Albani, *op. cit.*, pp. 24–46. Qadi 'Iyad states in his commentary on *Sahih Muslim* that the majority of jurists require a Muslim woman to cover up in public, except for her face and hands; *Sahih Muslim*, ed. M.F. 'Abd al-Baqi, 4 vols. Beirut: Dar al-Fikr.

[174] During 2007–8, the UK Department of Health introduced a 'bare below the elbow' policy for all medical and nursing staff in clinical contact with patients, in order to reduce the incidence of infections. While some Muslims opposed the policy, with some medical staff and students even leaving the profession, others supported it on the basis of the diversity of Islamic legal opinion on the matter of dress, plus the overriding Islamic legal imperative that values medical care and the saving of lives extremely highly.

[175] al-Jassas, *op. cit.*, p. 317.

[176] al-Tabari, *op. cit.*, vol. 9, pp. 303–7.

[177] al-Jassas, *op. cit.*, p. 287.

[178] *Ibid.*

[179] Mawdudi 1986.

[180] Jalal al-Din al-Mahalli and Jalal al-Din al-Suyuti (n.d.), *Tafsir al-Jalalayn*, Beirut: Dar al-Ma'rifah; p. 462.

[181] Al-Jassas, *op. cit.*, p. 291, where he fiercely contests this view, limiting the ruling only to other women.

[182] See, for example, *ibid.* p. 288.

[183] al-Albani, *op. cit.*, p. 44.

[184] al-Jassas, *op. cit.*, pp. 317 and 372.

[185] al-Qurtubi, *op. cit.*, vol. 12, p. 227.

[186] al-Jassas, *op. cit.*, p. 291.

[187] al-Tabari, *op. cit.*, pp. 331–2.

[188] Ghazzali, *al-Mustasfa min 'Ilm al-Usul.*

[189] Shatibi, in the introduction to his *Muwafaqat*, states that his work is an explicit synthesis of the principles of Ibn al-Qasim and Abu Yusuf, that is, of Maliki and Hanafi or traditionalist and rationalist principles of jurisprudence.

[190] Quoted in Jasser 2008.

[191] Muhammad 2001.

[192] 'Abdullah b. Bayyah (2007), *Sina'ah al-Fatwa* (*Crafting Legal Verdicts*). Beirut: Dar al-Minhaj; p. 319. Cf. Ibn 'Ashur, *al-Tahrir wa l-Tanwir*, vol. 18, p. 207.

[193] 'Abdullah b. Bayyah, *ibid.*

[194] '*Ibid.*, p. 320. The *hadith* is from Bukhari (2002), *Sahih, Kitab al-Jihad wa l-Siyar* (*Book of War and Military Expeditions*). Beirut: Dar al-Kutub al-'Ilmiyyah; p. 530, no. 2880.

195 Lord Carey, former Archbishop of Canterbury, raised this concern about Muslim women's dress in parts of the UK at the session on 'Islam–West Dialogue' at the World Economic Forum – Middle East, Sharm el-Sheikh, Sinai, Egypt, 2008.

196 Ibn al-Qayyim (1977), *I'lam al-Muwaqqi'in 'an Rabb al-'Alamin*, vol. 3. Beirut: Dar al-Fikr; pp. 14–70.

197 Muhammad b. Salih b. 'Uthaymin (d. 1421/2001), *Commentary on Sahih Muslim* (audio-taped lectures), Riyadh: Taybah Islamic Recordings.

198 Qur'an, *Surah al-Qasas* (The Story), 28:25.

199 This became a national political issue in the UK in 2007, when the Conservative Party complained about the increasing sexualisation of young girls in British society.

200 Prof. Javed Iqbal (son of Sir Muhammad Iqbal), public televised lecture on Islam and *Shari'ah*, Pakistan Television, Summer 2003.

201 Qur'an, *Surah al-Anfal* (Spoils of War), 8:60.

202 Interestingly, it is reported that the extremist Egyptian group, *al-Takfir wa l-Hijra*, followed just such a line of reasoning in the 1960s when they 'emigrated' from Cairo to the desert and encamped there, training for military action only with horses, which were no match for Nasser's tanks that decimated the would-be revolutionaries; Jasser, Auda (2008), 'Understanding the Spirit of Islamic Law', lecture at the City Circle, London, 16th May 2008.

203 Bukhari 2002.

204 *Ibid.*

205 al-Jassa, *op. cit.*, p. 313, quoting a *hadith* transmitted by Abu Dawud.

206 Bukhari, *op. cit.*, p. 83, *hadith* no. 362.

207 *Ibid.*, *hadith* no. 358.

208 *Ibid.*, p. 85, paragraph preceding *hadith* no. 372.

209 *Ibid.*, p. 82, paragraph preceding *hadith* no. 351.

210 *Ibid.*, *hadith* no. 351.

211 Wadud 2007, p. 219.

212 The focus groups were conducted with women aged between 16 and 45. They were somewhat different to the interviews, having a relaxed and informal atmosphere, in a group setting of between 5 and 10 women, with mostly structured questions.

213 The first, al-Judai, felt that the requirement of a female dress was of modesty, particular covering was required for the chest region, though this did not include the neck or the ears. It should cover most of the body, although in his opinion specificity of exactly how much of the arms, legs or hair was not provided by the texts. It was important also for some head covering to be worn, though that could take the form of a scarf or shawl; it could also be a hat or a bandana. The second, Raza, felt that the whole body of the Muslim female should be covered except the hands and face. The style of dress was up to the woman, according to her social context. The third, Momoniat, felt the ideal dress for a Muslim female was a complete covering, including the face and hands, although it was permissible for the face and hands to show in certain circumstances, depending on the choice of the woman.

214 According to self-description.

215 The *ahadith* are understood to be narrations of what the Prophet Muhammad

was said to have spoken about or acted upon. They are used as tools by traditional scholars to understand verses of the Quran.

216 The *hadith* about tearing the cloth and covering was mentioned. In response to this, another member of the group quickly remarked that this *hadith* referred to the head and not the face. However this misunderstanding has a place, as many interpretations of the *hadith*, more specifically the word *khimar*, are listed as the face, and not the head.

217 Asma (the daughter of Abu Bakr) entered the house of the Prophet and she was wearing (near) transparent clothes. The Prophet said: 'O Asma! When a woman comes to the age of menstruation she should only show this,' and he pointed at his face and hands (Abu Dawud, Chapter on Dressing, no. 3580).

218 Abu Dawud categorises its chain as *mursal* – the link between the successor and the Prophet is missing and therefore cannot be traced back to him with sufficient strength to qualify for legislative scrutiny. However, al-Albani chooses to use it as permissible evidence for the showing of the hands and face, as there are variant accounts of the *hadith* (Roald).

219 Gibb and Kramers 1974, p. 138.

220 The word does appear in seven verses: 7:46, 38:32, 41:5, 42:51, 17:45, 19:17 and 33:53, but they all have very different contexts. For example: in *Sura al-Araf*, 7:46, it is used to describe the separation of those in paradise from those in hellfire; in the next world they will be separated by a *hijab* (curtain/veil). In *Sura Fussilat*, 41:5, the unbelievers comment to the Prophet that there is a *hijab* between he and they. And in *Sura Shura*, 42:51, it is used to explain how it is not possible for man to speak to God unless by revelation or from behind a *hijab*. *Sura al-Ahzab*, 33:53, is the only verse that speaks of it in respect of women, more specifically to the wives of the Prophet, but even then it is not with respect to her requirement of dress.

221 'I know the word *hijab* is used, but it is not the best Islamic word to use for what you are looking for. People understand it to mean "covering" today, but it is not a word that is found in the Qur'an and *Sunna* [used in this way]. What I (know people) understand by the word *hijab* is the "covering". A covering that provides "protection" for the woman. But that covering is not described in (a specific) way in the Qur'an and *Sunna* clearly, and that is for a reason – for the "ease" of people. To make it easier for people to interpret it in whichever way they deem fit for their "protection" at any given time. So I refer to it as (dependant on) the "custom" also – the best thing in society to make you look good/presentable (according to custom), and at the same time protect you. (Interview)

222 The verse with the word *hijab* in reference to the Prophet and his wives is in *Sura al-Ahzab*. It reads: 'O you who believe enter not the Prophet's houses – until leave is given to you – for a meal, (and then) not so early as to wait for its preparation: but when you are invited, enter; and when you have taken your meals, disperse without seeking familiar talk. Such behaviour annoys the Prophet: he is ashamed to dismiss you, but Allah is not ashamed to tell you the truth. And when you ask his ladies for anything you want, ask them from behind a screen: that makes for greater purity for your hearts and for theirs. Nor is it right for you that you should ignore Allah's Messenger, or that you should marry his widows after him at any time. Truly such a thing is in Allah's sight an enormity.' (Qur'an, 33:53)

[223] Mernissi 1991, p. 85.

[224] Anas reports: 'I know (about) the *hijab* (the order of veiling of women) more than anybody else. Allah's Apostle became the bridegroom of Zaynab bint Jahsh whom he married at Medina. After the sun had risen high in the sky, the Prophet invited the people to a meal. Allah's Apostle remained sitting and some people remained sitting with him after the other guests had left. Then Allah's Apostle got up and went away, and I, too, followed him till he reached the door of Aisha's room. Then he thought that the people must have left the place by then, so he returned and I also returned with him. Behold, the people were still sitting at their places. So he went back again for the second time, and I went along with him too. When we reached the door of Aisha's room, he returned and I also returned with him to see that the people had left. Thereupon the Prophet hung a curtain between me and him and the Verse regarding the order for (veiling of women), *hijab*, was revealed.' (Bukhari 2002, 7:65:375)

[225] Mernissi, *op. cit.*, p. 92

[226] *Ibid.*

[227] Darsh 1995, p. 12.

[228] Interestingly, focus group 'a' (those who covered the face) held the *jilbab* in very high regard as an outer garment, and of similar description to that given by Momoniat – clearly a one-piece outer garment that needed to be worn over ordinary clothes. Some described it as literally 'a coat; to be worn outside'. For the *jilbab* to take this form was so important for them that they likened one who did not wear it to be like one without *hijab*, in other words not wearing a head covering at all (all group members agreed with this understanding). Where this specific classification came from was not clarified; but it would seem that the understanding of 'outer garment' had itself been translated in this way. Group 'b' (those who exposed the hands and face) disagreed, and held views similar to Judai's: as long as the chest was covered, the type and style of dress could vary, though they had similar requirements of looseness and transparency. But again, if Darsh's point about abrogation of verses is to be taken into account, how the word *jilbab* is understood doesn't really matter. As the verse is succeeded by *Sura al-Nur*, this in itself specifies the female dress requirements, and the understanding of *jilbab* is not required.

[229] On questioning people who are more familiar than me with the Arabic language, it appears that similar to the changes of application and meaning of the word of *hijab*, the meaning of the word *khimar* was originally the head-cover, but with the passage of time it is sometimes understood in language today to include the face-covering too.

[230] Wehr, Hans (1976), *A Dictionary of Modern Written Arabic*, New York: Spoken Languages Services; p. 261.

[231] I asked if the *khimar* could have been just a cultural aspect of the dress, and his response was: 'It is the language actually, not just tradition.' (One would have wanted to elaborate in this area more; however, due to shortness of time, this was unfortunately not possible.)

[232] Perhaps it is in this context, then, that Asad explains *khimar* as 'customary headcovering worn by Arabian women before the advent of Islam' (Asad 1980, p. 539).

233 When asked for an example of a *hadith* that clearly specifies this requirement, the *hadith* about Asma was given.

234 This is the plural feminine form.

235 Asad, *op. cit.*, pp. 538–9.

236 Wehr, *op. cit.*, p. 50.

237 Furthermore the Qur'an uses this word in *Sura al-Qasas* also – when Moses is described as putting his hand over his *jayb*. Here there is no dispute over this being the chest (even the heart region), and not the neck, face or ears. Therefore it is difficult to comprehend how the translation of the verse which specifies the *juyub* can be taken to include the neck, ears, and especially face region.

238 When I asked 'What if the covering itself causes attraction, as some feel it adds an air of mystery to a woman?', one lady agreed that her inspiration for initially wearing one was because she had felt a woman underneath must have been so beautiful. Some members of the group acknowledged that this could be a risk, especially in Britain. However, for others, this attention was not seen as negative but interpreted either as 'respect' or 'difference' with regard to who she was. Momoniat agreed with the latter point.

239 Asad, *op. cit.*, p. 539.

240 *Ibid.*

241 Another point of interest is a story about Fatima bint Ali ibn Abi Talib, the grand-daughter of the Prophet, narrated by Ibn Sa'd. He reports that Urwah ibn Abd Allah ibn Qushayr entered the house of Fatimah and watched as she donned two thick ivory bracelets on each wrist, a ring on her finger and a beaded thread around her neck. When Urwah questioned her about this apparent excess of adornment, she answered in a brief retort that it is a testimony to her pride in her femininity and her confidence that a woman's desire to beautify herself may not be contested. 'Women are unlike men.' (Alvi *et al.* 2003, p. 195).

242 *Fitna:* Arabic term meaning tribulation.

243 From all the individuals interviewed in the focus groups, only one woman felt that she had initially been forced to cover her head by her brothers. The end result was that she wore a head covering in front of them, and removed it when they were out of sight. She stopped wearing it completely after six months. Yet a year later, when she had learnt more about Islam for herself and understood more about the concept of covering, she chose to cover her head again, this time for herself, and she hasn't stopped doing so over the last 20 years. All the remaining women covered themselves out of personal choice from the outset. Interestingly, some women felt displeasure and pressure from their families to remove the covering (rather than the other way around). For example, one lady in focus group 'a' felt her in-laws did not like her to wear the face-covering, and her husband would often encourage her to remove it, though she would prefer to keep it on. Similarly, in group 'b', two ladies mentioned the anxiety of their families, who would like them to remove the head-cover at times to aid them in finding suitable marriage partners, who might otherwise be put off by a woman wearing a scarf.

244 Refers to the age before Islam – literally, the state of ignorance.

245 Barlas 2002, p. 55.

246 *Ibid.*, p. 54.

247 *Ibid.*, p. 55.

248 Equally essential was the ability to be recognised by fellow Muslims, 'who would now say *Salam* to you'.

249 Focus groups 'a' and 'b' were asked the question: 'If identity was so important for Muslims in Islam, where was the equivalent for a man? Did he not have to distinguish himself from other religions; be recognised by other Muslims; or wear something physical to remind him to watch his behaviour as he was an ambassador of Islam?' After vigorous debate about length of trousers and covering between the navel and the knee, both groups could only think of growing a beard as an equivalent to covering the head/face. Most, however, felt that growing a beard was not obligatory in Islam (only recommended) and that having a beard still did not necessarily identify you exclusively as being a Muslim.

250 A full-length outer covering.

251 A lady in group 'b' commented: 'Last week, there was a woman that was covering her hair but her trousers and top were really tight, and the builders couldn't take their eyes off her.'

252 Al-Qaradawi 1993, p. 79.

253 He also felt that, if men were not used to seeing women, this could lead to greater difficulty in self-control. That could be seen as an argument for removing the covering of the face. For, rather than taking the emphasis away from seeing the woman purely on a sexual basis, it appeared to make her more intriguing, and as a result the man was somehow less in control of his desires towards her.

254 This would explain again why the grand-daughter of the Prophet was content to decorate herself before going out.

255 An innovation, which is seen as an external accretion to the purity and integrity of Islam, and is hence viewed negatively.

256 This would also appear to fit in with some historians' description of society at the time: in pre-Islamic times, women used to cover their face and heads and leave their chests exposed.

257 Roald 2001, p. 275.

258 I also asked if this was because of slave status, but al-Judai did not feel it was primarily for this reason.

259 Unfortunately, time did not allow us to probe the issue further, but I intend to go back to this area of research to understand more fully this situation and make further studies in this area.

260 Slaves are mentioned here because they were an integral part of the Arabian society at the times of the Prophet. The author has shown elsewhere how Islam gradually eradicated the inhuman institution of slavery it had inherited (Translator's Note: see Ghamidi, Javed Ahmad (2010), *Mi#za#n* (Islam: A Comprehensive Introduction), trans. Shehzad Saleem. Lahore: Shirkat Press; pp. 448–51.)

261 Al Ghazali (1995), 'Breaking the two desires' trans. T. J. Winter, in *The Revival of the Religious Sciences*. Cambridge: The Islamic Texts Society.

262 Ibn Hazm (1994), *The Ring of the Dove* (trans. Anthony Arberry). Anglesey: Luzac Oriental.

263 *Ibid.*

[264] Fath al Bari, Sharh Sahih al Bukhari 8/489.

[265] Mernissi 1991.

[266] Thornwell, Emily (1856), *The Lady's Guide to Perfect Gentility*. New York.

[267] *Ibid.*

[268] Mawdudi 1986.

[269] *Ibid.*, p.146.

[270] *Ibid.*, p.144.

[271] Al Albani 1413 AH.

[272] Mawdudi 1986, p. 122.

[273] Bewley 1999.

[274] NVIVO 7 is useful as qualitative analysis software, which, like all such tools, comes with the caveat that it is the researcher who thinks about, analyses and interprets the data and *not* the software. In this research, semi-structured interviews were used so that participants' opinions and views were not constrained in any way. NVIVO 7 was initially used as a tool to give structure to interview transcripts. For the purpose of further analysis, NVIVO 7 was used to organise participants' responses under broad themes; for example, their comments about *hijab* were all collated under the broad theme *hijab*. Patterns and subthemes were then identified within broad themes; for example *hijab* as religious injunction; *hijab* as religious practice; *hijab* as symbolic of identity, modesty, etc. These sub-themes were used to identify and inform the arguments that this chapter makes.

[275] Carey, George (2008), *Balanced Immigration*. Available online at www.glcarey.co.uk/Speeches/2008/Balanced%20Migration.html

[276] For a more detailed discussion on the theological basis of the *hijab* see Roald 2001, pp. 254–94.

[277] Muslims consider the Qur'an to be a divinely revealed document and the unequivocal truth.

[278] The *Sun'nah* consists of narrated traditions from the lifetime of the Prophet (peace be upon him) that document various real-life situations and the advice that the Prophet (pbuh) gave in various situations. Muslims use this to further understand guidelines that they derive from the Qur'an.

[279] *Ijmaa* refers to the consensus of qualified Islamic scholars.

[280] Muslims believe that the practice of *hijab* is a divinely endorsed framework of modesty that has been enjoined upon men and women. *Hijab* is an Arabic word which can refer to the headscarf worn by a Muslim woman; it can also refer to the headscarf worn along with a long, loose outer garment called the *jilbab* (Arabic); another oft-repeated term is the *niqab* (Arabic) which refers to a piece of cloth used to cover the face; and finally *purdah* (an Urdu word) normally refers to a system that includes covering up and strict segregation for women. Most of these terms are used interchangeably or synonymously, depending on the cultural contexts in which they are used. Terms like *burkha* and *abayah* refer to various styles of the *jilbab* or outer garment. For practicality this research will use *hijab* to refer to all the various garments used by Muslim women to cover.

[281] Verse 24:31 of the Qur'an deals with Islamic frameworks for modesty.

[282] Cooke 2001.

[283] Bewley 1999.

[284] Afshar 1994, pp. 127–50; Alvi *et al.* 2003a, pp. xi–xxiv; Haddad *et al.* 2006; Syed 2005, pp. 515–30; Vyas 2008, pp. 15–19.

[285] Azim 1997.

[286] Ahmed 1992.

[287] Lambert-Hurley *et al.* 2007.

[288] Montagu 1837.

[289] Said 1978.

[290] Ahmed, *op. cit.*

[291] *Ibid.*; Bullock 2003; Afshar 2008, pp. 411–27.

[292] Lewis 1996.

[293] Bullock, *op. cit.*

[294] Clarke, L. (2003), '*Hijab* According to the *Hadīth*', in Alvi *et al.* 2003, pp. 214–86.

[295] Thanvi 1998.

[296] Mawdudi 1986.

[297] Khan 1995.

[298] Ahmed, *op. cit.*

[299] Clarke, *op. cit.*, pp. 214–86.

[300] Barlas 2002.

[301] El Saadawi 1980.

[302] Mernissi 1985; Mernissi 1997.

[303] The participant's name has been changed to protect her anonymity.

[304] *Assalam Alaikum* is an Islamic greeting that is commonly used in any Islamic context. It translates to 'May peace be with you'.

[305] *Muhajjabah* is an Arabic terms that refers to 'she who practises *hijab*'. *Hijabi* is a more commonly used term that means the same thing – one who practises *hijab*.

[306] Alvi *et al.*, *op. cit.*, pp. 214–86.

[307] Bullock, *op. cit.*

[308] Hall, Stuart (1992), 'The Question of Cultural Identity', in Hall, Stuart, Held, David and McGrew, Tony (eds), *Modernity and its Futures.* Cambridge: Polity Press; pp. 273–326.

[309] Hall and du Gay 1996, pp. 1–19.

[310] Badr, Hoda (2004), 'Islamic Identity Re-covered: Muslim Women after September 11th', *Journal of Culture and Religion*, 5.3, 321–38; Haddad *et al.* 2006; Williams, Rhys and Vashi, Gira (2007), 'Hijab and American Muslim Women: Creating the Space for Autonomous Selves', *Sociology of Religion*, 68.3, 269–87.

[311] The participant's name has been changed to protect her anonymity.

[312] Hussain, Dilawar (2004), 'British Muslim Identity', in Seddon, Mohammad, Hussain, Dilawar and Malik, Nadeem (eds), *British Muslims Between Assimilation and Segregation – Historical, Legal and Social Realities.* Markfield: The Islamic Foundation; pp 83–118.

[313] The participant's name has been changed to protect her anonymity.

[314] Hall, Stuart, 'Who needs Identity?', in Hall and du Gay 1996, pp. 1–19.

[315] Iqbal, Cameron (2007), 'The Understanding of Cultural Symbols such as the Veil and *Hijab* in Britain and France', *The International Journal of the Humanities*, 5.3, 13–40.

[316] Hall, *op. cit.*

[317] Göle, Nilüfer (2008), '*Le foulard, symbole d'émancipation?*', *Courrier International*, 905.

[318] *Le Monde*, 8.1.2004.

[319] '*La laïcité à l'école et dans la société française*', Presse Internationale, Dec. 2003–Jan. 2004. Available online at www.aidh.org/laic/eur-europ.htm

[320] Samary, Catherine (2007), '*Pour une alternative laïque contre l'étatisme "civilisateur"*', *Topics & Roses*, 15 December.

[321] *La Croix*, 21.5.2005.

[322] Bessis, Sophie (2001), '*L'Occident et les autres: Histoire d'une suprématie*', édition La Découverte.

[323] This philosophy for the *hijab* has been expounded by many writers, including: Dwyer, C. (1999), 'Veiled meanings: Young British Muslim Women and the Negotiation of Differences', *Gender, Place and Culture: A Journal of Feminist Geography*. 6.1, 5–27; Amiraux, V. (2003), 'Veiled discourse on Muslim women in Europe: The feminization of debates over Islam', *Social Compass*, 50.1, 85–96; and Afshar, H., Aitken, R. and Franks, M. (2005), 'Feminisms, Islamophobia and Identities', *Political Studies*, 53, 262–83.

[324] Following the revelations of verse 31 of *Surah An-Nur* ('And say to the faithful women to lower their gazes, and to guard their private parts, and not to display their beauty except what is apparent of it, and to extend their head-coverings (*khimars*) to cover their bosoms, and not to display their beauty') and verse 59 of *Surah Al-Ahzab* ('Say to your wives and your daughters and the women of the faithful to draw their outer-garments close around themselves; that is better that they will be recognized and not annoyed'), the Muslim women began covering themselves completely. This is the origin of the *hijab*.

[325] An extensive discussion on such studies is provided in Bullock 2003.

[326] A study conducted by Sherifa Zuhur (1992) in Egypt found that those who observed the head- and face-covering believed it was a sign of religious identity. Forty per cent of those interviewed who did not cover also stated that they believed it was a religious act.

[327] Examples include Algeria in the 1950s, Egypt following the Six-Day War with Israel in 1967, and Iran following the 1979 revolution. Details of studies in these countries are provided in Bullock, *op. cit.*, pp. 87–95.

[328] All of these reason are explored in Bullock, *op. cit.*, pp. 105–17.

[329] See for example, Ahmed, A. S. (2003), *Islam Under Siege*, London: Polity Press; pp. 36–9.

[330] In May 2004, FBI director Robert Mueller told a Congressional Panel in the USA that 532 attacks against Arabs or Muslims (or Sikhs mistaken for Muslims) had been investigated since 9/11. A study conducted in the USA by Bakalian and Bozorgmehr, looking at the 9/11 backlash against Muslims, details post-9/11 hate crimes against Muslims and how American Muslims responded to this. Bakalian, A. and Bozorgmehr, M. (2005), 'Muslim American Moblization', *Diaspora: A Journal of Transnational Studies*, Spring, 14 1, 7–43.

[331] Dodd, V. (2005), 'Muslim women advised to abandon Hijab to avoid attack', *Guardian*, 4 August.

[332] Cooke, M. (2008), 'Religion, Gender and the Muslim Woman', *Journal for Feminist Studies in Religion*, 24.1, 91–9.

[333] *Ibid.*

[334] *Ibid.*

[335] Silvestri, S. (2008), 'Unveiled Issues. Europe's Muslim Women's Potential, Problems, and Aspirations'. Research Report. A publication of the King Baudouin Foundation.

[336] *Ibid.*, p. 6.

[337] *Ibid.*

[338] *Ibid.*, p. 7.

[339] *Ibid.*, p. 66.

[340] Ahmad, F. (2008), 'Beyond the Hijab as Lodestone', *Journal of Feminist Studies in Religion*, 24.1, 99–101.

[341] Hussain, S. (2008), 'Muslims on the Map, A National Survey of Social Trends in Britain', *International Library of Human Geography*, Taurus Academic Studies; p. xiii.

[342] Cooke, *op. cit.*, p. 97.

[343] *Ibid.*, p. 2.

[344] For a discussion on the social and political reality for Muslims in Britain, see Rehman, J. (2007), 'Islam, "War on Terror" and the Future of Muslim Minorities in the United Kingdom: Dilemmas of Multiculturalism in the Aftermath of the London Bombings', *Human Rights Quarterly*, 29.4, 841–56.

[345] Hussain, *op. cit.*, p. 3.

[346] Ahmed, *op. cit.*, p. 116.

[347] *Ibid.*, p. 117.

[348] Anouar, Majid (2000), *Unveiling Traditions, Postcolonial Islam in a Polycentric World*, Durham: Duke University Press; p. 100.

[349] Safi 2003, p. 3.

[350] An example of a text that is currently being translated is a 40-volume biographic dictionary detailing the Muslim women in history who were *hadith* scholars. The preface is: Akram, M. (2007), *Al Muhaddithat, the Women Scholars in Islam*. Oxford: Interface Publications.

[351] See, generally, Evans, M. D. (1997), *Religious Liberty and International Law in Europe*, Cambridge: Cambridge University Press.

[352] Cases have been brought against the state from Turkey and Switzerland under this provision.

[353] McGoldrick, D. (2006), *Human Rights and Religion: The Islamic Headscarf Debate in Europe*. Oxford: Hart Publishing; p. 8.

[354] ECHR Application No 44774/98.

[355] *Ibid.*, at para. 93.

[356] McGoldrick, *op. cit.*, p. 12.

[357] Bullock, *op. cit.*, pp. 85–135.

[358] Grand Chamber, Judgement 10 November 2005, para 3, Summary Judgement.

[359] *Ibid*

[360] *Ibid.*

[361] R, on the application of Begum (by her litigation friend, Rahman) (Respondent) v. Headteacher and Governors of Denbigh High School (Appellants), U.K. House Lords 15 (2006) UKHL 15.

[362] Tristan, Pierre (2008), 'Moroccan Woman Denied French Citizenship for Her

Niqab', 19 July 2008. Available online at middleeast.about.com/b/2008/07/19/moroccan-woman-denied-french-citizenship-for-her-niqab.htm

363 Kahf, Mohja (2008), 'Spare Me the Sermon On Muslim Women', *Washington Post*, 5 October 2008, p. B01. Available online at www.washingtonpost.com/wp-dyn/content/article/2008/10/03/AR2008100301968.html

364 Bowen, John R. (2007), *Why the French Don't Like Headscarves: Islam, the State and Public Spaces*. Princeton: Princeton University Press; p. 177.

365 Razack, Shirene (2008), *Casting Out: Race and the Eviction of Muslims from Western Law and Politics*. Toronto: University of Toronto Press.

366 Bullock, *op. cit.*

367 Allievi, Stefano (2006), 'The Shifting Significance of the *Halal/Haram* Frontier: Narratives on the Hijab and Other Issues', in Karin van Nieuwkerk (ed.), *Women Embracing Islam: Gender and Conversion in the West*, Austin: University of Texas Press; pp. 120–1.

368 Tristan, *op. cit.*

369 *Ibid.*

370 Kahf, Mojha (2008), 'From Her Royal Body the Robe Was Removed: The Blessings of the Veil and the Trauma of Forced Unveilings in the Middle East', in Jennifer Heath (ed.), *The Veil: Women Writers on Its History, Lore and Politics*, Berkeley: University of California Press; p. 38.

371 Bowen, *op. cit.*, p. 69.

372 *Ibid.*

373 See the various essays in Jennifer Heath (ed.), *op. cit.*

374 Alvi *et al.* 2003a.

375 Bullock, *op. cit.*, p. 35.

376 Badran, Margot (2006), 'Feminism and Conversion: Comparing British, Dutch and South African Life Stories', in Karin van Nieuwkerk (ed.), *op. cit.*, p. 200.

377 Segal, Eliezer, 'Who Has Not Made Me a Woman: Different versions and parallels from classical sources and manuscripts provide an interesting perspective on this controversial blessing'. Available online at www.myjewishlearning.com/texts/liturgical_texts/Overview_Jewish_Prayer_Book/MorningBlessings3230/NotAWoman3232.htm

378 Bullock, *op. cit.*, p. 134.

379 *Ibid.*, p. 83.

380 See online at www.veil-project.eu/

381 Bullock, *op. cit*, ch. 2.

382 See online at www.turks.us/article.php?story=20060210122346765

Select bibliography

Abdullah, Yusuf 'Ali (2004), *The Meaning of the Holy Qur'an* (10th edn). Beltsville, Md: Amana Publications.

Abu' A'la Mawdudi (1947), *The Ethical Viewpoint of Islam.* Lahore: Markazi Maktaba Jam'at-i-Islami.

— (1971), *The Meaning of the Qur'an.* Lahore: Islamic Publications, p. 16.

— (1980), *Human Rights in Islam.* Leicester: The Islamic Foundation, pp. 262, 322

— (1986), *Purdah and the Status of Women,* trans. Al-Ash'ari. Lahore: Islamic Publications.

Abu Bakr al-Jassas (1986), *Ahkam al-Qur'an (Legal Rulings of the Qur'an),* vol. 3. Beirut: Dar al-Kutub al-'Arabi, pp. 317, 372.

Afshar, Haleh (1994), 'Muslim Women in West Yorkshire – Growing up with Real and Imaginary Values Amidst Conflicting Views of Self and Society', in Haleh Afshar and Mary Maynard (eds), *The Dynamics of Race and Gender – Some Feminist Interventions,* London: Taylor and Francis.

Aga Khan, Sultan Muhammad Shah (1954), *The memoirs of Aga Khan: world enough and time.* London: Cassell.

Ahmed, Leila (1992), *Women and Gender in Islam.* New Haven: Yale University Press, p. 154.

Akram, M. (2007), *Al Muhaddithat, the Women Scholars in Islam.* London: Interface Publications.

Al Albani Nasiruddin (1413 AH), *Jilbab Mar'atul Muslimah.* Jordan: Al Maktabah Al Islamiyyah.

Al-Qaradawi, Yusuf (1993), *The Lawful and The Prohibited in Islam,* Salimiah, IIFSO.

al-Qurtubi, Ahmad al-Ansari (1965), *al-Jami' li Ahkam al-Qur'an,* Beirut: Dar Ihya' al-Turath al-'Arabi.

Alvi, S., Hoodfar, H. and McDonough, S. (2003a), 'Introduction', in S. Alvi, H. Hoodfar and S. McDonough (eds), *The Muslim Veil in North America – Issues and Debates.* Toronto: Women's Press.

— (eds) (2003b), *The Muslim Veil in North America – Issues and Debates.* Toronto: Women's Press.

Asad, Muhammad (1980), *The Message of the Qur'an.* Gibraltar: Dar Al-Andalus.

Azim, Saukath (1997), *Muslim Women, Emerging Identity,* Jaipur: Rawat Publications.

Aziz, K. K. (ed.) (1998), *Aga Khan III: selected speeches and writings of Sir Sultan Muhammad Shah.* London and New York: Routledge and Kegan Paul.

Barlas, Asma (2002), *Believing Women in Islam – Unreading Patriarchal Interpretations of the Qur'an.* Austin: University of Texas Press.

Bewley, Aisha (1999), *Islam: The Empowering of Women.* London: Ta-Ha Publishers.

Bhimani, S. (2003), *Majalis al-'ilm: sessions of knowledge: reclaiming and representing the lives of Muslim women.* Toronto: TSAR Publications.

Blank, Jonah (2001), *Mullahs on the mainframe: Islam and modernity among the Daudi Bohras*. Chicago and London: University of Chicago Press.

Bowen, John R. (2007), *Why the French Don't Like Headscarves: Islam, the State and Public Spaces*. Princeton: Princeton University Press.

Braybrooke, Marcus (ed.) (1992), *Stepping Stones to a Global Ethic*. London: SCM Press.

Bukhari, Sahih (2002 [1423]), *Kitab al-Jihad wa l-Siyar (Book of War and Military Expeditions)*. Beirut: Dar al-Kutub al-'Ilmiyyah.

Bullock, Katherine (2003), *Rethinking Muslim Women and the Veil – Challenging Historical & Modern Stereotypes*. Herndon, Va: The International Institute of Islamic Thought.

Contractor, S. (2010), *Demystifying the Muslimah*. PhD thesis, University of Gloucestershire.

Cooke, Miriam (2001), *Women Claim Islam: Creating Islamic Feminism through Literature*. London: Routledge.

Darsh, Syed M. (1995), *Hijab or Niqab?* London: Dar al-Dawa.

De Souza, Eunice (ed.) (2004), *Purdah: an Anthology*. Oxford: Oxford University Press.

E Guindi, Fadwa (1999), *Veil, Modesty, Privacy and Resistance*. Oxford: Berg.

El Saadawi, Nawal (1980), *The Hidden Face of Eve – Women in the Arab World*. London: Zed Books.

Evans, M. D. (1997), *Religious Liberty and International Law in Europe*. Cambridge: Cambridge University Press.

Gibb, H. and Kramers, J. H. (1974), *Shorter Encyclopaedia of Islam*. Leiden: E. J. Brill.

Göle, N. (1996), *The forbidden modern: civilization and veiling*. Ann Arbor: The University of Michigan Press.

Gombrich, R. (1987), 'What Kind of Thing is Religion?', in *SHAP Handbook on World Religions in Education*. London: Commission for Racial Equality.

Haddad, Y., Smith, J. and Moore, K. (2006), *Muslim Women in America – The Challenge of Islamic Identity Today*. New York: Oxford University Press.

Hall, S. and du Gay, P. (eds) (1996), *Questions of Cultural Identity*. London: Sage.

Halstead, J. M. (1986), *The Case for Muslim Voluntary-Aided Schools. Some Philosophical Reflections*. Cambridge: The Islamic Academy.

Heath, Jennifer (ed.) (2008), *The Veil: Women Writers on Its History, Lore and Politics*. Berkeley: University of California Press.

Jackson, Roy (2009), *Mawdudi and Political Islam*. London: Routledge.

Jasser, Auda (2008 [1429]), *Maqasid al-Shari'ah – A Beginner's Guide*. London and Washington: International Institute of Islamic Thought.

Kamali, Muhammad Hashim (2001), *Issues in the Legal Theory of Usul and Prospects for Reform*. Islamabad: Islamic Research Institute, International Islamic University.

Khan, Wahiduddin (1995), *Women between Islam and Western Society*. New Delhi: Goodword Books.

Kjellberg, Eva (1967), *The Isma'ilis in Tanzania*, MA Thesis, University College, Dar es Salaam.

Lambert-Hurley, Siobhan (2007), *Muslim Women, Reform and Princely Patronage: Nawab Sultan Jahan Begam of Bhopal*. London: Routledge.

Lewis, Reina (1996), *Gendering Orientalism – Race, Femininity and Representation*. London, Routledge.

Majid, Anouar (2000), *Unveiling Traditions, Postcolonial Islam in a Polycentric World.* Durham, NC: Duke University Press.

Malti-Douglas, Fedwa (2001), *Medicines of the Soul.* Berkeley: University of California Press, p. 38.

McGoldrick, D. (2006), *Human Rights and Religion: The Islamic Headscarf Debate in Europe.* Portland, Or: Hart Publishing.

Mernissi, Fatima (1985), *Beyond the Veil: Male–Female Dynamics in Modern Muslim Society.* Bloomington: Indiana University Press.

— (1991), *Women and Islam: An Historical and Theological Enquiry.* London: Blackwell.

— (1997), *The Veil And The Male Elite.* Oxford: Blackwell.

Montagu, Mary (1837), *The Letters and Works of Lady Mary Worthley Montagu.* Edited by Lord Wharncliffe. London: Richard Bently.

Muhammad Nasir al-Din al-Albani (1385), *Hijab al-Mar'ah al-Muslimah (The Muslim Woman's Veil)*, 2nd edn. Beirut/Damascus: al-Maktab al-Islami, p. 24.

Mutahhari, Murtaza (1992), *Islamic Hijab.* Chicago: Kazi Publications.

Nieuwkerk, Karin van (ed.) (2006), *Women Embracing Islam: Gender and Conversion in the West.* Austin: University of Texas Press.

Papanek, H. (1962), *Leadership and social change in the Khoja Isma'ili community.* PhD thesis, Radcliffe College, Cambridge, Mass.

Rahman, Fazlur (1982), *Islam and Modernity: Transformation of an Intellectual Tradition.* Chicago: University of Chicago Press.

Razack, Shirene (2008), *Casting Out: Race and the Eviction of Muslims from Western Law and Politics.* Toronto: University of Toronto Press.

Ricoeur, P. (1974), *Political and Social Essays.* David Stewart and Joseph Bien (eds). Athens: Ohio University Press.

— (1987), *Lectures on Ideology and Utopia.* New York: Columbia University Press.

— (1992), *Symbolism of Evil.* Boston: Beacon Press, p. 387.

Roald, Anne Sofie (2001), *Islamic Female Dress in Women in Islam: the Western experience.* London and New York: Routledge.

Romain, Jonathan (1985), *The Jews of England.* London: The Michael Goulston Education Foundation.

Ruthven, Malise (2000), *Islam in the World*, 2nd edn. London: Penguin Books.

Said, Edward (1978), *Orientalism – Western Conceptions of the Orient.* London: Penguin Books.

Safi, Omid (ed.) (2003), *Progressive Muslims, on Justice, Gender and Pluralism.* Oxford: Oneworld Publications.

Sayyid-Vali, Reza Nasr (1992), *Islamization of Knowledge.* Islamabad: International Institute of Islamic Thought.

Seddon, M., Hussain, D. and Malik, N. (eds) (2004), *British Muslims Between Assimilation and Segregation – Historical, Legal and Social Realities.* Leicester: The Islamic Foundation.

Sultan Muhammad Shah (1977), *Message to the world of Islam*, 4th edn. Karachi: Isma'ilia Association for Pakistan.

Swider, Leonard (1999), *For All Life.* Ashland, Or: White Cloud Press.

Syed, Ali (2005), 'Why Here, Why Now? Young Muslim Women Wearing *Hijab*'. *Muslim World*, October, 95.4, 515–30.

Thanvi, Ashraf Ali (1998), *Bahisti Zawar or Heavenly Ornaments*, trans. Masroor Saroha. Delhi: Fahim Publishers.

Vyas, Sapna (2008), 'Identity Experiences of Young Muslim American Women in the Post 9/11 Era'. *Encounter: Education for Meaning and Social Justice*, Summer, 21.2, 15–19.

Wadud, Amina (1999), *Qur'an and Woman: re-reading the sacred text from a woman's perspective*. New York: Oxford University Press.

— (2007), *Inside the Gender Jihad, Women's Reform in Islam*. Oxford, Oneworld Publications.

Zuhur, S. (1992), *Revealing Reveiling: Islamist Gender Ideology in Contemporary Egypt*. New York: State University of New York Press.

Index

Lightning Source UK Ltd.
Milton Keynes UK
UKOW03f1006121113

220931UK00001B/15/P